Singing
FOR
DUMMIES®

by Pamelia S. Phillips, DMA

WILEY

Wiley Publishing, Inc.

Singing For Dummies®

Published by
Wiley Publishing, Inc.
909 Third Avenue
New York, NY 10022
www.wiley.com

Copyright © 2003 by Wiley Publishing, Inc., Indianapolis, Indiana

Published by Wiley Publishing, Inc., Indianapolis, Indiana

Published simultaneously in Canada

For general information on our other products and services or to obtain technical support, please contact
our Customer Care Department within the U.S. at 800-762-2974, outside the U.S. at 317-572-3993, or fax
317-572-4002.

Wiley also publishes its books in a variety of electronic formats. Some content that appears in print may
not be available in electronic books.

Library of Congress Cataloging-in-Publication Data:

Library of Congress Control Number: 2003101903

ISBN: 0-7645-2475-5

Manufactured in the United States of America

10 9 8 7 6

1O/RX/QW/QT/IN

is a trademark of Wiley Publishing, Inc.

About the Author

Dr. Pamelia S. Phillips is Chair of Voice and Music at CAP21 (New York University Undergraduate Drama Department in the Tisch School of the Arts). Pamelia earned her Doctorate of Musical Arts and Master of Music in Vocal Performance from Arizona State University and a Bachelor of Music Education from Arkansas State University. Her performances range from contemporary American Opera premieres to guest performances with major symphonies.

Dr. Phillips has also taught at Wagner College, Arizona State University, Scottsdale Community College, and South Mountain Community College.

Performances include title roles in *Carmen*, *Tragedy of Carmen* and *Lizzie Borden*, the Witch in *Hansel and Gretal*, Giulietta in *Tales of Hoffmann*, Dorabella in *Cosi fan tutte*, Mum in *Albert Herring*, Constance in the world premiere of *She Stoops to Conquer*, Lady with a Hat Box in *Postcard from Morocco*, Frau Bauer in *Dora*, Beatrice in the stage premiere of *Garden of Mystery*, Mrs. Cornett in *Tobermory*, staged performance of *From The Diary of Virginia Woolf*, Gloria Thorpe in *Damn Yankees*, Gymnasia in *...Forum*, Liebeslieder singer in *A Little Night Music,* and Lady Thiang in *King and I*. Symphonic performances include Berlioz' *Le mort de Cléopâtra* with the Bronx Symphony, Mahler's *Fourth Symphony* with the Centré Symphony, *Das Lied von der Erde* and Mahler's *Third Symphony* with the New York Symphonic Arts Ensemble, and guest artist with Phoenix Chamber Symphony, Scottsdale Fine Arts Orchestra, and the National Chorale.

Dedication

For George and my family. And to every one of you who is the world's best shower singer. My hat is off to you for daring to improve your technique out of the comfort zone of the shower.

Author's Acknowledgments

The author gratefully acknowledges Project Editor Jennifer Connolly for always being of sound mind and great imagination, the Acquisitions Editor Natasha Graf for believing in me and for being a great singer herself, Technical Editor Margaret Ball for being crazy enough to believe that I should write a book, Copy Editor Esmeralda St. Clair for her humor, and Martha Sullivan for creating the musical examples.

Thank you to my parents, Holmes and Darlene, for all the lessons you paid for, the hours you had to listen to me practice, and the many miles you drove to attend my concerts.

Eternal thanks to my students (and a few colleagues) who sang so beautifully on the recording, and to my students and colleagues who offered advice and support.

Special thanks to my voice teachers Julia Lansford, Jerry Doan, and Norma Newton.

Publisher's Acknowledgments

We're proud of this book; please send us your comments through our Dummies online registration form located at www.dummies.com/register/.

Some of the people who helped bring this book to market include the following:

Acquisitions, Editorial, and Media Development

Project Editor: Jennifer Connolly

Acquisitions Editor: Natasha Graf

Copy Editor: Esmeralda St. Clair

Acquisitions Coordinator: Holly Grimes

Technical Editor: Margaret Ball

Media Development Specialist: Kit Malone

Editorial Manager: Christine Beck

Media Development Manager: Laura VanWinkle

Editorial Assistant: Melissa Bennett, Elizabeth Rea

Cover Photos: © Ghislain & Marie David de Lossy/Getty Images/The Image Bank

Cartoons: Rich Tennant, www.the5thwave.com

Production

Project Coordinator: Nancee Reeves

Layout and Graphics: Seth Conley, Carrie Foster, Joyce Haughey, Mary Gillot Virgin

Proofreaders: John Greenough, Susan Moritz, Angel Perez, Brian Walls, TECHBOOKS Production Services

Indexer: TECHBOOKS Production Services

Special Help: Jennifer Bingham, Christina Guthrie, Greg Pearson, Chad Sievers

Singers on the CD: Rachel Anton, Margaret Ball, Suzanna Neeley Bridges, Jared T. Carey, Maria Couch, Natasha Graf, Robert Hunt, Eric Noone, Skie Ocasio, Jeffrey Sheets, Martha Sullivan, and Pam Phillips

Pianist and recording: Brian Suits

Publishing and Editorial for Consumer Dummies

Diane Graves Steele, Vice President and Publisher, Consumer Dummies

Joyce Pepple, Acquisitions Director, Consumer Dummies

Kristin A. Cocks, Product Development Director, Consumer Dummies

Michael Spring, Vice President and Publisher, Travel

Brice Gosnell, Publishing Director, Travel

Suzanne Jannetta, Editorial Director, Travel

Publishing for Technology Dummies

Andy Cummings, Vice President and Publisher, Dummies Technology/General User

Composition Services

Gerry Fahey, Vice President of Production Services

Debbie Stailey, Director of Composition Services

Contents at a Glance

Introduction *1*

Part 1: Exploring the Mechanics of Singing *7*
Chapter 1: So You Want To Sing 9
Chapter 2: Getting in the Right Frame of Spine 17
Chapter 3: Breathing for Singing 27
Chapter 4: Toning Up the Voice 43

Part 11: Discovering Your Singing Voice *57*
Chapter 5: Matching Voice Types: More Than Your Average Dating Service 59
Chapter 6: Acquiring Beautiful Tone 69
Chapter 7: Exploring Resonance 79
Chapter 8: Shaping Your Vowels for Clarity 87
Chapter 9: Exercising Consonants for Articulation 95

Part 111: Developing Your Technique *105*
Chapter 10: Developing a Practice Routine 107
Chapter 11: Discovering the Parts of Your Singing Voice 121
Chapter 12: Raising the Roof on Your Range 137
Chapter 13: Guys and Dolls: What's Unique about Your Voice 149
Chapter 14: Tuning Up Your Speaking Voice for Belting 159
Chapter 15: Finding the Right Voice Teacher for You 171
Chapter 16: Training for Singing 183

Part 1V: Singing in Performance *199*
Chapter 17: Selecting Your Music Material 201
Chapter 18: Mastering the Musical Elements 211
Chapter 19: Acting the Song 227
Chapter 20: Confronting Your Fear of Performing 239
Chapter 21: Auditioning a Song for Musical Theater 249

Part V: The Part of Tens *265*
Chapter 22: Ten Performers with Good Technique 267
Chapter 23: Ten FAQ about Singing 271
Chapter 24: Ten Tips to Maintaining Vocal Health 275
Chapter 25: Ten Tips for Performing Like a Pro 281

Part VI: Appendixes 289

Appendix A: Suggested Songs to Advance Your Singing Technique 291

Appendix B: About the CD 301

Index 307

Table of Contents

Introduction 1

  About This Book 1

  How to Use This Book and the CD to Improve Your Singing 2

  How This Book Is Organized 2

    Part I: Exploring the Mechanics of Singing 3

    Part II: Discovering Your Singing Voice 3

    Part III: Developing Your Technique 3

    Part IV: Singing in Performance 4

    Part V: The Part of Tens 4

    Part VI: Appendixes 5

  Icons Used in This Book 5

  Where to Go from Here 6

Part 1: Exploring the Mechanics of Singing 7

Chapter 1: So You Want To Sing 9

  I Love to Sing! What Singing Is Really All About 9

  What You Want to Know Right from the Beginning 10

    Correcting posture for a better sound 10

    Knowing the keys to proper breathing 10

    Locating the notes on the staff 10

    Finding your tone and resonance 12

  Developing Your Singing Voice 12

    Determining your voice type 12

    Fine-tuning vowels and consonants 13

    Warming up your voice — practice makes perfect 13

  Working the Different Parts of Your Voice 13

    Strengthening your middle, chest, and head voice —

      a complete vocal workout 14

    Working as guys and gals 14

  Applying Your Technique 14

    What to look for in a voice teacher 14

    Choosing appropriate singing material 15

    Feeling comfortable with the music and text 15

  Applying Technique to Performance 15

    Overcoming performance anxiety 15

    Auditioning for a singing role 16

Chapter 2: Getting in the Right Frame of Spine **17**

   Evaluating Your Posture 17

   Creating Correct Posture 18

      Moving into correct alignment 19

      Going to the wall 19

      Walking and maintaining posture 21

      Projecting confidence through posture 21

   Releasing Tension 22

      Melting into the floor 22

      Limbering up 23

      Shaking, rattling 'n' rolling 24

      Stretching like a rubber band 24

Chapter 3: Breathing for Singing **27**

   Breathing Basics 27

      Discovering your singing breath 28

      Posturing yourself for breathing 29

   Practicing Inhalation 33

      Panting like a pooch 33

      Dropping your breath into your body .34

      Sipping through a straw 34

      Singing "Happy Birthday" 35

   Practicing Exhalation 35

      Blowing out a candle 36

      Trilling for exhalation 36

      Moving air with consonants 38

      Raising your arms to feel rib expansion 38

   Advancing Your Breath Control 39

      Extending the breath: Singing slowly .39

      Opening your ribs 40

      Puffing like the magic dragon 41

Chapter 4: Toning Up the Voice **43**

   Defining Tone 43

   Flexing Your Singing Muscles 44

      Discovering your own bands 45

      Making the first sound 45

      Putting your larynx into position 46

   Matching Pitch Whether You're Tone Deaf or Not 47

      Sliding up and down on pitch 48

      Developing muscle memory 49

      Recording yourself and singing along .50

   Releasing Tension for Better Tone 50

      Checking for neck or jaw tension 51

      Dropping the jaw, not the chin 52

Watching for strain 53
Bouncing the tongue and jaw 53

Part II: Discovering Your Singing Voice 57

Chapter 5: Matching Voice Types: More Than Your Average Dating Service 59
Sifting through the Ingredients to Determine Your Voice Type 59
Identifying the Fab Four 61
Highest range of the dames: Soprano 61
How low can she go: Mezzo 62
Highest range of the dudes: Tenor 64
He's so low: Bass 65
Casting Call 66
Determining Your Voice Type 67

Chapter 6: Acquiring Beautiful Tone 69
Creating Tone 69
Starting the tone 70
Creating back space 71
Coordinating air with tone 71
Sighing your way to clarity 72
Releasing Tone 73
Inhaling to release tone 73
Letting your throat go 74
Sustaining Tone 74
Connecting the dots with legato 74
Trilling the lips or tongue 75
Ascending and descending with scales for length of tone 75
Finding Your Vibrato 76
Understanding vibrato 77
Moving from straight tone to vibrato 77
Imitating your favorite singer with vibrato 77

Chapter 7: Exploring Resonance 79
Good Vibrations 79
Exploring your resonators 80
Ringing it out 81
Eliminating Nasality 81
Getting the feel for soft palate work 81
Coordinating your soft palate and tongue 82
Moving air through the nose 83

Debunking Common Misconceptions 84
   Resonating tone in your sinuses 84
   Placing every tone in the same location 84
   Keeping your tongue completely flat 85
   Opening your mouth wide 85
   Don't worry about your soft palate 86
   The more forward the sound, the better 86
   Smiling to stay on pitch 86

Chapter 8: Shaping Your Vowels for Clarity **87**
  Getting Your Backside into Shape — Back Vowels, That Is 88
   Exploring the shape of back vowels 88
   Lipping around your back vowels 89
   Singing the back vowels 90
  Mastering the Front Vowels 90
   Exploring the shape of front vowels 91
   Speaking the front vowels 92
   Singing the front vowels 93

Chapter 9: Exercising Consonants for Articulation **95**
  Making Tip Consonants 96
   Shaping tip consonants 96
   Singing tip consonants 98
  Making Soft Palate Consonants 98
   Shaping soft palate consonants 99
   Singing soft palate consonants 99
  Working Lip Consonants 100
   Shaping lip consonants 100
   Singing lip consonants 101
  Working Combination Consonants 102
   Shaping combination consonants 102
   Singing combination consonants 103

Part III: Developing Your Technique............................105

Chapter 10: Developing a Practice Routine **107**
  Knuckling Down to a Practice Plan 108
  Getting Answers to Your Practicing Questions 109
   Where should I practice? 109
   What's the best time to practice? 109
   How long should I practice? 110
   What do I need besides my voice? 110
  Warming Up 111
   Stretching to warm up your body 112
   Warming up your voice 113

Exercising Your Voice 114
    Picking exercises that work for you 115
    Breaking it down 116
Practicing Correctly 117
    Charting your practice 117
    Taping yourself 117
    Applying information and exercises 119
    Using the CD to practice exercises 119

Chapter 11: Discovering the Parts of Your Singing Voice 121
Finding Your Middle Voice 122
    Noting your middle voice range 122
    Singing in middle voice 123
Checking Out Your Chest Voice 126
    Zeroing in on your chest voice range 126
    Feeling your chest voice 127
Aiming High with Head Voice 129
    Finding your head voice range 129
    Feeling head voice 130
Making a Smooth Transition 132
    Working around chest voice 132
    Working around head voice 134

Chapter 12: Raising the Roof on Your Range 137
Tactics for Tackling Register Transitions 138
Working on Your Range 138
    Taking your range higher 139
    Varying the dynamics throughout your range 140
    Mixing it up: Combining registers for a comfortable sound 141
Taking Your Agility to New Levels 143
    Moving along the scale 143
    Picking up the pace 144
    Skipping through the intervals 145
Improvising for a Better Pop Sound 146
    Mastering patterns in pop music 147
    Singing pop riffs with chords 148

Chapter 13: Guys and Dolls: What's Unique about Your Voice 149
Doing It for the Boys 149
    Singing through puberty 150
    Figuring out falsetto 150
    Frying tones 155
You Go Girl! 156
    Getting into the mix 156
    Singing wicked high notes 157
    Laughing up high 158

Chapter 14: Tuning Up Your Speaking Voice for Belting **159**

Playing around with Pitch 160
    Talking to yourself 160
    Chanting and speaking 161
    Rapping for pitch exploration 162
    Finding your optimum speaking pitch 162
    Using body energy to find clarity of tone 163
Defining Healthy Belting 164
    Knowing your limits as a beginner belter 166
    Noting the difference between the sexes 166
    Coordinating breath and energy 167
Preparing for Belting 167
    Being bratty to feel resonance 167
    Calling out to a friend 168
    Increasing your speaking range 168
    Trying out a belt 169

Chapter 15: Finding the Right Voice Teacher for You **171**

Yes! — A Voice Teacher Is Right for You 171
Searching for the Best Voice Teacher 172
    Finding a prospective voice teacher 172
    Identifying what you want 173
    Interviewing a prospective teacher 174
Knowing What to Expect from the Teacher 178
    Feeling good when you leave the lesson 178
    Working with imagery and other tools 179
    Applying tried-and-true singing methods 179
Knowing What to Expect from Yourself 180
    Developing your own practice process 180
    Avoiding overworking your flaws 180
    Performing in recitals 181
Making Your First Lesson a Success 181

Chapter 16: Training for Singing **183**

Defining Training Requirements 183
    Opting for opera 183
    Making your mark in musical theater 185
    Crooning as a country singer 185
    Performing pop and rock 187
    Jazzing it up 188
Training to Sing at Any Age 189
    Recognizing differences between young singers and teens 189
    Developing long-term technique in teenagers 190
    Understanding that voices change with age 191

Training with a Choir 192
    Enjoying the benefits of singing in the choir 192
    Singing in the choir versus going solo 194
    Picking the perfect fit 195

Part IV: Singing in Performance *199*

Chapter 17: Selecting Your Music Material 201

Choosing the Song 201
    Finding songs at your level 201
    Determining the appropriate key for you 205
    Selecting a suitable song style 206
    Singing to your strengths 207
Shopping for the Hard Copy 207
    Finding retail outlets 208
    Downloading sheet music 209
    Flipping through compilation books 209
    Checking out music at your local library 210

Chapter 18: Mastering the Musical Elements 211

Tackling a Song in Steps 211
    Memorizing the lyrics as text 212
    Tapping out the rhythm 213
    Singing out the melody (without the words) 216
    Putting words and music together 217
Reading Musical Notation 217
Using Vocal Technique in Your New Song 219
    Giving voice to vowels 220
    Backing into phrases 221
    Breathing heavy — fogging up the windows 222
    Changing the tone for each section 224

Chapter 19: Acting the Song 227

Seeing the Song as a Story 227
    Chatting it up before I sing 227
    Voicing the text 228
    Musical responses 229
    Accounting for interludes 229
Exploring Character 229
    Characterizing your character 230
    Discovering your character's motivation 231
    Planning actions to get something done 232
    Finding the character's tempo 232

Getting Physical 233
    Figuring out where to focus 233
    Hands up 234
    Gesturing appropriately 235
    Movin' and groovin' with my song 236

Chapter 20: Confronting Your Fear of Performing **239**

Facing the Symptoms 239
Alleviating Anxiety through Preparation 240
    Practicing well 241
    Playing to your strengths 242
    Managing your thoughts 242
    Getting up the nerve 243
    Building performance focus 243
Performing to Build Confidence 244
    Devising a game plan 245
    Evaluating your performance 247

Chapter 21: Auditioning a Song for Musical Theater **249**

Getting Some Tips on Musical Theater 249
    Strutting your stuff 249
    Doing your homework 250
Selecting Your Songs 251
    Adding variety to spice up your style 251
    Dramatizing your lyrics 252
    Avoiding the wrong song 253
Getting Yourself and Your Music Ready 254
    Adjusting the key if you need to 254
    Making a 16-bar cut 255
    Marking the music 256
    Preparing your book 256
    Taking your songs to an accompanist 258
    What do you wear? 259
What Goes On at an Audition? 259
    Who'll be there 260
    Working with the audition pianist 260
    Directing your focus 263

Part V: The Part of Tens *265*

Chapter 22: Ten Performers with Good Technique **267**

Eileen Farrell 267
Frederica von Stade 267

Luciano Pavarotti 268
Audra McDonald 268
Brian Stokes Mitchell 268
Karen Carpenter 269
Elvis Presley 269
Luther Vandross 269
LeAnn Rimes 269
Garth Brooks 270

Chapter 23: Ten FAQ about Singing **271**
Is belting bad? 271
Why doesn't my voice work sometimes? 271
What's the difference between a coach, voice teacher,
    and an accompanist? 272
If my voice is scratchy, do I have nodes? 272
Do I have to be fat to have a big voice? 272
What's the best singing method? 273
Do I have to speak Italian to sing well? 273
Can I have a few drinks before the
    performance to calm my nerves? 273
Why can't I eat ice cream before I sing? 273
What do I do if my voice is husky, breathy, strident, muffled,
    and hooty? 274

Chapter 24: Ten Tips to Maintaining Vocal Health **275**
Figuring Out Everyday Abuses 275
Incorporating Healthy Speech into Your Singing 276
Getting the Skinny on Weight 277
Keeping Yourself Hydrated 277
Getting Plenty of Shut-Eye.............................277
Making Sure You're Well-Nourished 278
Preventing a Sore Throat or Infection 278
Medicating a Sore Throat 279
Keeping Your Emotional Life in Check 280
Paying Your Voice Teacher 280

Chapter 25: Ten Tips for Performing Like a Pro **281**
Rehearsing to Beat the Band 281
Wearing the Right Duds 282
Finding Your Stance 282
Singing with a Piano, Organ, or Band 283
Making Your Entrance 284
Roping in Your Audience 284
Ignoring That Mosquito 284
Handling Those Hands 285
Using the Mic 286
Taking Your Bow 287

Part VI: Appendixes *289*

**Appendix A: Suggested Songs to Advance Your
Singing Technique** *291*
Classical: Ten songs for soprano 291
Classical: Ten songs for mezzo 292
Classical: Ten songs for tenor 292
Classical: Ten songs for baritone or bass 293
Musical theater: Ten songs for soprano 293
Musical theater: Ten songs for mezzo 294
Musical theater: Ten belt songs for women 295
Musical theater: Ten songs for tenor 295
Musical theater: Ten songs for baritone/tenor 296
Musical theater: Ten belt songs for men 297
Country: Ten songs for women 297
Country: Ten songs for men 298
Pop: Ten songs for women 298
Pop: Ten songs for men 299

Appendix B: About the CD *301*
Finding the "On the CD" Icon 301
Finding the tracks on the CD 302
Tracks on the CD 302
Troubleshooting 306

Index *307*

Introduction

I'm so happy that you chose this book! If you're a shower singer or secretly desire to sing on a stage, this book is for you. The book is full of helpful information covering all aspects of singing from posture and breathing to vocal health and increasing your range. Absolutely no experience is necessary! If you know zero about singing, you're going to have a great time exploring your singing voice.

About This Book

You can't develop your singing voice overnight; it takes time. Some people are born with a voice ready to sing at the Hollywood Bowl, but the rest of the people who like to sing have to work on their voice to prepare it for the first performance. Whichever category you fit into, this book has some valuable information for you. If you have singing experience, I've added some challenges to keep you on your toes and help you to improve your technique. For the beginners, however, I wrote every single page with you in mind.

Exercising the singing voice is the ticket to improving your technique. The exercises in the book are similar to what you may encounter in a voice lesson or a class about singing. You may think that exercises aren't productive to improving your sound in your favorite song. By working on exercises, you give your body a chance to figure out exactly how to make the sounds. After you get the technical details cooking, you can apply that information to your songs and sound even better.

Another misconception is that you can't get anything from a book to help you with singing. You may not have someone there listening to you as you practice, but you can find suggestions throughout the book on how to listen to your voice and critique it for yourself, so you improve every time you practice.

How to Use This Book and the CD to Improve Your Singing

This book is designed as a reference guide, not a tutorial, and includes many exercises to help you improve your singing. Flip through the book and look for parts that interest you. (For that matter, you can go through the parts that don't interest you, and who knows what you may discover about your singing voice!) What's important to remember is that you don't have to read this book from cover to cover to improve your singing; just look for the topics that you need and use the exercises as well as the CD to develop your best singing voice.

The CD is an important partner for your book. The CD's exercises work the technical info that you read about in the book. You hear a pattern played for you on the piano, a singer demonstrates the pattern for you, and then the pattern is repeated several times for you to sing along. Just singing songs is cool, but you want to work on technique to help your songs sound great. If you work on the articulation exercises on the CD and then apply that information and skill to songs, you can sing with great skill and be understood. If you've never had lessons before, you may not see the benefit of the exercises in the beginning, or they may seem difficult. Keep trying them during your practice sessions, and you can see how quickly the exercises can help you to sing.

You can check out Chapter 10 for some ideas on developing a practice routine to coordinate all the information that you read in the book with what you hear on the CD. After you plot out your practice routine, you want to keep the CD handy, so you can choose which tracks to practice. Storing the CD in the back of the book in the plastic cover is the safest place for it. You may want to put the CD in your car to sing along with as you drive to work. That's cool as long as you remember to pay attention to your driving.

Because many people respond quickly to imagery, I include ways to use imagery to help you improve your singing. Knowing the mechanics works well for some singers and others prefer just to know what to think about or visualize as they sing. For singers who prefer knowing what to listen for, I give you that information as well. One last way that the exercises are explained is by having you do something physical. Sometimes, just feeling the movement in your body gets the idea across. Whatever way you prefer to use, you'll find it in this book.

How This Book Is Organized

The book is organized into six parts with each part containing specific types of information about singing. You explore the mechanics of singing before working on your technique. For those of you who have no experience singing, you may find that the first part is especially helpful.

Part I: Exploring the Mechanics of Singing

The three huge singing topics — posture, breathing, and tone — are covered in Part I. You want these skills to be rock solid. If you have a grasp on these three important topics, you can increase your singing capability. You may find yourself coming back to these chapters often to solidify these skills. Take your time as you work through these first four chapters. You may want to add the exercises you find in this part to your practice chart. By working on these skills everyday, you can see steady improvement.

Part II: Discovering Your Singing Voice

The main topics in Part II are tone, resonance, vowels, consonants, and voice types. If you have always wanted to know the difference between a soprano and a mezzo, Chapter 5 is waiting for you. You can even find more information than you need just so you can keep up with the conversations with your singer friends. Tone is a big topic, too, so Chapter 6 offers you even more information to get you sounding really good when you sing. After you figure out what tone really is all about, you can find out about the resonance of your tone in Chapter 7. If you aren't sure what resonance is all about, you can read all about the misconceptions of resonance in Chapter 7. Chapters 8 and 9 get your vowels and consonants moving and grooving, too. By articulating the vowels and consonants correctly, your audience can easily understand you no matter what style of music you sing.

Part III: Developing Your Technique

In this part, you can move on to information that'll help you to apply singing technique. Chapter 10 is all about practicing and developing a routine to improve your singing voice and apply all the information in the book. Chapter 11 takes on the registers of the voice: middle voice, chest voice, head voice, and Chapter 12 discusses range. You may have heard people talking about the chest voice but may not be quite sure what that means. Head to Part III, and you can find out more than you ever dreamed about the registers of the voice.

In Chapter 13, I separate the boys from the girls. Not because you can't get along and sing together, but because some things are unique about each gender. Even though some of the exercises in this chapter are designed for one gender or the other, everyone can sing along to any exercise. Just look at the information in the chapter to help you sing along.

Chapter 14 helps you with your speaking voice and belting. Though you may think that your speaking voice and singing voice are entirely different, you may be surprised how much your speaking voice can help or hinder your singing.

This part also provides some solid suggestions for finding the right voice teacher. And you can also find out more about the various musical styles — country, classical, musical theater, and jazz.

Part IV: Singing in Performance

After you have your technique working well, you may want to test it out in public. Before you walk onto the stage, check out this section for some great advice on how to prepare before the big debut. Chapter 17 helps you figure out how to choose songs that enhance your technical skills and where to find those lovely tunes. After you find the tune, you want to explore Chapter 18 for help with that new song. Trying to figure out the song alone may seem over-whelming, but Chapter 18 has some helpful hints to make the task manageable.

That new song needs some spice both from the music and the words. Just looking gorgeous on the stage isn't enough. You want to give the audience something to think about as you sing. Chapter 19 explores acting the song while singing; two skills that are important to use together. If you aren't sure you're ready to get out on the stage because of butterflies in your stomach, check out Chapter 20 on performance anxiety. Being nervous is okay, but you can explore ways to help you with the anxiety so your sweaty palms don't bother you as you sing beautifully. If you think your butterflies are a sign that you're excited, Chapter 21 gives you some sound advice on taking the song to a musical theater audition. Many people dream of auditioning for a show but have no idea how to prepare. The answers to your questions and preparation advice are waiting for you in Chapter 21.

Part V: The Part of Tens

If you listen to the top ten songs in your favorite category of music, do you know which singers have good technique? Because the industry tends to be about making big bucks over talent, find out which singers really have good technique to back up their fame. You may see some surprises on the list. Handling yourself on stage takes some practice if you've never been in the spotlight. In this part, you can find ten singers who use wonderful technique.

You may also have some questions about singing that you just didn't know whom to ask, so I also made a list of the ten most frequently asked questions that my students bring in to their lessons. You may find the answer to that question that's been nagging you.

Part VI: Appendixes

Appendix A has a really cool list of songs for you to explore when you're ready. The songs include classical, musical theater, pop, and country. No matter what style of songs you like, you can find some on the list to try out your new skills as you work through the chapters of the book. The songs are all chosen because of the benefits the song provides for your technique. You may not find the top hits of today on the list, but you can find some songs that are great for working on singing technique no matter what the style.

Appendix B has a chart to coordinate the information on the CD tracks. You can use the chart in Appendix B to help you locate the skills you want to practice today. By working slowly through the exercises on the tracks, you give your body time to figure out how to correctly sing the exercises and apply that information to the songs in Appendix A.

Icons Used in This Book

When you see this icon, you find information specifically for the male voice. The male voice is a bit different than the female voice, and you want to know how to handle your voice like a man. You're welcome to sing along, and the information following this icon tells you all you need to know.

Along with this icon, you find information strictly for the female voice. Your voice needs your undivided attention in certain areas and this icon helps you sort through those tougher places to make great sounds.

This icon tells you that a track on the CD corresponds to the information in the chapter.

This information is so helpful that you should store it in your memory bank.

This icon highlights detailed explanations that you may find really interesting or you may just want to skip right over.

The Tip icon emphasizes good advice from someone who has already made the mistake and wants to save you the trouble.

To avoid making a blunder or injuring your voice, pay attention to what these paragraphs have to say.

Where to Go from Here

If you have zero singing experience, you may want to start with Chapter 1 and work your way through the chapters in order. However, this book is designed in such a way as to allow you to jump in anywhere you want and start swimming through information that's completely understandable. For those of you who have some experience with singing, go ahead and choose whatever chapter appeals to you. You may have to refer to other chapters occasionally if you missed a definition, but otherwise, you're free to roam the chapters at your own pace and in any order.

As you work through the exercises in this book, you want to have the basic technical skills of breathing (see Chapter 3) and tone (see Chapters 4 and 6) readily available. If you find yourself struggling, perhaps you'll want to go straight to Chapter 2 to make sure you have proper singing posture. You can also check out the cheat sheet at the beginning of the book for a quick reference as you practice, too.

Part I
Exploring the Mechanics of Singing

The 5th Wave   By Rich Tennant

Okay, this time try not to take such a deep breath.

In this part . . .

In this part, you can check out interesting info about posture, breath, and tone. These three areas are the biggies. You want great posture to get your body lined up and ready to sing at your best, and you need some air moving in and out of your body to keep the glorious sounds coming out. Working on tone allows you to improve on the glorious tones that you're already making or to tweak your tone just a little if your engine knocks rather than hums.

Take your time as you read through these chapters. You may even want to come back to the exercises on a regular basis just to maintain a smooth running vocal engine.

Chapter 1

So You Want To Sing . . .

In This Chapter

▶ Examining the contents of this book

▶ Exploring what you need to know and when

▶ Finding out how to use the materials in the chapters

So you're curious about singing. Congratulations on being brave enough to pick up this book and improve your singing skills. Whatever musical background and experience you have or don't have, this book has something to offer you. The book contains great exercises and even a CD that allows you to hear the exercise and sing along. If you're a beginner, welcome aboard. You can find out all kinds of cool info about singing in this book. This chapter provides an overview of all the great stuff that you can encounter in the book.

I Love to Sing! What Singing Is Really All About

Singing is one of the coolest means of expression out there. If you stop and think about it too long, singing may not make much sense, but it really feels good. Singing well is about knowing how to work the parts that create the sound for singing. The chapters that you encounter in the book outline what you need to know in just the right sequence. You don't have to read them in the order written to get what you need. Some of the later chapters may be a little difficult if you don't have any singing experience. The only way to know is to jump right in and start reading on whatever topic interests you.

What You Want to Know Right from the Beginning

Before you choose the date for your first big concert or recital, you want to find out about singing before you step out onto the stage. The first part of this book provides you with the big picture. First, you want to get yourself aligned — that is, line up all your body parts to get ready to sing and then explore your breathing. Breathing while singing isn't that much different from how you breathe normally, but you have to take in more air and use more air. When you get the air flowing, you can explore the tone of your voice.

Correcting posture for a better sound

Posture is important to sing well. If all the parts for singing are lined up correctly, you stand a really good chance of getting wonderful sounds to come flying out of your body. Knowing how to stand isn't rocket science, but it may take a little adjustment on your part. If you aren't used to standing tall all the time, you may feel a bit awkward at first. Chapter 2 explores posture for singing.

Knowing the keys to proper breathing

The big key to great singing is knowing how to use your breath to make the sounds. You may not know how to get much breath in your body and then make it last throughout a long phrase. If you check out Chapter 3, you can find all kinds of exercises and explanations of how to work on your breath, so you can sing those long phrases in your favorite song.

Locating the notes on the staff

Voice types are probably easier to figure out if you know where to find the notes on a musical staff. (See Figure 1-1 in this chapter.) The treble clef spaces correspond with the notes F, A, C, and E. Beginning on the bottom of the staff and going up, it spells *face*. You can use sentences to remember the other notes. Again, starting on the bottom line and moving up, the notes on the lines of the staff are E, G, B, D, and F, letters that begin the words of the sentence, *Every good boy does fine.* For the bass clef, the spaces are A, C, E, and G, the letters that begin the words *All cows eat grass* or *All cars eat gas.* The lines in the bass clef are G, B, D, F, and A, which correspond with *Good boys do fine always.* If you prefer animals, then use *Great big dogs fight animals.*

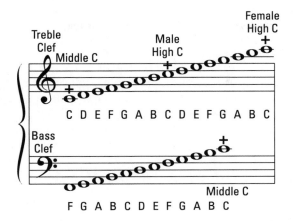

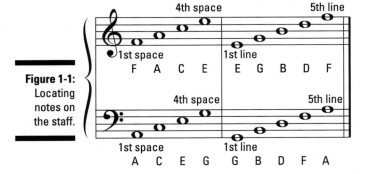

Figure 1-1:
Locating
notes on
the staff.

If I say that a singer's range is Middle C to high C, I have to use ledger lines to notate those two notes, because they're not within the five-line staff. Ledger lines are extra lines added above or below the staff for those notes that are higher or lower than the notes on the staff. When you find Middle C in Figure 1-1, you can see the extra line added below the staff. The easiest way to find Middle C on the piano is to look at the brand name printed on the lid covering the keys. If you find that brand name, the C right in the middle of that name or just to the left, is usually Middle C.

Middle C is called *Middle C,* because it's in the middle of the keyboard that contains 88 keys. Middle C is also called C4, because it's the fourth C on the keyboard. The names of the notes are A, B, C, D, E, F, and G. Those notes repeat over and over on the piano. If Middle C is C4, then the next C above is C5 and so on. C is the note just to the left of the pair of black keys. The distance between the two Cs is called an *octave*. If you start counting at the first *C* and count eight white notes up, you find another C. That means the E just above Middle C (C4) is E4. Easy enough but not every person you encounter knows this system, so I stick to what works: Middle C.

You also encounter the words *flat* and *sharp* in this book. *Flats* lower a pitch one-half step and a *sharp* raises the pitch one-half step. F-sharp is the black key on the piano between F and G. The same black key between F and G can be called G-flat.

Finding your tone and resonance

Vocal tone is important, because you want the best sounds to come out of your mouth. By exploring exercises on tone, you can make changes to your sound. People often tell me that they want to change the way that they sound. To change your sound, you need to know how you create sound. The two chapters on tone, Chapters 4 and 6, give you quite a bit of information about how to start a note and then what to do to make the note sound a specific way.

Developing Your Singing Voice

After you have the basic information swimming around in your head, you can start to work on your singing voice. Chapters 5 through 9 offer you more specific information about how to create a sound that's unique to you. Sometimes, singers try to imitate their favorite famous singer. What you want to do is sound like yourself. Your voice can be just as fabulous as that famous singer. You just have to practice to develop it.

Determining your voice type

Most singers want a category to belong to. You may have heard of the categories of singers — soprano, mezzo, tenor, and bass. If you aren't sure which one applies to your voice, explore Chapter 5. You can find explanations of what makes a soprano different than a mezzo or a tenor and a bass. You don't have to figure out your voice type today, but you can explore the chapter so you know what to listen for as you sing.

Fine-tuning vowels and consonants

A long time ago in grade school, you had to work with vowels and consonants. Well, you can refresh yourself in Chapters 8 and 9! By making your vowels and consonants specific, you can make yourself easily understood when you're singing. You've probably heard someone sing but couldn't understand a word they said. It's even worse when the song is in English or a language that you speak. By knowing how to articulate vowels and consonants, you can create specific sounds that your audience can follow.

Warming up your voice — practice makes perfect

After you discover all this great information about singing, you need to make a plan of practicing it on a regular basis. If practicing seems like a foreign concept to you, check out Chapter 10. The whole chapter is devoted to helping you figure out what to do when you warm up and how to apply the exercises that you read about in the book to your daily practice routine. Because you can explore so much, make a list of what you want to accomplish today and then add more to that list each time that you practice.

Working the Different Parts of Your Voice

Your goal is to make your singing voice sound like one smooth line from top to bottom. Your voice may have a few bumps and wiggles as you work your way up and down. That's perfectly normal, but help is right at hand. Chapters 11 through 13 work with specific areas of the voice called *registers* — chest voice, head voice, middle voice, and falsetto. In these chapters, you can discover what each part of the voice feels like and what to do with it.

Strengthening your middle, chest, and head voice — a complete vocal workout

The first step in the workout for the voice is to find the different registers of the voice and then notice what each feels like. After you find them, you want to try and smooth out the transition between the registers. You may find that your chest voice and head voice feel miles apart. The exercises in Chapters 11 and 12 are designed to help you smooth out the bumps. You may not think the exercises are easy in the beginning, which is good. I don't want you to be bored. Even if you've never explored any vocal sounds, you can figure out these exercises and get your voice in good working order, which just takes some time and patience.

Working as guys and gals

The exercises in this book are for both male and female voices. In Chapter 13, you can find some exercises that help either gender and that are unique about your voice. Guys have a register called *falsetto* but the girls don't. Don't feel bad ladies, you can still sing along with the exercises that are for the male voice. I give you plenty of ideas for working the exercises.

Applying Your Technique

After you explore your technique through the exercises that I provide, you need to take the next step. Chapters 15 through 19 are about applying your technique. At some point, you want to apply that healthy technique to songs. You also want to maintain your healthy technique and a healthy voice at all times.

What to look for in a voice teacher

Finding a voice teacher can be tricky. After you find the teacher, the experience can be rewarding. If you aren't sure how to go about finding a teacher, explore the tips and suggestions in Chapter 15. Finding the teacher may be the most difficult part. After you answer the questions in Chapter 15, you have a better idea of what you want from voice lessons.

Choosing appropriate singing material

Finding new songs to sing can be overwhelming. You have so many choices, but how do you know what works for you? The clues are in Chapter 17. The lists there offer you suggestions of what to look for and what to avoid when choosing songs. Whether you want a song to sing for your own pleasure or a song for a specific function, you want a song that accentuates your strengths. After exploring the technique chapters earlier in the book, make a list of what your voice does well. For more suggestions of songs, you can explore Appendix A for a list of suggested songs for enhancing your singing technique. The songs cover different styles of music from classical to country.

Feeling comfortable with the music and text

After you choose the song, you need to know how to decipher and digest what you see on the page. Listening to a recording can be deceiving, because the artist may not be singing what's on the page. Look at the page and feel confident that you can conquer the melody, rhythm, and the text. Don't worry if you can't read music. You don't have to. You can explore the steps in Chapter 18 to get you singing the song in a shorter amount of time. You can take this skill a step further in Chapter 19 and explore acting to combine with your singing. Sounding good when you sing is great, but you want to sound good and understand the story behind the music. You don't have to know anything about acting to explore this chapter. It's all right there for you.

Applying Technique to Performance

After your technique is really cooking, you can explore Chapters 20 and 21 about taking your technique into a performance situation. Performances can be big or small. Whatever the size of the audience, you want to look like a pro and feel good about what you're doing onstage.

Overcoming performance anxiety

If your daydreams of singing are clouded with anxiety about singing in front of an audience, Chapter 20 is just for you. By confronting your fear and taking charge, you can make progress and let go of the anxiety. You only add pressure to your performance if you assume that you're supposed to be totally calm. Many famous performers get nervous before a performance. After exploring Chapter 20, you know that it's fine to be nervous, but you can still sing while nervous.

Auditioning for a singing role

So many singers dream of auditioning for a Broadway show that I wrote a whole chapter about it. Chapter 21 has information for you about what to expect at the audition, who may be there, what you may have to sing or do, and how to prepare for the audition. Because an audition for a musical is different than an audition for an opera, you want to know what's kosher and what's not.

Chapter 2

Getting in the Right Frame of Spine

In This Chapter

▶ Checking out your carriage and bearing

▶ Striking the right stance to help you sing

▶ Lengthening, limbering, and getting ready to sing

*T*o sing efficiently, you need to line up all your body parts that are involved and get them ready to do their job with as little tension as possible. If you're all slumped over, you have more trouble taking the breath that you need to sing because posture and tension directly affect the muscles. Tension in your body also prevents you from taking a deep breath and makes singing more difficult. In this chapter, you discover how to create correct, tension-free posture so that you can project confidence and sing your best.

Evaluating Your Posture

In front of a full-length mirror, look at your posture. Notice the way that you hold your body, especially your head, chest, hips, knees, arms, and hands. More than likely, after you looked in the mirror, you changed your posture. Did you change your posture because you thought that your body may *work* better or because you thought you may *look* better? For singing, you should evaluate your posture for both reasons. Aligning your body properly puts all the muscles that help you to sing in the right position. This helps you to sing better, and proper alignment makes you appear confident and professional.

Look at Figure 2-1 and see which posture looks best for singing. You probably prefer the illustration of erect posture — correct alignment — and not the slumped over figure. Notice the alignment of the body in the diagram with correct posture. The spine is a steady line from the top to the bottom. The shoulders are down and back, and the head is centered over the shoulders. This kind of posture is ideal for singing, because it not only gives the visual impression of confidence, even if you aren't confident on the inside, but it also improves the way you sing.

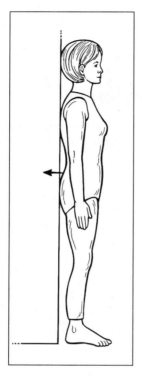 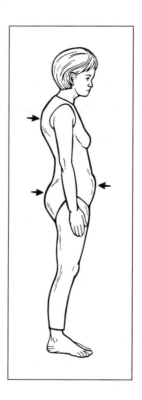

Figure 2-1:
Right and
wrong
posture.

Creating Correct Posture

Creating correct posture means finding out what correct posture looks like and feels like, so you can quickly make whatever changes you need. By changing your posture, you can control what kind of impression you make on others — whether you're on the stage singing or at the audition vying for the show's lead. Good posture keeps energy flowing so that your energy isn't trapped in one body part and aligns your body for correct breathing. See more information about breathing for singing in Chapter 3.

Nervous ticks, such as constantly wiggling your fingers, frequent shifting of weight from one foot to the other, and roaming eyes, are examples of energy that isn't freely flowing throughout the body. If you catch yourself twisting your hands or wiggling your fingers frequently while singing, watch yourself in the mirror to become aware of the movement. Then allow yourself to move around as you sing to use that excess energy. After you move around, stand still but maintain that same freedom in your body as if you may move at any moment. Freely flowing energy keeps you looking confident and singing well.

Using your acting skills also gives your body something specific to do and the random wiggles and twitches often subside. Acting and singing is what Chapter 19 is all about.

Moving into correct alignment

To see what changes you need to make to properly align your body, stand in front of the mirror, so that you can view your body. You don't have to sport your birthday suit but put on something, so you can see the outline of your posture.

The first step for finding correct alignment is lengthening the back of your neck. Lengthening your neck keeps your head centered over your shoulders, so the singing muscles in your neck are placed in their proper alignment. To lengthen your neck

1. **Put your head in its normal position.**

2. **Put your hand on the back of your neck.**

3. **Move your neck back toward the palm of your hand or lie on the floor and feel your neck expand into the floor.**

   Notice how this length also enables you to keep your chin level with the floor when your mouth is closed. This posture may feel odd at first, but it helps you make your best sounds.

Going to the wall

Practice singing against the wall to find the correct alignment of your body; notice the position of your head especially when you sing. Stand with your back to the wall. Put your bum, shoulders, and the back of your head against the wall. If you have rounded shoulders, don't worry about putting the top of your shoulder against the wall. You also don't have to smash in the small of your back unless you need to explore the alignment of your spine. Your feet can be several inches away from the wall to make a nice comfy "chair" against the wall. In this position, practice your breathing for a few moments to feel the movement in your body. When you find your alignment against the wall, sing part of a song. Next, move away from the wall and compare your posture and breathing. Going to the wall is also helpful if your head bobs around as you're singing. Being against the wall helps you feel any extra movement of your head and allows you to rest your head against something solid to keep it steady. Try to feel the energy flowing throughout your entire body and not just trapped in your neck.

Now that you lengthened your neck, your head is in the correct position — centered over your shoulders. Finding the correct position for your chest is the next step for exploring correct posture.

Chest

Having a wide chest and open ribs allows you to breathe fully and positions your chest properly for singing. However, lifting your chest too high can create tension in your neck exactly where it affects singing, and collapsing the chest puts your head out of alignment and prevents you from fully expanding your body for breath. In order to open your chest for breathing:

1. **Hang your arms by your side with your hands released.**
2. **Move your shoulders back but down and released.**

   If you aren't sure about the placement of your shoulders, roll them forward and back until you find the center. Lift the shoulders too high and then drop them down. Press them down and then release them to find the center resting position.

After you find the correct position for your chest — expanded wide — you need to find the center for your hips.

Hips

Keeping your hips centered aligns your back, so you can breathe easier. Where your hips should be may seem obvious, but some people get a little carried away and push out their derrière or tuck their hips too far under to straighten their back. Doing so creates tension in your back in the exact place that you need to release and expand for breath. To find the center of your hips, rock your hips (pelvis) too far forward and then rock back to the center. Rock your hips too far behind you and keep rocking until you find the center.

Knees

After you find the center for your hips, don't forget to unlock your knees. You need to keep your knees loose so that your lower back can expand when you breathe. When you lock your knees, your knees are pushed backward as far as they can go, and your lower back also locks, which prevents your lower back from expanding when you breathe. So unlock your knees — not bent so much that you're squatting — but keep your knees just loose enough to wiggle. Choir directors suggest unlocking your knees, so you don't faint and fall off the risers.

Feet

At the root of good posture is the position of your feet. By placing your feet no wider than your shoulders with one foot slightly in front of the other, you can evenly distribute your weight. Balancing your weight on the balls (middle) of your feet rather than on your heels gives you a sense of forward motion and helps keep your knees unlocked.

Keep in mind that I'm nagging you about posture so that you become physically aware of your body. In some of the exercises that come up later in the book, you must find your alignment, open your body for breath, drop your jaw, find the correct shape for the vowel, move the breath to begin the tone, and look like you're having a great time. That's plenty to think about. Take some time now to really understand how your body moves and recognize tension, so you won't be so frustrated later when I ask you to do ten things at one time!

Walking and maintaining posture

Maintaining your posture while you walk actually makes a big difference. You may actually have to sing while walking around the stage. Choirs sing as they process, and backup singers groove to the music as they dance. What if you have to cross the stage? You want to look glorious for the entire time that you're onstage and not just when you land in place next to the piano. To maintain your posture while walking, look out as you walk. By looking out, you can still see where you're going without looking at the ground. By walking this way, you can maintain that correct posture that you found in the "Moving into correct alignment" section, earlier in this chapter.

Projecting confidence through posture

Projecting confidence onstage is important, because you want to feel good about your performance, and you want the audience to be comfortable watching you perform. Audiences are usually apprehensive about performers who project fear and not confidence. Luckily, that's not a crime, or I would've been shot by a firing squad as a young singer. Projecting confidence is about finding your correct posture and maintaining that throughout a performance. If you maintain that posture and a calm expression even when you forget the words, many people probably won't even notice. I have seen it many times; the performer is onstage making up the words but just looks terrific as if he intended to sing those words. By maintaining poise and posture, the performer projects to the audience that everything is fine and not to worry, as if to say, "I'll get back to the original words in a moment." The performer also walks away feeling good, because he stuck to a basic singing rule: Good posture enhances good singing.

Singing for others offers you an opportunity to be the temporary center of attention. Many of you are comfortable with that attention and positively crave it. For those of you that don't crave that attention, decide to accept it. Your singing may bring great joy to your loved ones and yourself. Why deprive yourself of that joy? Each day, work on your posture and body language to project confidence, and eventually, you'll recognize it as a normal part of who you are.

To explore how correct posture exudes confidence, pretend that you're a king or queen and notice your posture. Strut like you own the place. Now, pretend that you're really sick and ache all over your body. Wouldn't a king carry himself differently than someone who is ill? It's possible that a king could be ill but not in this scenario. He would walk tall, carry himself with great dignity and grace, and glide around the room. The sickly person would barely stand much less project confidence. In this scenario, which one are you? Are you the king with a dignified posture or are you stooped and closed off from the world? You're probably somewhere in the middle between the king and the sickly one. Strive to be the king or queen when you sing.

As you continue to evaluate your own posture, notice the posture of others. Observe their movements to better understand what you need to do to change your own alignment.

Releasing Tension

Releasing tension in your neck allows for a more open sound and releasing tension in your back makes breathing easier. You may notice that I don't ask you to relax. If you relax, you may fall limply on the couch to watch your favorite sitcom. *Releasing* means to keep your body in a state of readiness: ready to move, breathe, and crawl out of your comfort zone and sing for the world. Think of body movement as fluid motion even when you're still.

Melting into the floor

I highly recommend that you go through the numbered sequence in this section for releasing tension. You can feel each body part without worrying about holding yourself up and take your time working through each part. This exercise that follows walks you through the entire body very methodically.

To do this exercise, lie on the bed or the floor and find a comfortable resting position. Don't go to sleep on me! If lying down makes you drowsy, do the exercise standing up. Working from the bottom to the top, you can release the tension in your muscles and joints. Follow the directions given in the numbered list that follows or just work your way up from your toes feeling length and movement in each joint of your body. Imagine each muscle growing loose and longer and creating space and width in the joints. Allow your body to melt into the floor and widen. Please continue to breathe deeply as you work your way through your body.

1. Let your toes and ankles feel heavy. Wiggle them to release any leftover tension. Feel the distance between your foot and ankle. Imagine the joint growing longer.

2. Work your way up to your knees and let them melt into the floor (or bed if you chose something soft). Feel them loose and ready to move.

3. Keep going up to your hips and feel your legs and upper body moving away from each other. Allow your hip joint to grow longer.

4. Notice your lower back. Sometimes, the lower back holds tension when standing. Let that tension melt away and feel each vertebra lengthen and grow taller.

5. Feel your shoulders loosen; wiggle them to release any tension. Melt your shoulder blades into the floor to release their grip on your lower back.

6. Feel the openness of your chest. Notice the width and height of your chest as your ribs open during breathing.

7. Notice your head position that you worked earlier to find the length in the back of your neck. Allow your neck to grow longer and move your head taller on your body.

8. Before you get up, notice all other body parts and let the tension float away. Pretend that you're bread, and the kneading machine is working its way over your body.

9. When you're ready, stand up.

One common area that generates tension is the forehead. Having a flexible face as you sing is best. By preventing facial tension, you can keep the muscles inside the mouth freely moving. You can find more information about the muscles in the mouth, such as the soft palate, in Chapter 7. If you notice your forehead wrinkling as you sing, put a piece of clear tape vertically on your forehead between your eyebrows. You can feel the tape move when you tighten up your forehead. It's normal for your eyebrows to move as you sing or speak, but keeping your forehead free of tension is the goal.

Limbering up

Lying down and releasing tension feels great, but you can't stay on the floor. It's time now to find that same free flow of energy and release of tension when you're standing up, too. Because of gravity pulling you toward the floor or bed, you may have felt a release of tension from the exercise that you did in "Melting into the floor" section, earlier in this chapter. You can find that same feeling of release while you stand.

1. Pretend that you're a rag doll or Pinocchio the marionette. Rag dolls wouldn't have any tension in their body. They can move in any direction and are quite limber.

2. Drop over from the waist and take a few deep breaths. As you breathe, notice the flow of energy in your body. Remember that feeling of fluid motion from lying on the floor. Keep your knees bent to take the pressure off your back. You can also rest your elbows on your knees for support until you feel more comfortable dropping over farther.

3. Release any leftover tension and slowly roll back up. As you stand back up, imagine stacking each vertebra on top of the other, so you can feel lift and height in your body.

4. If you were a marionette, you'd have strings attached to your head and body. Feel that string attached to the crown of your head and grow taller without even moving until you're standing back up with correct posture.

Shaking, rattling 'n' rolling

For releasing tension, this exercise is the quickie. On those days that you don't have 20 minutes to go through the motions of lying on the floor, just shake it out. When I say shake it out, you may get confused and think I mean dancing the night away as you do at a disco. Nah, I mean wiggle, squirm, jiggle, shake, or any other verb that means to move your bod around and let out the starch. If you're dignified during your business day, I recommend rolling around in your sweats to let go of that stuffed-shirt feeling.

Stretching like a rubber band

If you still can't find that sensation of releasing tension in your body, try this exercise. Imagining moving like a rubber band gives you something to visualize as you stretch.

1. **Pretend that you're made of rubber.**

   This exercise isn't so that you can stretch yourself in a million directions but to allow you to feel fluid motion in your body. If you were made of rubber, your body could stretch upward and relieve any pressure on your joints.

2. **Try to feel that sensation of moving upward.**

   You don't have to lift up on your tiptoes but just imagine your body growing taller.

3. **Now tighten up your body to feel the opposite of rubber.**

   Ouch. That's different, isn't it?

4. **Feel the rubbery motion of your arms stretching a little longer in their socket as you open your arms to the side.**

5. **Notice that your back feels spongy instead of locked and straining to hold you up.**

6. **Pretend that you have a long, rubber neck.**

   Let it lift up from your shoulders while still supporting your head. Visualize your head being filled with helium and let it float.

Whichever exercise you choose, the goal is to feel fluid motion in your body as you maintain correct alignment for singing. By releasing the tension, you may be more aware of how each part of your body is energized yet still.

Chapter 3

Breathing for Singing

- -

In This Chapter

▶ Getting down to the brass tacks of breath control

▶ Inhalation and expansion of your body

▶ Exhalation and extending the breath

▶ Discovering how your body moves while breathing

- -

*H*ow you manage your breath when you sing can drastically change the sound of your singing voice. If you try to hold your breath and sing, it just won't work. You also can't sing a loud phrase without using some air. Exhaling is what I mean. Most people think of exhaling being about air and not sound. When you sing, exhaling is about both happening at the same time. Without using a consistent flow of air, you have to squeeze in your throat, which creates a tighter sound, or use air to make a louder, more open sound. Although breathing is natural — you don't even have to think about it — when you sing, you need to train your body to breathe in a certain way so that you breathe efficiently throughout an entire song. You don't want to run out of breath in the middle of a word. The exercises in this chapter can help you master breath control, so you can sing through all those long phrases in your favorite songs with ease. You'll be so windy that you'll blow out those birthday candles no matter how large the flame is on the cake.

Try not to push yourself too quickly when you're working on breath. Work slowly for a week or two. Get the movements described in this chapter to become a natural habit.

Breathing Basics

When you breathe normally, you automatically make a shallow inhalation and an even exhalation followed by a pause before it all starts again — you don't even need to think about it. On the other hand, when you sing, you not only need to inhale quickly and exhale slowly as you sing the phrases of a song, but you also need to maintain proper posture. (See Chapter 2 for more information on posture.) Breathing in this manner provides you with the breath control that you need to sing efficiently. However, because controlled breathing doesn't come naturally to you, you need to train your body to breathe for singing. Keep reading to walk through the breathing basics.

Discovering your singing breath

The easiest way to find out how you should breathe for singing is simply by feeling it. Being able to visualize and feel the proper way to breathe helps make the process more natural for you, too.

Inhalation refers to air moving into your body — breathing in. *Exhalation* is when you exhale or blow out the air. You exhale when you speak or sing.

Inhaling to sing

Singing songs requires getting a full breath quickly — a quick inhalation — because the orchestra can't wait five minutes for you to find the air. So knowing how your body feels when you inhale helps you to get air in your body quickly to sing the next phrase. Use the following exercise to explore your own inhalation. Get a feel for how your body should move when you inhale and exhale.

1. Pretend that air is really heavy as you inhale. Visualize it weighing 50 pounds and let it fall low into your body.

2. Let it fall lower than your belly button. Explore this sensation.

3. Then let the breath fall in faster. Still visualize it being heavy but let it fall quickly into your body.

4. You can also fill your lungs as if you were going to blow up a balloon. You will feel your abdomen and lower back expand.

This sensation of quickly filling your lungs with air is how you properly inhale for singing.

Yawning happens all the time when working on breath control. The body gets confused with the different amount of air coming in, and you yawn. My students yawn plenty during lessons and are embarrassed at first. I have to tell them it's okay to yawn when we're working on breath.

Exhaling to sing

Singing means that you have to control your exhalation. You want to have a sustained and smooth exhalation. This control helps you to sing those demanding high notes and long slow phrases.

Breathing like a bellows

Attached to your ribs, your lungs are made of pliable tissue — not muscle. When you inhale, the muscles in between the ribs *(intercostals)* move the ribs up and out as the lungs expand downward. When the intercostal muscles relax back inward, the lungs move back to their normal resting position. Another muscle that helps you to breathe is your *diaphragm* — a dome-shaped muscle located underneath your lungs and attached to the ribs and the spine. When you inhale, the diaphragm flexes downward and moves back upward as you exhale. If the diaphragm flexes downward as you inhale,

the organs below your diaphragm have to move out of the way. The organs move down and out, which is why your abdomen moves out as you inhale. As you exhale, the organs gradually move back to their normal resting position.

This is where the importance of good posture and breathing for singing connect. If you stand in a slouch or a rigid military-like position, your diaphragm locks, and it can't descend when you need to inhale. This prevents your lungs from getting the full breath that they need for you to sing.

To explore exhalation, blow a feather around the room. If you have a spotless house, you'll have to use an imaginary feather.

1. Try to blow the feather really high up in the air and use a long stream of breath to get it up.

2. Try not to collapse your chest as you blow the feather.

3. While chasing the feather with your breath, notice what moves in your body as you exhale. You should feel that your abdomen has slowly returned to normal and that your chest has stayed in the same position the whole time.

4. At the end of the exhalation, you should feel the need to immediately inhale again.

Posturing yourself for breathing

Breathing efficiently when you sing is a combination of great posture (see Chapter 2) and skillful inhaling and exhaling. (See the sections "Practicing Inhalation" and "Practicing Exhalation," later in this chapter.) Remember the importance of good posture; it allows you to get a deep, full breath. If you slouch or you're too rigid, your diaphragm locks and prevents you from getting a correct breath for singing. (See the "Breathing like a bellows" sidebar in this chapter.) If your breathing and your posture work together as a team, you can improve your singing.

Are you an innie or an outie?

I'm talking about breathing, not belly buttons. Breathing can be confusing for a singer who's just starting out, because you have to pay attention to so many things at one time. Also, different people who know something about singing may tell you something about yet another breathing method that you should use for singing. You may have a friend who says that his teacher asks him to leave his abdominal muscles out and distended as he exhales, and another friend may tell you that the abdominal muscles must move in when you exhale. Who do you believe? Both of them. Being an innie or an outie can refer to how you breathe as well as your belly button. Either method can work if you understand how breath works in your body. Everything I've described up to this point is the innie method. I wanted you to understand how breath naturally moves in your body before you take on too much information. However, see the "Advancing Your Breath Control" section, in this chapter, for more details about being an "outie."

To sing your best, you want to develop good posture while you breathe. When your body is aligned correctly, taking and using an efficient breath is easier.

Your own two hands can help you to maintain great posture while breathing. As you work through the breathing exercises in this chapter, place one hand on your chest and the other hand on your abs. As you inhale, use your hand to feel whether your chest stays steady; you want it to stay in the same position for both the inhalation and the exhalation. (If your chest rises during inhalation, you create tension in your chest and neck.) With your other hand, feel it moving out with your abs as you inhale and back in toward your body as you exhale.

Positioning your body to feel breath

Different body positions also help you to feel your breath movement. Moving through different positions can help you feel the movement of breath.

Start flat on the floor and gradually work your way up to standing. It's great to work your breath on the floor, but you can't perform on the floor. You have to get up sometime and breathe correctly, so it may as well be right away. By starting out on the floor, you're able to totally focus on breathing and the movements in your body. By gradually working your way up, you can continue exploring the same movement of breath while working your way up to standing. Some singers have trouble finding the right movement for breathing when they stand. When they begin on the floor, they often find a sense of release in their body and can really feel the movement.

Lying on the floor

1. Lie down on the floor or bed with a heavy book on your abdomen.

2. As you inhale, you should see the book rising up then lowering back down as you exhale. If you don't see the book moving, notice what's moving as you breathe. Feel the sensations in your body. When you inhale, your lungs expand and take in air. Your body, specifically your abdomen, moves out as you inhale.

3. As you exhale, the air is leaving your body, and you should see or feel the abs moving back in. This movement happens because of the air moving and not because I told you to move your abs. You can bounce your abs without breathing, but that won't improve your singing.

Getting down on your hands and knees

1. Get down on your hands and knees. Yes, you need comfy clothes to survive reading this book. In this dignified position, take some slow breaths and notice what you feel moving in your body.

2. During inhalation, your abs fall toward the floor.

3. During exhalation, your abs move back in with the outgoing air. If you feel just the opposite motion, try it again.

4. Your chest should stay steady and not collapse.

5. Notice how your back expands out with the inhalation.

When you're successful and feel the correct movement of your body and breath, try the exercise in "Squatting down," the next section in this chapter.

Squatting down

Squatting is just as exciting as getting down on your hands and knees, and it requires comfy clothes, too.

1. **Squat down on the floor.**

   You can keep your heels on the floor or lift them up off the floor. You can also place your hands on the floor to steady your balance. Don't fall over!

2. **As you inhale, notice the movement across your back.**

   What you want to feel is your abs moving out and your lower back expanding as you inhale. If you're not sure about this breath movement, change your position just a bit. You don't have to be in a squat exactly.

Breathing jargon

If you have had some singing lessons, you may be confused by all the phrases and terms that singers use to describe breathing. Your voice teacher or choir director may have said, "Support that note," or "Sing on breath!" If those commands make sense to you, congratulations! I always thought they were confusing, because the word *support* can mean so many things.

✔ **Support** probably became a popular term for breathing for singing, because the Italians use the word *appoggio,* which means *to support* or *to lean your body into the breath.*

✔ **Appoggio** also implies that singers flex their body or ribs open as they sing and leave the body open during exhalation. (This is similar to the outie method mentioned in the "Are you an innie or an outie?" sidebar in this chapter, and the "Advancing Your Breath Control" section, in this chapter.) This may

sound confusing to you, but it should make more sense as your understanding of your own breathing habits develop with practice.

✔ **Singing on breath** is what you're supposed to do all the time. If someone says, "Sing on the breath," what he probably means is connect the breath to the tone or start the sound by connecting air. You can grunt and make a sound, but that's not applying air or singing on the breath. You can also blow too much air and make a breathy sound, which isn't what it means to sing on the breath. The process in between those two is what you're looking for. In the future, ask the person to be more specific if you're confused by the phrase.

But it's okay if you don't know every singing cliché. How could you know them all yet? There are just too many.

Slumping over

Slumping is illegal among singers, but don't tell anyone.

1. Stand up and slump over. Yes, I know. I told you not to do this in Chapter 2. And right after this exercise, you won't do it again — promise.

2. As you're slumped over, feel the movement in your body as you breathe.

3. Release your neck so that your back can stay pliable for breathing.

4. Notice that when you take in the air, you can feel the lower abs moving out, because they're all flabby from being slumped over. Those of you who are really thin, you may not feel your abs move much in the beginning. That's okay. You can still acquire great breathing habits for singing.

5. Notice also that your lower back opens as you inhale. Try to let your ribs close slowly as you exhale instead of collapsing right away.

These charming, physical positions help you to feel the breath moving in your body. Try standing tall and notice what your body does when you take a breath.

It's okay if you're really confused right now or feel short of breath. Feeling short of breath when you begin working through these exercises is normal. Be really patient, and you'll begin breathing efficiently. It takes a while to create a new habit in your body, and breathing for singing is definitely new. Your inhalation was perfect when you were a baby. If you watch an infant breathe, they know exactly what to do. As you age and your life becomes more complicated, stress affects your body. You start to carry unnecessary tension in various parts of your body, which can prevent you from breathing correctly. Your body gets stressed out. But not in this book! Stress busters are on the way!

Practicing Inhalation

Although inhaling may be natural for everyone, you need to practice the correct way to inhale while maintaining correct posture in order to breathe your best while singing. Correct inhalation means keeping yourself properly aligned, your body free of tension, your throat open, and your shoulders steady to allow the most air to fall into your body. Try the following to feel the difference between incorrect and correct inhalation:

- If you gasp, you can feel a tight sensation in your throat as you try to squeeze air in while your vocal cords are closed. However, if you pretend that you're hiding and don't want anyone to hear you breathing, you leave your throat open and can take in plenty of air.

- If you inhale and intentionally raise your shoulders, you can feel that as your shoulders rise, your neck gets tense. However, if you keep your shoulders steady and inhale, you get more breath into your body.

Panting like a pooch

When you mimic the panting that a dog does, you can feel the motion of breath going into your body without worrying about how you're doing it. If you have a dog, watch him breathe for a few minutes. Notice how his body moves. His body expands as he inhales and contracts when he exhales. If your dog is visiting his friends this afternoon and is unavailable for observation, then pretend! The following exercise helps you to take a tension-free, quick inhalation.

1. Watch a dog breathe.

2. Pant like a dog. Pretend that you're a dog on a really hot summer afternoon and pant. As you pant, notice what's moving in your body. Gotta love those doggies!

3. During inhalation, the abdominal muscles move out. As you continue panting, slow down the rate of your inhalation.

4. As you slow down, feel the steady movement of your body as you breathe, expanding out as you inhale and relaxing back in as you exhale.

5. During exhalation, the abdominal muscles move back inward.

Dropping your breath into your body

You explored dropping heavy air into your body in the "Discovering your singing breath" section, earlier in this chapter. Taking too much air in is called *overbreathing,* which can cause adverse tension in the body. After you get used to breathing for singing, you can judge how much air you need to take in for each phrase. The exercise that follows allows you the same opportunity to let breath fall into your body, helping you to develop a deep inhalation that's not forced.

1. Exhale.

2. Hold your nose and silently count to ten while holding your breath. Do not inhale while you're counting to ten.

3. After counting to ten, release your nose and inhale. Most likely, you need the breath so badly that it just falls right into your body.

4. Notice the movement of your body as the air comes rushing in. Your throat opened to allow the air to rush in, and your lower body released, so the air could drop in.

After expelling all your air on a long musical phrase, let that air that you need just drop into your lungs naturally.

Sipping through a straw

I'll bet that when you were a kid, your mom told you not to suck air through your straw. Right? It makes that horrible slurping noise after all the liquid is drained from your glass. Now you need a dry straw that doesn't have any leftover milkshake stuck inside. Breathing through a straw enables the air that you breathe to drop low into your body, making it easy to feel your abdomen expand as you breathe. You also can't gasp or suck in air too quickly with a straw.

1. Find a straw and cut it down to three inches.

2. Insert one end in your mouth.

3. Breathe through the straw, making sure not to raise your chest or shoulders, and notice how low the breath drops into your body.

Singing "Happy Birthday"

Inhaling properly should now be fairly easy for you. Singing "Happy Birthday" tests your ability to inhale correctly and then sing a song. Before you start the song, feel the breath moving into your body. When you're in the groove, go for it.

1. Sing through the song "Happy Birthday."

2. Take a deep breath and sing one phrase.

3. Pause.

4. Before you sing the second phrase, remember all that you just recently discovered about inhalation. Take your time and find the correct way to take in that breath. You don't have to rush.

5. Calmly take the breath back in.

6. Take the time to find the correct motion of the breath and then sing the next phrase.

7. Repeat this series of steps until you have finished the song. Remember to get the breath right instead of rushing to the next phrase or gasping for air.

Each time that you try this exercise, it gets easier. Try it the next time that you sing a new song to coordinate your breathing properly whenever you sing it.

You're so normal if you feel like you don't remember how to breathe. Your body gets confused putting all this information into practice, so just work the inhalation until it's easy for you and then move on to another exercise. Go back and reread the explanation about how the breath works in the body and then try some of the exercises again. You may find that they're easier now that you can picture the movement of the air as well as feel it.

Practicing Exhalation

When you sing and exhale, you need to remember not to collapse your body too quickly. You want to keep the same aligned position that you had for your inhalation, the chest should be steady, and your abdomen will gradually move inward as the breath is released. When you aren't singing or speaking and as you go about your everyday business, you normally exhale much quicker than you should when you sing. It doesn't take much breath to speak either. When you sing, however, you have to inhale quickly and extend the flow of air over a longer period of time. It takes practice to be able to sing a long phrase without breaking it to breathe. Practice a steady, controlled exhalation while maintaining good posture

Blowing out a candle

The object of the exercise is to make the flame flicker by exhaling and not blasting hot wax onto your hand! Make sure that you exhale with a steady, slow stream of air — just enough to bend the flame. This helps you to develop the control needed when you sing a long phrase of music. Just in case you don't have a candle handy, you can blow air across the top of a hot cup of cocoa, tea, or just use your imagination. You can work this exercise with your imagination, or you can actually light a candle. Please be careful with the candle if you use a real one. Hold or set down the candle in a holder that's at least eight inches from your mouth, so you don't burn your eyebrows.

1. Light a candle and hold it eight inches away from your face.

2. Take a deep breath, keeping your shoulders and chest nice and steady.

3. As you exhale, blow gently on the flame to make it bend but not flicker around wildly.

4. Continue the steady stream of air to keep the flame bent, counting silently to see how long you can bend the flame.

Be careful that your body doesn't collapse quickly as you exhale during this exercise. Instead, feel a steady movement in your body during the exhalation. If you can bend the flame for the count of five the first time, try to make it to six the next time. Bend the flame for six counts several times in a row before you try for seven. Each time, make sure that you notice what's happening in your body.

Trilling for exhalation

A *lip trill* is an itchy exercise, but it's great for feeling the movement of the exhalation. Why is it itchy? The vibrations of your lips may make your nose itch after a few minutes. No problem. Scratch your nose and keep going. What's a *lip trill*? Ever see a horse blowing air through his lips? The horse's lips flap in the breeze. This may seem silly, but it's a great test of your exhaling endurance. Take a low breath and send the breath between your lips and let them vibrate. If your lips don't vibrate like Mr. Ed, it's probably because your lips are too tight. Loosen your lips and just let them hang free as you blow air between them this time. If your lips are tight, place a finger at the corners of your mouth and gently push the corners toward your nose as you do the lip trill.

1. Practice trilling your lips. After you have the lip trill moving easily, start counting silently.

2. Sustain the lip trill for four counts. Inhale slowly and repeat the cycle. Make sure that you take a good breath before you begin. As you count to four, notice what moves in your body as you exhale. Try not to collapse your chest as you exhale. Let your lower body do the work.

3. Sustain the lip trill for four counts again, but this time, inhale on one count and repeat the cycle.

4. Sustain the lip trill for longer periods of time as your endurance improves. When you can easily do the lip trill several times in a row, increase the number by two counts. The object of the exercise isn't to count to 50 but to work the endurance of the breath and make sure the body is working properly as you exhale.

When the lip trill is a piece of cake for you, add a tune. That means lip trilling to a song. You can easily lip trill "Happy Birthday." Let each note connect to the other without a pause or without pushing your tongue against your teeth for each note. In other words, make it *legato* (smooth and connected).

To practice more lip trills, check out Figure 3-1.

1. Sing through the lip trill pattern in Figure 3-1.

2. Play the track again, and this time, try a tongue trill. Many people find that they can make good sounds with a tongue trill. The tongue trill works like the lip trill. Leave your tongue loose in your mouth and blow air between your tongue and the roof of your mouth. Make sure that your tongue is released, or this won't work. As the air moves over the tongue, the tip of the tongue will raise and vibrate against the roof of your mouth.

   Play the track for a third time, alternating between the tongue trill and singing on the given notes. You can easily go right from the tongue trill to a vowel. For example, sing the first two notes on the tongue trill and the last two notes on *ah*. Make a smooth transition from the tongue trill to the *ah*. See if the airflow remains the same.

Figure 3-1:
Lip and
tongue trills.

TRACK 2

1. Lip trill   Br _____
2. Tongue trill   Tr _____
3. Tongue trill to "ah" Tr _____ ah _____

Moving air with consonants

Consonants require airflow. If you put your hand in front of your mouth and say the consonant *K,* you should feel puffs of air each time you pronounce the consonant. Place one hand in front of your mouth to feel the puff of air and one hand on your abdominal muscles or just below your belly button to feel what moves as you say the consonant. For most people, saying the consonants helps them understand the coordination of breath that's required to generate the sound. Other consonant sounds that can help you to feel the movement of air are *T, SH, F, H,* and *J.* Instead of saying the name of the consonant, put the consonant before a vowel. For example, *to, shoe, foot, ha,* and *jaw.*

1. Inhale. Repeat the consonant *K* four times without inhaling until the end of the four consonants. Inhale slowly and repeat.

2. Change to other consonants, such as *T, SH, F, H,* and *J.*

3. Practice saying the consonant and inhaling quickly while taking in the same amount of air.

If you're unsure about how your abdominal muscles are supposed to move during exhalation, then cough. When you cough, your abs contract to move air out of your body and dispel any phlegm that's lodged in your throat.

Raising your arms to feel rib expansion

Sometimes, you can get so carried away with noticing one detail of singing that you forget another. As you've been working on all this breath, have you been aware of your posture? I hope so! If not, take some time and check your posture. See Chapter 2 for an overview of posture. The reason that I want you to move your arms in the exercise that follows is so that you can feel the opening of your chest and ribs:

1. Raise your arms over your head. Feel your ribs open.

2. Keep your chest stable. You don't need to raise your chest but merely let it open.

3. Try singing part of a song with your arms over your head.

4. Move your arms out in front of you as if you were reaching out to grab something straight out in front of you.

5. Flex your back open. Keep your chest steady as you explore the opening of your back.

6. Put your arms out to your side, parallel with your shoulders. Keep your chest open. If you're having trouble opening your chest, keep your arms at the same height but move them behind you.

7. Feel the opening of your chest as your arms move behind your body.

Each time that you go through this exercise, you can drop your arms from the position that you've been holding and maintain that sense of openness in your chest or ribs. Singing with your arms in various positions is fine. I do it all the time.

Advancing Your Breath Control

If you've been working on the exercises in this chapter, you've probably explored your inhalation and exhalation enough so that you know what should be moving and grooving as you breathe and sing. To give yourself an opportunity to work on more advanced breathing exercises, keep on reading and working through the exercises. They aren't too advanced for you, especially if you've been exploring other exercises and are comfortable with what moves as you breathe.

If you're new to singing, moving too quickly to the advanced exercises without practicing the basics won't give you an opportunity to make the movement a habit. It took some time for me to make correct breathing a habit, but now, I don't have to worry about changing gears when it's time to sing. I breathe in the same manner when I sing as when I speak, because the movement has become so natural for me.

Extending the breath: Singing slowly

Up until now, I suggested simple tunes, such as "Happy Birthday," so that you could easily concentrate on many details at one time. However, it may be time for you to try a tougher song. Think of a song that gives you trouble when it comes to managing the long phrases. It can be a hymn or familiar tune in which you just can't quite conquer the phrases. Some familiar tunes with long phrases are "Danny Boy," "Come Unto Him" from *The Messiah*, and "Over The Rainbow." Sing the song through to refresh your memory of the words and the tune. When you're ready, sing through the song at a slow pace. You want to sing slower, so you extend your exhalation. By singing slower, you have to figure out how to extend your breath over a longer period of time. Singing faster songs with short phrases doesn't require a long exhalation, and it doesn't require that you control your exhalation over long phrases.

Practice the exercise that follows to move on to the next level of breath control so that you can manage your breath easily during longer phrases.

1. Sing the song slowly.

2. Inhale slowly before the beginning of each phrase. Sing through each phrase with a consistent exhalation, which gives you a smooth connected line.

3. Sing through the song again slowly, but inhale quickly, while taking in the same amount of air that you did when you were inhaling slowly.

4. Be careful not to gasp; open your throat and allow the air to come in. Gasping prevents you from getting the air in quick enough.

The innie method focuses on moving the abdomen in gradually during exhalation. The outie method means the singer focuses on keeping the abdomen out during exhalation. For many singers, the outie method is helpful, because it's hard for beginners to prevent the abdomen from moving back in too quickly during exhalation and the visual of the abdomen staying out helps them slowly move back in. After their abdomen moves back in, some singers squeeze their throat to continue singing. You can explore the outie method to see if the visual of your body staying wide during the exhalation helps you to slow down the movement of your abdominal muscles and extend your breath. I want you to remember that more than one method of breathing is available, and you need to explore what works for you and understand why. You'll encounter someone who thinks they have all the answers about breathing, and I want you to be familiar with your own breathing to understand your options.

Opening your ribs

Because your lungs are housed within your rib cage, allowing the ribs to open as you inhale and letting them stay open as you exhale is beneficial. This is what's also known as *outie* breathing or *appoggio* (that's Italian for *support* or *lean*). Don't *force* your ribs to stay open but *allow* them to stay open. Even if the words *force* and *allow* seem similar, they're different. Forcing the ribs to stay open results in pressure being put on your body and a tight sound.

After you've been working with breath for some time and can easily manage quick, efficient inhalation and have some control over longer exhalation, then try the exercise that follows.

1. Practice flexing open your ribs. Stand in front of the mirror and try to open your rib cage. You want to open your ribs on the side of your body and not raise your chest. Watch the movement in your body to make sure you're not lifting your chest. It may take a few tries before you can

figure out how to open the ribs. After you know how to move them, allow the ribs to open as you inhale. The area that you're trying to move is at the bottom of the rib cage.

2. Inhale and open your ribs. Practice inhaling and allow your ribs to open. If you aim the breath at the lowest rib, you can open the ribs without forcing your chest to rise.

3. Work for a time just allowing your ribs to open when you inhale and to close as you exhale. As this becomes easier, allow the ribs to stay open longer on the exhalation.

4. Inhale and allow your ribs to open. Leave the ribs open as you exhale. Take the next breath and allow your abdominal muscles to expand out.

5. Now that your ribs are open and your abdominal muscles are expanded, exhale. As you exhale, allow the abdominal muscles to move in as the ribs stay out.

6. As you reach the end of your breath, allow the ribs to close or collapse back to their normal position.

7. Exhale moving your abs first and then your ribs.

The long-term goal of this exercise is to provide you with the option of opening the ribs as you inhale and letting them close by choice, depending on the length of the phrase that you're singing. I keep my ribs open if I have to sing a really long phrase. This motion may take up to a month or more to master. Keep trying.

 Sometimes, you'll be asked to sing and dance at the same time. Because dancers have to keep their body moving while singing, they can't always let their abdominal muscles release as far as I can. But dancers can allow the ribs to open when breathing. If a dancer allows his ribs to open upon inhalation and slowly lets them close upon exhalation, he won't have to worry so much about letting the abdominal muscles be loose. Practice breathing as I described at the beginning of this chapter in the section called "Discovering your singing breath" first. After you understand the way that the body was designed to breathe, then take it a step further and practice working with your ribs for dancing while singing.

Puffing like the magic dragon

The following exercise develops the coordination between your inhalation and exhalation using the consonant sounds for *H, F, SH, V, J, S* or *Z*, try this sequence. This will make it easier for you to sing long phrases with great breath control.

1. Say the consonant sound four times vigorously as you exhale. Inhale slowly. Repeat. When this pattern is easy, move on to the next step.

2. Repeat the same sequence but take the breath more quickly this time. You can keep time in your head and inhale in one count. Inhaling quickly requires that you get the same breath in your body, but quickly, to make the next phrase of your song.

3. Say the consonant sound eight times as you exhale. Inhale slowly. Repeat.

4. Repeat the eight-count sequence, inhaling in one count.

5. Now, try holding out the consonant sound for two counts each time without inhaling in between. At the end of saying the consonant sound slowly for four times, inhale in one count.

6. When that's easy, say the consonant sound eight times (two counts each) and inhale in one count.

7. If you feel lightheaded, sit down immediately.

Gaining weight or losing weight quickly can totally confuse your body. If your body is used to moving a certain amount of weight around, it affects your breathing. You have to slowly get used to your body being a different size after the weight change, especially if you've gained weight. Take your time when you lose weight to allow your body to slowly adjust.

Chapter 4

Toning Up the Voice

In This Chapter

▶ Changing the tone of your voice

▶ Discovering your larynx and vocal cords

▶ Exercising to improve your tone

▶ Working out the chinks in your song system

*Y*ou can't see your singing voice, but you can become familiar with the parts that work together to create sound. Now, you may be wondering what *parts* a singing voice has. After all, if you're like most people, you may think that a singing voice just moves up and down to a melody. The truth is, though, that a singing voice actually does have different parts that you can discover how to control.

In this chapter, you discover what to release to help you create that gorgeous tone, and even find a little *vibrato* (the variation of a sustained pitch) along the way. I also include some helpful exercises for those of you that are *tone deaf* (not able to accurately distinguish between differences in pitch). Relax. By the time you finish this chapter, not only will you be better at controlling your singing voice, but you'll also be able to locate some fun body parts to brag about at your next family gathering. "Hey, want to feel my larynx?"

Defining Tone

If you turned on the radio, would you recognize your favorite singer? Elvis, Roy Orbison, Ethel Merman, Little Richard, Luciano Pavarotti, or Marilyn Horne? You probably would. How? If you answered, "By their voices," you're partly right. More specifically, you recognized your favorite singer by the *tone* of his voice. *Tone* is what's known as the *color* or *timbre* of your singing voice, and every voice has a specific color, which can be described as warm, dark, or strident. Two singers singing the same song in the same key may sound different — the reason is tone.

Here's the pitch . . . and it's good! Or is it warm?

Whether you sing just for the fun of it or you dream of performing professionally, you can count on meeting up frequently with three terms: *pitch, note,* and *tone.* These three terms are often used incorrectly or interchangeably, but I can show you their true relationship to one another, which may make your journey through the world of singing less confusing.

✔ **Pitch** is the high or low frequency of a sound. When you sing, you create pitch, because your vocal cords vibrate at a certain speed. For example, a foghorn emits a low frequency or pitch, and the sound your smoke detector emits when you press the test button is a high frequency or pitch. In singing, when your vocal cords vibrate at a faster speed, you sing a higher pitch than when they vibrate slower. The A just above Middle C vibrates at 440 cycles per second. That means your vocal cords open and close 440 times per second.

✔ **Notes** are musical symbols that indicate the location of a pitch.

✔ **Tone** is the *color* or *timbre* of pitch and can be described by many different words such as warm, dark, brilliant, ringing, rich, lush, shrill, or strident. (See the section, "Defining Tone," earlier in this chapter for more information.) An example of a singer with a warm tone is Karen Carpenter and a person with a strident tone is Steve Urkel from the television show "Family Matters."

Based on these definitions, it makes more sense to say that one is pitch deaf rather than tone deaf. You may also hear singers say that they're afraid to sing high notes when they should say that they're afraid to sing high pitches. Although knowing the exact definition of these terms is good, I doubt that anyone will correct you if you mix up the words *tone* and *pitch.*

Your tone of voice changes with your moods or emotions. You know if someone has had a bad day just by the tone of her voice. Didn't you know you were in big trouble just by the way your mother said your name? When you sing, your tone changes with the emotional journey of the song and the style of the music.

Flexing Your Singing Muscles

Within your head and neck, groups of muscles and various other body parts help to create tone. At the same time, the brain sends a message to the muscles that create your singing voice: The air in your lungs begins moving out, and the vocal cords move into position to create the pitch. The color of the pitch is the tone. Does it seem complicated? Well, it isn't — this is exactly what happens every time you speak.

To change the tone, you change the space in your mouth and throat, your posture, and the amount of breath moving as you sing. The exercises in

Chapter 6 help you to create the right tone and adjust the space in your mouth and throat in order to change your tone and make your voice sound great. (Chapter 2 gives you pointers on posture, and Chapter 3 provides information to help you make the most of your breathing.)

Discovering your own bands

Many different parts of your body influence how you sing, but understanding how they all work together to produce the best sound is the key to great singing. Chapters 2 and 3 in this book are devoted to the big anatomical influences, such as breathing and posture, but knowing where those tiny little bands of tissue called *vocal cords* — your muscles for singing — are located and how they make tone is just as important. When developing good vocal technique, you need to understand how your breath, posture, and tension affect how your vocal cords work.

Your vocal cords are inside your *larynx* (pronounced *lar*-inks, not *lar*-nicks), which is the source of your singing voice. Your vocal cords are two small bands of tissue stretching across your larynx that vibrate to create pitch.

Your vocal cords coordinate with your breath to release a pitch by opening and closing (vibrating) as air (your breath) passes through. Each vibration is called a *cycle of vibration* or *glottal cycle*. If you're singing the same note that an orchestra plays to tune their instruments, your vocal cords are vibrating at 440 cycles per second — yes, that fast. So, in order to make those fast vibrations, you need to keep your breath flowing; otherwise, you run out of air and can't sustain the tone. (See Chapter 3 to discover techniques that improve your breathing.)

In addition, we have to make sure our posture is correct (See Chapter 2 for information about improving your posture.) If we are not standing correctly, our breathing mechanism doesn't work well, so we can't get the air moving for singing. Allowing ourselves to get too tense also prevents the body from working efficiently which in turn can affect the vocal cords. Tense jaws, chests, and locked knees all make it impossible to breathe and produce good tone

Making the first sound

You can make singing sounds without even realizing it. Working through the sounds in the steps that follow can start you on the road to singing. Making these sounds helps you discover how to make tension-free sounds that explore your entire singing range.

Make the following sounds:

1. **Try sighing first — a nice long sigh.**

   A sigh is that sound you make as you feel the warmth of the whirlpool or the relaxation of your body as someone massages your shoulders. As you sigh, make the sound as long as possible. Start higher and gradually slide lower.

2. **Next, imitate a siren.**

   If you frequently hear sirens then you'll probably slide up and down or around in circles a few times exploring high and low pitches. Those pitches in the siren are the same pitches that you will sing in the exercises later in the book.

3. **Have you ever whooped with joy?**

   Another way to explore the first sounds is by using that wonderful imagination. Pretend that someone just told you that you won the lottery. Instead of screaming, try whooping with joy. That wasn't so bad was it?

Putting your larynx into position

The first step to controlling your singing voice is to know where your larynx is. The larynx can move up or down, but the position affects your tone. A low larynx helps to create a full, open sound. Raising the larynx creates a tighter and more strident sound.

Place your fingers on the middle of your throat underneath your chin. Now, swallow: As you swallow, you should feel something move up and then down. That's your larynx.

The bump in the middle of the larynx is called the *Adam's apple*. Because men usually have a larger, more pointed larynx than women, guys can feel their Adam's apple more easily.

Keep your fingers on your throat and yawn. Feel that? The larynx went way down. Feeling your larynx may have been difficult, because it went so low. When you sing, you want the larynx to be in the middle of your neck, (a neutral position) or lower. A low larynx helps to create a nice full, open sound. Raising the larynx creates a more brassy sound.

Nonsingers usually have a high-resting larynx. That's because the majority of the muscles in the neck are designed to keep the larynx high — which isn't what you want for singing. Because this is the opposite of what you want, you have to figure out how to keep the larynx in a more neutral or lower position in your throat.

Throughout this book, you'll explore different sounds that you can make with your singing voice. Knowing where the larynx rests in your throat makes it easier for you to tell if your larynx is too high or too low.

Because you can't see your voice, feeling the sound is important. It seems strange to say, "Feel the sound," but that's common singing lingo. Your singing voice makes vibrations that you can feel in your body and hear resounding out in the room. Trusting the feeling of good technique is important, because each room that you sing in has different acoustics. If you always practice in a lively room and hear the sound bouncing back to you and then sing in a concert hall or big room that doesn't have the same acoustics, your ear will be totally confused. You'll try in vain to push out the sound to get that reverb back. Because you know where your larynx is, put your finger there again to feel the tonal vibrations. With your finger in the middle of your throat, hum a few bars of your favorite song. The buzzing sensation that you felt is your vocal cords vibrating and creating tone. Awesome! You may have felt that buzzing sensation in your lips or around your nose. You can even feel the vibrations on the crown of your head.

Within your body, six groups of muscles raise your larynx and three groups lower it. The natural resting position of the larynx is high. The larynx was designed to prevent food from going down the wrong way. For that reason, the larynx raises each time you swallow. The muscles that raise and lower the larynx also raise and lower your soft palate, drop your jaw, and raise your tongue. In other words, it's a skill to lower the larynx for singing and then move your soft palate and tongue without the larynx bouncing back up.

Matching Pitch Whether You're Tone Deaf or Not

You may be familiar with these phrases: "He can't carry a tune in a bucket." Or "She's tone deaf." If that sounds familiar, I have some good news. You can develop a sense of pitch, so you *can* carry a tune in a bucket, a shower, or a choir.

Being able to hear a pitch in your head or from an external source, such as the radio or a piano, and then sing it is called *matching pitch*. The first step to matching pitch is figuring out how to hear the pitch in your head, so you can match it. The second step is matching it with your voice. Matching pitch is a skill. Perhaps that's not your strongest skill today, but you can improve with some practice. Using my suggestions in this section, you can improve your ability to match pitch and join in at the next campfire sing along.

Perfect pitch

Perfect pitch is naming a note and singing it without hearing the pitch first. For example, someone with perfect pitch can sing Middle C correctly without hearing it first. They can also pick up a piece of music that they've never heard and sing all the correct notes without hearing the first note. You can't develop perfect pitch nor does it mean that the singer automatically sings every note in tune. Relative pitch, however, can be developed. *Relative pitch* is guessing at the note and usually getting close to the exact pitch. Most singers develop relative pitch from singing their scales or even a certain song over and over. They often begin on the correct note just by knowing the way it feels. Perfect pitch may sound cool, but it's not necessary for good singing.

Sliding up and down on pitch

Sliding up and down on pitch gives you the chance to hear a pitch from an external source, such as a piano, and then singing that pitch or sliding around until you match it. Sliding away from the right note allows you to hear the vibrations of your voice clashing with the wrong note and then matching the right note.

With practice, you'll be able to match any pitch, but start in the middle part of your voice and then work your way up.

1. Play a note on any instrument. After you play the note, feel it in your body. Visualize yourself singing the note, before you actually sing it.

2. Play the note again and sing it. If you didn't match the pitch, slide up and down until you match it. You can keep playing the note on the piano until you match it. How will you know when you match it? You'll hear that the vibrations of your voice and the vibrations of the note sound similar. The sounds will blend together.

3. Play a different note. Visualize it and hear the note in your head before you sing it. Now, sing the note. If you miss again, slide up and down until you match the pitch.

Matching pitch may be tricky for you in the beginning. If you've never been able to do it, matching pitch won't happen instantly, but you can improve with some practice. Be patient and keep trying!

If you did sing the correct note after some practice, good for you. Play the note again. This time, intentionally slide above the note or higher than the note and then slide back down and match it again. The next time, try sliding below the pitch and then back up to match it. This will train your ear to hear the matching vibrations of your voice and the instrument.

You can also ask someone to sing a note and hold it out. Allow yourself to listen to them sing the note for a moment and then try to match their pitch. Make sure the note isn't too high. Matching pitches that are close to your speaking range is easier than matching pitches that are outside of your speaking range. As your buddy sings, try sliding around until you match his pitch. If you still aren't sure, ask him to tell you when you get it right. This buddy system is beneficial for you, because your buddy can be the pitch monitor. It's usually easier to match the pitch when your buddy is the same gender. When you can match pitch, you'll be able to sing along with your buddy but as you explore pitch, find a buddy of the same gender.

On Track 3, listen to the note played on the piano and the singer sliding above and below the pitch. This will help you understand what I mean about the vibrations of your voice matching the correct pitch. You'll hear the clashing of the sounds when the singer is too high or too low, and you'll hear the matching vibrations when she matches the pitch.

Developing muscle memory

For some folks, a link is missing between hearing the pitch and singing it. Developing what's called muscle memory can bridge the gap, however. *Muscle memory* means that your voice remembers how it felt to sing a certain note or exercise, so you can recall that feeling the next time that you sing that note. Practice the following exercise, so you can develop muscle memory for matching pitch.

1. Find a quiet place and hear your favorite tune in your head. Take a few moments and listen to it.

2. Now, take a moment and try to feel the pitch in your body. What does that mean? If I asked you to imagine yourself speaking, you could feel or imagine the sensation in your body. You hear the sound of your speaking voice all the time in your head when you're rehearsing that funny joke for the dinner party or practicing your acceptance speech for the big award banquet. Right now, I want you to feel the sensation of singing the tune that you hear in your head.

3. Visualize yourself singing the notes in the first few lines to process the message that your brain sends to your vocal cords.

4. Sing a few lines of the tune. Were you close? If you got part of the song but not the high notes, try singing the song again in a lower key that's more suited to your voice.

5. If you hit most of the notes on target but missed a few, go slower. Take more time between hearing the pitch in your head and singing it. You can even sing a nursery rhyme that isn't as complicated as your favorite tune.

Recording yourself and singing along

Another way of discovering how to match pitch is to record your singing along with another recording. Recording yourself singing along to a familiar song allows you a chance to hear the notes you sing as compared with the notes that the singer on the recording sings. Listening to yourself sing on a tape is different from listening to yourself singing live. You can be more objective and hear the difference between what you sang and what was on the original recording.

1. Get out your favorite singer's latest CD and find your hand-held cassette tape recorder, a minidisc recorder, or DAT tape recorder.

2. Press the button that says *Record* on the tape recorder and press the button on the CD player that says *Play*. Hold the tape recorder near your mouth and sing along with the CD. Sing at least half of the song.

3. Stop the CD and rewind the cassette. Be brave and play the tape. Were you close to matching the pitches? Did you hit most of the notes? Missing only the high notes is fine for now. You can read more about singing higher notes in Chapter 11 and 12. Not liking what you hear on the recording is normal. Don't give up yet! You'll get used to hearing your voice on tape. Comparing your sound to the CD isn't fair, because the artist probably spent thousands of dollars for a sound engineer to make her sound incredible.

4. If you missed most of the notes, go back and review the previous two exercises. You can also get your buddy to help you with this exercise. Ask your buddy to tell you when you miss the notes.

If you go online to www.visualizationsoftware.com/voicetools.html, you can purchase a software program entitled *Match pitch*. With a little bit of effort and a little extra equipment, such as a microphone attached to your computer, you can monitor your singing pitch. You'll need to read music just a little to monitor your singing pitch. You can review the information in the sidebars about reading music or pick up a copy of *Piano For Dummies* by Blake Neely (Wiley Publishing, Inc.), which has a large segment about reading music.

Releasing Tension for Better Tone

Anytime you sing, be aware of how your body moves to create tone. When you sing, you want your body to be relaxed so that you create that round, full sound. For example, if you're singing and your body is tense and your throat is really tight, the sound will be tight, thin, or strident. You don't want that.

The following exercises in this section help you to discover how to release tension from your neck, jaw, and tongue to create that beautiful tone. But before you try those exercises, get your entire body into alignment by starting from the bottom and working your way up:

- ✔ **Feet** are placed no wider than your shoulders, one foot slightly in front of the other.
- ✔ **Knees** are unlocked.
- ✔ **Weight** is evenly distributed on both legs.
- ✔ **Shoulders** are back but down and relaxed.
- ✔ **Chest** is wide.
- ✔ **Head** is centered over your shoulders.
- ✔ **Chin** is level with the floor.
- ✔ **Arms** are relaxed at your side.

For more information on posture and alignment, take a look at Chapter 2.

Checking for neck or jaw tension

Having a loose jaw and flexible tongue is important. The tighter your jaw, the tighter the sound, and the tighter your tongue, the more difficult it is to make your song understood.

Become aware of the back of your neck and jaw as you sing, so you can monitor whether you have a flexible jaw and tongue by following these steps:

1. As you step into alignment, notice what you feel in the back of your neck. Massage the back of your neck to release any tension. As the tension melts away, notice how easy it is to move your head without tension in the back of your neck. Feel your head floating on your shoulders.

2. After your neck is feeling free of tension, notice what your jaw is doing. Without even realizing it, most people clamp down on their jaw. Everyday stress can lead to clenched teeth and clamped jaws. To relieve this cramped feeling, let your jaw hang loose as if you were asleep. I know that you have seen someone snoring away with his jaw hanging wide open for any old bug to fly right on in. Allow yourself to explore this feeling of release and openness in your jaw.

3. When you feel the fluid motion, try singing a few lines of a song. Combine correct posture and breathing and open space in the throat and mouth with fluid motion of the jaw and neck. Whew! That's plenty to think about, but you can do it.

Dropping the jaw, not the chin

When you sing, you have to drop your jaw much farther than you do in everyday conversation. If you don't drop your jaw and open your mouth, the sound gets trapped inside your mouth and won't make it past the first row of the audience.

Your neck and jaw should be free of tension and ready to move. If they aren't, check out the exercise in the "Checking for neck or jaw tension" section, earlier in this chapter, to release tension from your neck and jaw.

In order to properly drop the jaw for singing, you need to feel around a bit first. Place your finger on your chin and trace your jaw line back to your ear. At the back of the jaw, you'll feel a curve under your ear. This is the area that I want you to focus on when you drop your jaw. Instead of trying to drop your chin, when it's time to drop your jaw, I want you to drop it from the area right underneath your ear.

To practice dropping the jaw:

1. Make sure that all the muscles around your face are free of tension. You can massage them again to make sure they're ready to open.

2. Try yawning and dropping your jaw at the same time. Remember that you want to drop the jaw and not just move the chin down. Your chin will move, but you want to open the space in the back by your ear (back space) and not just the front (front space).

3. Inhale slowly as you drop your jaw if the yawning isn't helpful. Dropping your jaw is important, because you need to inhale, drop the larynx and jaw, and open the back space all at the same time. The muscle groups that perform all these functions are connected, and you want them to perform the right task.

Another way to practice dropping your jaw is by pretending that you're biting an apple. Just follow these steps to feel the correct movement of the jaw:

1. **Imagine that you're about to take a bite out of an apple.**

2. **Hold the apple in your hand and bring it to your mouth.**

   You probably won't bite into the apple with your bottom teeth going in first. Your top teeth are in front of the bottom teeth. Keeping the top teeth in front is really helpful when you sing, because pushing your bottom teeth forward causes jaw tension. You don't need that when you sing.

3. **As you open your mouth to bite the apple say "Ah."**

   You should be able to fit two fingers in the space between your teeth.

4. **Bite the apple one more time and sing a few lines of your favorite song.**

Maintain that space in the back of your mouth as you sing to create a free, open tone.

Watching for strain

The best way to observe what your body is doing when you sing is to watch yourself in the mirror. The mirror is a great tool, because you can see exactly what's happening from the breath to the release of the tone.

The two exercises in the section "Checking for neck or jaw tension," showed you how to release tension in your neck and jaw, and the following exercise makes sure that you remain free of tension as you sing an entire song. After you see yourself free of tension, you can remember how it felt to be released while singing. When you're standing in front of an entire audience or just trying to belt out a song in the shower, you can hold onto that released feeling and create a full, rich sound.

To eliminate strain and tension while you sing, follow these steps:

1. Stand in front of the mirror and sing several lines of your favorite song. Watch your body in the mirror as you sing. Please don't worry about your hair or your outfit. You look fine! Concentrate on your upper body movements when you sing. If your neck muscles are bulging, you're straining too hard to make the tone.

2. Release the muscles in your neck and move your head around. Maintain that feeling of release when you begin the song again. Let the air help to start the tone. You don't have to push anywhere in your neck to create tone. For help coordinating the tone and breath, see Chapter 6.

3. Feel the free movement of your neck without tension before you begin each segment of the song.

Bouncing the tongue and jaw

To create great sound, your tongue should be just as released as the rest of your body while you sing. The tongue is a huge muscle, and if it's tense or bunched up in the back, it blocks the tone or squeezes the tone, making it sound tight. Your tongue should just lie like a rug — relatively flat — in your mouth except when you're making consonant and vowel sounds that require you to arch your tongue. (Exercises for singing vowels are in Chapter 8, and consonant exercises are in Chapter 9.)

Isolating the movement of the tongue and jaw is important, because you don't have to press your tongue down to move your jaw or move your jaw when your tongue moves. They're members of the same team, but they don't have to play at the same time. You can do the following to make sure that your tongue is released and working on its own:

1. Without moving your jaw, say, *Yuk*. Saying the *y* allowed you to move the back of your tongue.

2. Again, without moving your jaw, say, *Ya-ya-ya-ya-ya*. Did you notice how your tongue was bouncing?

3. Bounce your tongue again and then let it rest in your mouth. Notice what the tongue feels like when it's resting in your mouth. It's not tense or pushing up or down. It's just lying in your mouth.

This time, I want you to bounce your jaw and say *Ya-ya*. Say *Ya-ya* several times and let your jaw bounce or move up and down as you say it. Notice how it rests in place after you say the syllables. You want your jaw, like your tongue, to hang loose, ready to move at any moment — but not tense.

Use the musical pattern in Figure 4-1 to practice the following exercise:

1. Sing *yah* on each note to feel the movement of your tongue as you sing. For now, don't move your jaw. Just use your tongue to sing the *yah*.

2. After you've explored that sensation, sing the pattern again, but sing an *ah* with your tongue resting in your mouth. Notice how released your tongue can be when you sing the *ah* vowel.

3. Sing the pattern again, and this time, bounce your jaw and sing, *yah-yah*. Allow the jaw to move as you sing. You'll still be able to sing.

4. Sing the pattern again, and sing the *ah* vowel and let your jaw be still. Notice that the jaw is hanging loosely, and it's open.

5. The last time, sing the pattern four times following the sequence in Figure 4-1. Don't forget to step into your alignment and breathe.

Figure 4-1:
Bouncing
the tongue
and jaw.

TRACK 4

1. yah - yah - yah - yah - yah - yah - yah - yah - yah
2. ah _____

In the musical example in Figure 4-1, notice how the syllables are divided underneath the note. The *Ya-ya* is written underneath every note, but the *ah* has a line moving off to the right. That line indicates that you sing *ah* and hold it out for the length of the pattern. You don't have to re-sing the *ah* vowel for each note. Get out some music to see how the syllables are divided for some familiar words. Understanding this process helps you to master a new song, because you can guess which note and which syllable belong together.

Part II
Discovering Your Singing Voice

The 5th Wave   By Rich Tennant

"My vocal range? Well, I'm a soprano in the shower, a coloratura calling my son for dinner, and a real contralto arguing with my husband."

In this part . . .

The meat and potatoes of technique are in this part. You can find out about different voice types and figure out which category fits your voice. Tone is an important topic, so you have more information in this part to keep you moving in the right tonal direction. Because resonance seems to be a misunderstood phenomenon, you can debunk all the myths that you hear and find out the real story. Inquiring minds want to know, and it's all in this book waiting for you to gobble up.

The big workout in this part is for vowels and consonants. Being understood is tough if your vowels and consonants aren't distinct. That won't be a problem for you, because the exercises in Chapters 8 and 9 get your vowels and consonants whipped into shape, so tongue twisters, such as "Peter Piper's pickled peppers" and "Sally's seashells by the seashore" can become your best party trick.

Chapter 5

Matching Voice Types: More Than Your Average Dating Service

In This Chapter

▶ Looking at all the ins and outs of voice types

▶ Discovering just what those categories are

▶ Finding out where you fit in

Matching voice types is one of the big singing riddles. It's a riddle, because several ingredients combine to create a voice type. You don't have to know your voice type if you're singing for your own enjoyment. Out of curiosity, you may want to figure it out. If you aspire to sing professionally or do some professional auditions, you want to know your voice type. You'll be asked at the audition, so you want to know that answer before they ask. You can find information about auditions in Chapter 21. Determining your *voice type* — soprano or mezzo for women, tenor or bass for men — enables you to find out what songs are most appropriate for you. After you figure out what category you fit into, check out Appendix A for a list of songs appropriate for your voice type. Read on to explore what each voice type sounds like and how to determine where your voice fits in.

Sifting through the Ingredients to Determine Your Voice Type

Think of a voice type as a series of ingredients that are mixed together to create a unique tasting dessert. For singing, the ingredients are combined to create a unique sounding voice. The four common voice types are *soprano, mezzo, tenor,* and *bass*. The five ingredients that determine a voice type include:

✔ **Age:** Many singers are assigned a voice type as young singers, but their voices change with age. In Chapter 13, you can read about the growth of the male-singing muscles up to the age of 20. All voices continue to grow and develop with age. Think about the last time you made a phone call and heard the sound of a stranger's voice. Even if you didn't know the person on the other end, you could guess their age just by listening to their speaking voice. Because speaking voices and singing voices change with age, wait until your body is finished growing to determine your voice type.

✔ **Range:** All the notes in between and including the highest note and the lowest note that a singer can hit. Beginning singers usually have a shorter range than more advanced singers, because the high notes or low notes get stronger with practice. As you practice the exercises with this book and accompanying CD, your range will expand no matter whether you're a beginner or an advanced singer. Knowing your range helps you figure out your voice type, because a bass can sing lower than a tenor, or a soprano can sing higher than a mezzo. Although several factors help determine voice types, the two big factors that most affect how you determine your voice types are range and register transitions.

✔ **Register:** A series of adjacent notes that sound similar are produced in a similar fashion and have a similar tonal quality. The notes sound similar, because they're produced by the same muscles and often vibrate in a similar location in a singer's body. You want to know about registers, because the transitions between the registers can help you determine what voice type you are. Keep reading this chapter to find out where each voice type feels transitions to help you decide if your voice does something similar. Keep in mind that the transitions in your voice may change as your voice develops.

✔ **Tone of voice:** Each voice has a specific tonal quality or color. Color is also called *timbre*. Words that describe tone include *strident, dark, brilliant, metallic, ringing,* or *shrill.* Your neck or head size affects your voice's tone quality. When determining a voice type, the voice tone helps you further determine your category. The tone of voice for a tenor is often much brighter than a bass.

✔ **Voice strength:** Knowing your voice's strength also helps you determine your voice type. Sopranos and tenors have a stronger head voice than a mezzo or bass. Likewise, the mezzo and bass have a stronger, meatier middle voice than the soprano or tenor.

Don't classify yourself too quickly based on the preceding factors. For the general purposes of singing, focus on building great technique and see how your voice responds. Your voice tells you what voice type it really is; you just have to know how to look and listen. The "Determining Your Voice Type" section, later in this chapter, explains how to do just that.

Do you have the personality for it?

Knowing your voice category may give you insight into your personality — if tendencies in the opera hold true, certain personality types seem to fit certain voice types. Sopranos and tenors seem to be higher strung than mezzos and basses, but that's good. If the tenor weren't high strung, he'd never sing all those high notes to impress the girl and win her heart by the end of the performance. If sopranos weren't wildly devoted to their art, they would never leap to their death at the end of the last act. Mezzos and baritones are the ones chatting it up with their competition right before the final number where the soprano does herself in. Basses are the guys who can drink beer and play poker all night with the buddies, because a little swelling that may panic a tenor only makes the bass sound deeper and sexier. Sopranos and tenors tend to be type-A personalities, too, and mezzos and basses tend to be type B. Thank goodness for these personality differences among singers, because it makes for exciting chemistry in the theater. Variety is the spice of life!

The range of the voice where a singer should be most comfortable is called *tessitura.* If you hear the word tessitura used in a discussion about a song, in that case, *tessitura* means the area where most of the notes lie in the song. The tessitura of a Stevie Wonder song is quite high, because he's comfortable singing high notes. The tessitura for "God Bless America" and most folk songs is lower. Knowing where your voice is most comfortable, as well as where it's uncomfortable, is a determining factor when it comes to voice type.

Identifying the Fab Four

The four voice types are *soprano, mezzo, tenor,* and *bass.* Even though these names sound like characters in a mob movie, I promise you that they're nothing to be afraid of. Under each voice type heading, you discover specific traits about each voice type: the range, register transitions, voice tone, and any subdivisions of that voice type, as well as the names of a few famous singers to help you put a sound with the voice type.

Highest range of the dames: Soprano

The *soprano* has the highest range of the female voice types. The following aspects are characteristic of her voice type:

✔ **Range:** Often Middle C to High C although some sopranos can vocalize way beyond High C and much lower than Middle C (See Figure 5-1).

A soprano is expected to have a High C and many sopranos can sing up to the G or A above High C. Choral directors or musical directors listen for the singer's comfort zone when determining if the singer is a soprano. Although a mezzo can reach some of these higher notes, a soprano is capable of singing high notes more frequently than a mezzo.

✔ **Register transitions:** Because not all sopranos are the same, the register transitions don't occur on just one note. The transitions usually occur as the soprano shifts out of chest voice around the E-flat just above Middle C and into her head voice around F-sharp (fifth line on top of the staff) in the octave above Middle C.

✔ **Strength:** A soprano's strength is a strong head voice.

✔ **Voice tone:** The soprano voice is usually bright and ringing.

✔ **Weakness:** Sopranos have a harder time projecting in middle voice.

✔ **Subdivisions:** High, higher, highest — okay, that's not exactly technically accurate, but most other voice types have subdivisions that fill in the gaps. I just didn't want to leave the sopranos out!

✔ **Common Performance Roles:** The soprano is usually the lead in the show, such as Ariel in *The Little Mermaid,* Marian the Librarian in *The Music Man,* and Mimi in *La Bohème.*

✔ **Naming Names:** Famous sopranos you may know include Dolly Parton, Julie Andrews, Sara Brightman, Maria Callas, and Olivia Newton John.

Figure 5-1:
Soprano
range.

Middle C (C4) to High C (C6)

How low can she go: Mezzo

The difference between a *mezzo* (mezzo is the abbreviated term for *mezzo-soprano*) and a soprano is often tessitura. (Tessitura refers to where most of the notes lie in a song — the notes that a voice feels most comfortable singing.) Many mezzos can sing as high as a soprano, but they can't stay as high as a soprano. For example, some roles in operatic literature require the mezzo to sing as high as the soprano lead, but the mezzo doesn't have to remain that high as long as a soprano does — thank goodness — because the mezzo comfort zone is usually different than the soprano; mezzos prefer to live in their middle voices. On the other hand, a soprano hates to live in her middle voice all day, preferring to sing high notes and soar above the orchestra.

To further confuse you, many sopranos sing mezzo repertoire. How dare they! That's not fair, but it's a fact. As in other aspects of life, after the soprano becomes famous, she sings repertoire that she enjoys and that may be music written for somebody else, such as mezzos. So just because a soprano sings a song doesn't mean it's a soprano song. You have to look at the details, such as range of the song, and decide if that range fits your voice. You can find more information about selecting appropriate songs for your voice in Chapter 17 and a list of songs for each voice type in Appendix A.

✔ **Range:** The mezzo range is usually G below Middle C to a High B or High C. Many mezzos vocalize as high as a soprano but can't handle the repetition of the upper notes (See Figure 5-2).

✔ **Register:** The register transitions for the mezzo usually occur at E or F (first space) just above Middle C and the E or F (fifth line) one octave above that.

✔ **Strength:** Mezzos have a strong middle voice.

✔ **Voice tone:** The mezzo voice is usually darker or deeper than her soprano counterpart.

✔ **Weakness:** A mezzo's head voice is often her weakness.

✔ **Subdivisions:** One subdivision of mezzo is *contralto*. Less common than mezzos, *contraltos* can usually sing from F below Middle C to about an F (fifth line) below High C. A contralto can vocalize or sing higher and has an even darker, richer color and is more at home in the lower part of her voice. Sometimes singers darken their voices intentionally to make themselves sound like contraltos. The contralto may take her chest voice dominated sound up to a G (second line) above Middle C and shift into head voice around the D (fourth line) an octave above Middle C. Examples of contraltos include Marian Anderson and Maureen Forrester.

✔ **Common Performance Roles:** The mezzo is often the mother, witch, or the sleazy girl in town. Her roles include such fun ones as Miss Hannigan in *Annie,* Mrs. Pots in *Beauty and The Beast,* Carmen in the opera *Carmen,* and Aunt Eller in *Oklahoma!*

✔ **Naming Names:** Famous mezzos you may know include Marilyn Horne, K.D. Lang, Lorrie Morgan, Patsy Cline, and Karen Carpenter.

Figure 5-2:
Mezzo
range.

G below Middle C to B (B5)

Highest range of the dudes: Tenor

Thanks to the Three Tenors, The Irish Tenors, and even Three Mo' Tenors, you probably have a good idea of what a *tenor* sounds like.

✔ **Range:** The tenor range, shown in Figure 5-3, is about two octaves with many singing a little lower than C (second space in bass clef) and a little higher than the male High C (third space treble clef).

✔ **Register:** The tenor voice doesn't make a huge transition from his lower voice to his middle voice. His transition into his middle voice occurs around Middle C (or the E just above Middle C) and then a transition into head voice around F-sharp or G above Middle C.

✔ **Strength:** The tenor's strength is his head voice.

✔ **Voice tone:** The tenor voice is usually bright and ringing.

✔ **Weakness:** His weakness is often his lower voice.

✔ **Subdivisions:** In the musical-theater world, a subdivision of the tenor, called the *bari/tenor,* reigns. This voice type is someone with the power to project in the middle voice and the higher ringing money notes of the tenor. The other voice type that you frequently hear of in the opera world is the *countertenor* — a male singer who sounds like a female. This voice type sings in the same range as the mezzo (sometimes soprano) and sounds similar. When you've heard the countertenor singing enough, you can distinguish him from a mezzo. Until then, just enjoy the unique quality that these gentlemen bring to the singing world.

✔ **Common Performance Roles:** The tenor is almost always the lead, winning the girl at the end of the show. Examples include Rodolfo in *La Bohème,* Don José in *Carmen,* Tony in *West Side Story,* Billy in *Chicago,* and Rolf in *The Sound of Music.*

✔ **Naming Names:** Famous tenors you may know include Luciano Pavarotti, Placido Domingo, and José Carreras, whom you may recognize as the Three Tenors, as well as John Denver, Enrico Caruso, Daniel Rodriguez (the Singing Cop), Elton John, and Stevie Wonder.

Castrato sings with vibrato!

A *castrato* was a male singer who was castrated before reaching puberty. Beginning in the 16th century and continuing until the early 1900s, young male singers (mostly in Italy) were castrated in the hope that they would maintain their high voice. You can decide for yourself how painful this must've been without anesthesia, Tylenol, or even ice. The castrato maintained the ability to sing high notes while growing to a full-sized man who had enormous breath power. He had enormous breath power, because his larynx remained small due to castration, but his chest grew large, as he became a man. Big lungs + small larynx = great breath power. The downside of all this was that not all boys remained good singers. Boy singers are now safe to keep everything they came into the world with, so the mezzo or countertenor sings these roles today.

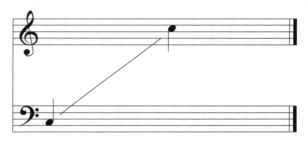

Figure 5-3:
Tenor range.

C one octave below Middle C to C one octave above Middle C

He's so low: Bass

Bass is the lowest of the voice types. The bass is the guy that sings all the cool low notes in the barbershop quartet.

- ✔ **Range:** His range is usually F (below the bass clef staff) to E (first line treble clef) but can be as wide as E-flat to F (See Figure 5-4).
- ✔ **Register transitions:** The bass changes from chest voice into middle voice around A or A-flat just below Middle C and changes into head voice around D or D-flat just above Middle C.
- ✔ **Strength:** His low voice is his strength.
- ✔ **Voice tone:** His voice is the deepest, darkest, and heaviest of the male voices.

↙ **Weakness:** His high voice is his weakness.

↙ **Subdivisions:** Filling in the middle between tenor and bass is the *baritone*. The baritone can usually sing from an A (first space bass clef) to F (first space treble clef) below the male High C. The bass-baritone has some height of the baritone and some depth of the bass and his range is usually A-flat (first space bass clef) to F (first space treble clef) and sometimes as high as G below the male High C. The baritone's register transitions usually occur at the A or B just below Middle C and the D or E above Middle C.

↙ **Common Performance Roles:** The bass or baritone (see next section) is often the villain, father, or older man. Examples include Ramfis in *Aïda*, the Mikado in *The Mikado*, and Jud Fry in *Oklahoma!* Some exceptions to this villain image are King Arthur in *Camelot*, Porgy in *Porgy and Bess*, and the Toreador in *Carmen*.

↙ **Naming Names:** Famous basses you may know include Samuel Ramey, James Morris, José Van Dam, Tennessee Ernie Ford, and Barry White.

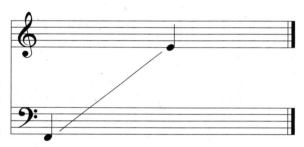

Figure 5-4:
Bass range.

F about an octave and a half below Middle C to
E above Middle C

Casting Call

In classical music or the opera world, the four voice types can be further divided into categories based on the size and agility of the voice. If you just want to know about your voice type without worrying about what happens at the opera, skip the following paragraph. The first four terms are in order like the soda sizes at the fast-food joint. Light is the small, lightweight cup, and dramatic is the cup so large that it won't fit in the cup holder in your car.

↙ **Light:** A bright, youthful, agile voice.

↙ **Lyric:** A medium-sized voice with a warm color that's comfortable singing long, even phrases. Lyric is appropriate for a romantic character.

✔ **Full:** A louder, stronger voice that doesn't necessarily sing fast lines as easily as a light voice.

✔ **Dramatic:** A voice that's even louder than a full voice and sings a heavier repertoire, such as Wagner. Dramatic voices are those that can peel the paint off the wall from 50 paces. These voices are big and heavier than full lyric voices, and they aren't known for subtlety but for power and strength.

✔ **Coloratura:** A flexible voice that moves easily through fast lines in the music.

A singer can be a mix of the terms in the preceding list. For example, a light lyric coloratura refers to a medium-sized light voice that moves easily. Seeing the words combined to describe a voice type isn't so confusing if you understand the definition of each descriptive word. However, only in the classical world is it important for you to know your voice category. Don't worry about the specific kind of category you happen to be in until you get some training. You may encounter the names of following subdivisions:

✔ **Soprano subdivisions** include light lyric, full lyric, light lyric coloratura and full lyric coloratura, light dramatic coloratura and full dramatic coloratura, light dramatic soprano (or spinto) and full dramatic.

✔ **Mezzo subdivisions** include light lyric coloratura or full lyric coloratura, light lyric or full lyric, and dramatic. The dramatic mezzo is similar to the dramatic soprano. To be fair to the sopranos, I confess that dramatic mezzos sometimes sing roles written for the dramatic soprano. You go girls!

✔ **Tenor subdivisions** include light lyric or full lyric, dramatic, or heroic. The heroic tenor is also called a dramatic tenor — the guy that has a large voice with great stamina. Don't challenge him to a singing contest at the local pub.

✔ **Bass subdivisions** include the comic bass (funny guy in the show), as well as lyric and dramatic bass. His subdivision buddy, the baritone, also comes in different shapes and sizes: light lyric baritone, full lyric baritone, and bass baritone.

Determining Your Voice Type

You may be confused after reading about all the voice types. Please remember that it's not absolutely necessary to name your voice type today. If you've read the descriptions of the voice types in this chapter, you may be ready to vote soprano over mezzo or bass over tenor for the time being. Try that range for a while and see if it fits well.

Listen to recordings of singers and read about what they've sung during their careers. If you know of singers that have voices similar to yours, look at the roles they sang. When you have gathered that information and when you know a bit about your own singing voice, then answer these questions.

- **Where are the register transitions for your voice?** Vocalize according to the information and exercises in Chapters 11 through 13 and write down the notes where transitions occur in your voice.

- **What's the timbre of your voice?** Is the tone more steely than chocolaty? Steely isn't a negative adjective; it's merely fact. Very often the steely voice is the character audiences love, but they don't want to rush up and put their arms around her and rescue her.

- **Is your voice light and flutelike?** Is your voice loud and heavy even when you're lightly singing? Heavy means the sound that you're making is loud even when you're singing comfortably.

- **What is your singing range and tessitura?** The difference between a mezzo and a soprano often is tessitura. The mezzo can sing the high notes but doesn't want to live up there, and the soprano wants to sing one high note after another.

- **Are you able to move your voice easily?** Do you enjoy the fast passages in the song and think of them as fun? If the fast notes are easy for you, you can add coloratura to your vocal description.

- **What do you consider the general or overall strengths of your voice — strong middle voice, weak head voice, and so on?** Your vocal strengths change as you practice.

As you work through the exercises in the book, jot down answers to these questions and see how they apply to the different voice types in this chapter. If you're new to singing, determining your voice type by yourself may take a few months. Your voice changes with practice. So have fun sorting through all the different types.

Chapter 6

Acquiring Beautiful Tone

In This Chapter

▶ Using space and breath to create tone

▶ Letting go of tone

▶ Maintaining that beautiful tone

▶ Discovering your own vibrato

*T*o create your own beautiful, engaging tones, you need to make space for the tone to resonate, and you need to apply the breathing skills that you picked up in Chapter 3. Space and breath are great partners in tone production. If you invite space to the singing party and don't invite breath, the space closes down. So think of those two factors as a team and keep them working together. This chapter gives you all the tools that you need to create your space and breath team while creating and sustaining beautiful tone and vibrato.

Creating Tone

When you sing, you want to create tones that are clear and ringing. You can't beat the sound. But making a clear tone takes practice and know-how. You need to know how to control your muscles and the movement of air through your mouth. What you don't want are breathy tones and tight tones:

 ✔ **Breathy:** A breathy tone is fuzzy and unfocused. To get an idea of what a breathy tone sounds like, pretend that you're whispering a juicy secret to a friend. The fuzzy tone that you use when whispering isn't clear or ringing. When you sing with a breathy tone, you lose plenty of air. It takes much more air to sing a breathy tone than it does a clear one.

> ✔ **Tight:** When your muscles are so tight that they squeeze the sound out, you get a tight tone. If you've ever watched a tennis match, then maybe you can recall the sound that the players make when they hit the ball. That grunting sound is from the exertion of energy that flows through their body as they hit the ball. Imagine if you had to use that sound to sing an entire song. Whew! That would be tiring.

What you want to do is move air (exhale) to create a free, large, colorful, open tone. Using too much physical pressure (which feels like squeezing) in the throat creates a tight, constricted sound, and not connecting enough air creates a fuzzy or airy tone. You need to find the happy medium, a tone that's connected to air and sounds clear. By coordinating the flow of air from the breathing skills you developed in Chapter 3 and by keeping the space open in your throat, you can control the quality of your tone. Keep reading for an explanation of how to start the tone and create enough space to ensure that you're creating the best tone possible.

Starting the tone

Starting a tone for singing is called *onset of tone*. You can start a tone two ways: with physical force or with air. The physical force is similar to the grunting of the tennis player when the muscles in the throat press together with very little air flowing. By starting the tone with a consistent breath flow and an open throat, you create a tone that has a different quality. Starting the tone with air is the same as the lip trill (see Chapter 3) or tongue trill. When you start the lip trill, the air passes between your lips and suction pulls them together, and they flap in the breeze. Your vocal cords do the same when you start the tone by coordinating a consistent flow of air.

The easiest way to start the tone, *humming,* means singing or making tone with your lips closed (as you may already know). Think of humming as a prolonged *M.* Try it. If you aren't sure if your tone was clear, say "Uh-huh," with your mouth closed — the sound you make when you're reading the newspaper and someone asks you a question. Say "Uh-huh" again and hear and feel the clarity and then use that same feeling to hum part of a song. The clarity of tone from your "Uh-huh" was different from the whisper you used to explore breathy tone. You can feel the difference in vibrations between a breathy tone and a clear tone. The clear tone creates stronger vibrations in your throat, mouth, and nasal passages. You may feel vibrations in all three locations or the vibrations may vary depending on how high or low you're singing or speaking.

When you start a tone, you want to rely on the feeling and not the sound. The sound may be different in each room, so you want to rely on the feeling, which should be more consistent from room to room and day to day in your singing.

By hearing that the "Uh-huh" was clear, you then can become aware of the feeling and start the tone again and explore that feeling. When you explore the feeling enough, you'll be able to start the tone, because you remember the feeling.

Creating back space

In the olden days, before computers, you often heard the phrase back space, referring to moving the carriage of a typewriter back one space. In singing, *back space* refers to the space in the back of your mouth and in your throat. Just opening your teeth or the front of your mouth (front space) shows off your gorgeous pearly whites, but it doesn't do enough for your tone. Yes, you do have to open your teeth to create enough back space, but the big opening has to be in the back of your mouth and your throat. For space and breath to work together, you need to open the space quickly and then move the breath. (See Chapter 3 for more information about breathing.) Try the following exercises to create the open space necessary for great tone.

To feel the open space in your mouth and throat, yawn inside your mouth and throat with your lips closed. The end of a yawn can be tense or the muscles can be tense. Remember how your mouth feels before the muscles stretch too far and become tense — that's the open space you need. Practice this a few times, so you can feel the space open.

Another way to feel space inside your mouth is to pretend that you have an egg in the back of your mouth. You can use other images, such as a golf ball if you don't like eggs. Compare the feeling of the space when it's closed and when you have the egg sitting on the back of your tongue. By imagining that the egg is in your mouth, practice moving that space quickly. Moving your tongue against the roof of your mouth would close down the space. But if you move the air while singing, this "egg" space stays open.

Try singing part of your favorite song. Find the openness of the yawn or feel the egg in the back of your mouth and begin singing with the throat and the back of your mouth open. Remember to find the same clarity that you had when you were humming. You can compare the tone change by singing with the throat and back of the mouth closed and then sing the same way with the space open. If you aren't sure about the difference in the sound, record yourself and listen back.

Coordinating air with tone

A good laugh has no comparison. Who knew that laughter is a great excuse to connect tone and breath? In the exercise just ahead, you and Santa get an opportunity to feel the connection of breath as you start a tone. Connecting the flow or air to the start of the tone is important for finding that open tone.

Laughter should be about the connection of air with the start of the tone, but sometimes you may get carried away and laugh by pressing in your throat. If your laughter makes your singing muscles too tired to sing or if your throat feels scratchy, your laugh may be too taxing on your throat and you need to start the tone with a more consistent flow of air. If your laughter is too taxing on your throat, try laughing like Santa, using a hearty "Ho, ho, ho!" Take a few minutes and explore that feeling of boisterous laughter. You can even bounce around on an "Ah" or "Ha" if Santa is too much of a stretch for you. Let the sound vary in pitch and change to higher and lower pitches as you extend the laughter. Notice the movement in your body as you laugh. More than likely your body moves exactly as described in Chapter 3. That means your lower *abs* (that's short for abdominal muscles) move in as you exhale to make the "Ho" sound. Another way to create this same coordination of breath and tone is to imitate the sound of a gorilla. You really have to coordinate the air and the tone to imitate the primates. They might be great singers if they knew how to elongate those tones.

You can even slow down the laughter to really feel the movement in your body as you laugh and move air, and this should be similar to what you do when you sing. After you explore laughter and movement of breath, try singing part of a song to notice the flow of your air as you start the beginning tone of each phrase. You want the air to be moving consistently the entire time that you sing, and the open space to remain open as you sing.

Sighing your way to clarity

Certain styles of music don't require clarity in the tone, but you should be singing a breathy tone by choice rather than having no idea how to make it clear when you really want to. Sighing helps you focus on finding this clarity of tone. It allows you to make sounds without worrying about singing precise pitches, which you shouldn't bother with for right now.

Start a sigh at a comfortable pitch and maintain the sound of a sigh as you slide down pitches. If the sigh was clear, continue your exploration and move to higher pitches or slide around on the sigh to hear the clarity of tone. If your tone wasn't clear, try to make a more energetic sigh. Adding more energy to the sigh means connecting your body to the sigh. Engage your entire body in sighing by moving as you sigh. Move your body in such a way (leaning, bending, stretching, and bouncing) that you feel as if your entire body is surging and singing. Using this exertion of energy when you sing also helps you find clarity in your tone. Your breath will be flowing to complete a specific physical movement, which will help the onset of tone. The vocal cords don't vibrate as easily with a tiny little breeze; they need a strong wind blowing to encourage them to make clear tone. Filling a room with a clear tone is easier than filling it with a fuzzy tone. Without a microphone, you'll need a clear tone to be heard when you sing.

Younger singers often have a breathy tone. While they have the ability to make a clear tone, they need to make the tone clear with the correct technique and not by adding pressure. A breathy tone is usually caused by lack of coordination, which means you need to get the breath ready and then add the energy that I just described. So if you have a breathy tone, work on your breathing skills (see Chapter 3) to help you understand that movement in your body. When the breathing skills are ready, focus on tone production. The tone may also continue to change as you mature, which is also normal. Just remember what good technique feels like and keep working to make it a habit in your body.

If you aren't sure if your tone is clear, record your practice session and compare the tone to Marilyn Monroe's unfocused tone when she sang "Happy Birthday, Mr. President" and then imitate Pavarotti to find clear tones. Knowing what your tone sounds like is the point and knowing when a clear tone is appropriate is important. You can use a breathy tone if that is the style and sound you want. Norah Jones has a breathy tone, but she's an example of someone singing pop and jazz music, using that tone on purpose.

Releasing Tone

Most people think of singing and enjoying themselves. Releasing a tone doesn't sound nearly as important as singing the tone. You sing a tone and then release it. Singing requires that breath move out of your body (exhale) and releasing the tone simply requires that you inhale. That sounds easy doesn't it? Practice the following two exercises a few times to get the feeling in your body. In the heat of the performance, you want your body to remember how to let go of the tone, so you can get in that next breath quickly.

Inhaling to release tone

An easy way to practice releasing tone is to inhale. Sing an *ah* vowel and when you're ready to stop the tone, simply inhale. The first few times that you try this, it may feel funny. You may think that you haven't done it right, because it was too easy. Practice singing the *ah* and releasing several times in a row: *ah,* inhale, *ah,* inhale, *ah,* and inhale. Although this exercise may have you momentarily sounding more like a sex kitten than a professional singer, it allows you to feel that singing is exhaling, releasing a tone is inhaling, and the breath is always in motion, whether going in or out. Remember that when you inhale, you want to release the muscles in your throat. If you keep the muscles tight, you'll gasp, because the air is trying to pass through a tight space.

Letting your throat go

After you explore inhaling to release the tone, try letting your throat go. That means releasing all the muscles in your throat. Just think of releasing in your throat by letting go of all the muscles and the tone stops. You may end up inhaling, but you didn't have to worry about that action, because your body took care of it. As a young singer, I was afraid to sing higher pitches, because I didn't know how to stop them without choking on the consonant. Think of the release being a lift off from the tone or a liftoff from the consonant and don't worry about stopping the tone.

Sustaining Tone

Sustaining tone is a singing must. Have you ever run out of air before the end of the phrase in your song and then had to sneak in a breath? Sneaking in a breath is legal when you sing, but I want you to sneak a breath because you choose to and not because you have to. Among the times that you ran out of air, you may even have had to take a breath in the middle of a word. Yikes! That's not a federal crime, but you came to the right place for some tips on applying your breathing skills to sustain tones.

Connecting the dots with legato

Those gorgeous lines that professionals sing so effortlessly happen, because they know how to connect the dots. By dots, I mean the pitches of a song. Singers sometimes sing a melody one pitch at a time, not thinking of them as a continuous line. To make the phrases *legato* (smooth and connected), you need to think of the pitches as having no empty space in between. The sound should flow from one pitch to the other, and the feeling in the throat is a continuous sound even while you change pitches. Singing a long line of tone happens because of breath control. If you haven't read Chapter 3 on breath control, please do so now, so you can apply those skills as you attempt to sing legato lines.

While singing the pattern in Figure 6-1, focus on making the sound legato and concentrate on the connection between pitches. Find your alignment, practice the breath a few times, open the back space, and begin.

Figure 6-1: Creating a legato line.

Trilling the lips or tongue

The lip trill is an exercise that's explained in Chapter 3. This time, you're going to really let those lips trill as you sustain pitches. Remember that the lip trill is making the sounds like Mr. Ed, the talking horse, or flapping your lips due to the air flowing between them. The purpose of using the lip trill is to monitor the flow of air. You can't continue the lip trill without the air flowing. By making the pattern longer, you get an opportunity to sustain the tone longer. If that lip trill is just too much for you, feel free to use a tongue trill. The principle is the same: trilling the tongue but maintaining a consistent flow of air.

Focus on creating a legato line as you sing the pattern in Figure 6-2. Find your alignment, prepare your breath, and begin.

Figure 6-2: Trilling a long, legato line.

Ascending and descending with scales for length of tone

Because you've been such a hard worker up to this point, how about a chance to put some of the exercises in this chapter together and strut your stuff? The pattern that you see in Figure 6-3 gives you the chance to sing and put your eggs all in the basket. Instead of playing the exercise faster, I slow it down to make it harder, so you really have to work the breath. Think through all the exercises that you can do so far (great posture, open space in your throat and mouth, and getting breath in your body), so you're ready to put it all together when you sing this pattern.

The pattern you see in Figure 6-3 is played slowly to allow you to lengthen your breath and sing long legato lines. You have time between each repetition to get your breath. Remember to find your alignment, open the back space, allow the breath to drop in your body each time and keep your chest steady throughout the pattern.

Figure 6-3:
Managing
long
phrases.

TRACK 7

1. oh _____
2. *ah* _____

Finding Your Vibrato

Vibrato, the variation of tone or pitch, is one of the differences between a folk singer and an opera singer's voice. *Vibrato* is the variation of a sustained pitch with a normal vibrato rate being five to eight pulses per second.

Exactly what causes vibrato is a mystery at this point in the research of singing. Many scientists speculate that it's the undulation of the cords as they open and close, and others claim that it's the undulation of the tissue on the walls of the throat.

The source of vibrato (or even what vibrato really is), however, isn't as important as the sound. Vibrato can be faster or slower depending on the singer. A really slow vibrato is sometimes called a *wobble,* which is often created, because breath coordination is lacking. Vibrato that's too fast is called a *tremolo* and is usually caused from too much tension somewhere in the throat or neck area. Keep reading to find out what exercises can help you find your vibrato and discover the difference between *straight tone* (no variation in pitch) and vibrato.

Straight tone is a choice that you can make when you sing. Straight tone has no vibrato and no variation in the tone. You can use straight tone when you sing various styles of music, but you want the straight tone to be a choice, because it's a different sound. Knowing how to move from straight tone to a tone that has vibrato is important to having variety in your singing tone. Young male singers (before they hit puberty) don't have vibrato, but most everyone has it or can acquire it.

Understanding vibrato

One way to understand vibrato is to listen to other singers, especially classical singers. Almost every classical singer has vibrato. Listen to the pitches as the singer holds them out to hear the variation of the tone. After you spend some time listening to others, record yourself singing a song that has slow or long pitches. Listen back to the recording of you singing. Notice the variations of your tone as you hold out the pitches. You may find that the vibrato was there all along and you just didn't know it or didn't know what it was called.

Moving from straight tone to vibrato

When you sing, you can choose to create tone that has variation in pitch (vibrato) or not (straight tone). There is absolutely nothing wrong with straight tone singing as long as that's your choice. Your choir director may have asked you to sing straight tones when performing some styles of music. Many people sing with straight tones, because they have too much tension in their neck or throat. You don't have to squeeze in your throat to create straight tone; it's actually just the opposite. You need to keep the throat open for a tone with or without vibrato.

On Track 8, listen to the singer demonstrate the difference between a tone with and without vibrato as well as moving from straight tone to vibrato. You try it. Sing a tone that has vibrato and then sing a tone that has no vibrato. Now try starting the tone without vibrato and sliding into a tone with vibrato. As the vibrato begins, you feel something release and the movement of the vibrato begins. It's not a huge difference but subtle. Try this several times in a row to feel the difference. If you still aren't sure which sound you're making, try whining. Whining usually is made with a straight tone. Compare the sound when you whine your way through part of a song and then open up and really sing.

Imitating your favorite singer with vibrato

Singers who have good coordination of breath and open space usually have vibrato. Think of a singer (probably someone you've heard singing opera or classical music) who makes a huge sound when they sing. Now imitate them.

Find a quiet place where you can make plenty of sound. Hear the singer's voice in your mind and then imitate that singer. If it helps, open your arms wide, hold a white towel or stand on a chair, so you feel enormous. Imitating someone with good technique doesn't hurt your voice. You may discover that you can make some pretty big sounds yourself.

If you imitate a singer with vibrato, then you can probably figure out how to imitate their vibrato, too. After you do, continue to explore that sound and notice what your voice sounds like. You can even tape yourself just to prove that you made that much glorious sound.

If you didn't find a different sound, imitate a different singer. This time choose a larger-than-life opera singer. Be flamboyant and pretend that you've been called in to sing, because the star is ill. Fake it and sing some of their songs, even make up the words.

The key to singing with vibrato is making the sound happen naturally, not forcing it. Explore different kinds of sounds and work with space and breath to find vibrato.

You may be tempted to create vibrato by bouncing your abdomen — but don't. Bouncing your abs doesn't consistently produce vibrato; instead, rather than forcing it, let the vibrato happen so that you keep air consistently flowing as you did in the exercises in Chapter 3. Ham it up and enjoy vibrato!

Chapter 7

Exploring Resonance

In This Chapter

▶ Separating the truth from fiction

▶ Putting your sound out where folks can hear it

▶ Knowing what resonance is not

▶ Moving your soft palate to achieve the best vocals

*H*ow do all those singers project so much sound without microphones? They take advantage of *resonance* — the vibrations that create tone — the glorious magic that allows a singer to fill a large hall with sound without electronic amplification. Creating tone is the first step in the singing process. (See Chapter 4 for more information on creating tone.) The next step is to make a ringing, resonant tone.

Sound vibrates in canyons, and you need to take advantage of the small canyons in your body called *resonators,* such as your throat, mouth, and nasal passages. Chapter 4 discusses how to open the space in the throat and mouth to get the most benefit from those resonators. And by lifting the soft palate, you adjust the resonance in the nasal passages. (For more on your soft palate, see the section "Eliminating Nasality" later in this chapter.)

In this chapter, you explore the sounds and feeling of resonance and discover where sound can resonate in your body.

Good Vibrations

Resonance is vibrations creating tone through and within your mouth, throat, and nose. So you know what it is. And you know what it isn't. (If you don't, read the section "Debunking Common Misconceptions" later in this chapter.) So you can begin exploring how to create your own resonance by moving the tone forward. Tone needs to move forward when you sing in order for everyone to hear you; otherwise, you just have your own private concert for one inside your head.

Moving the sound forward means taking advantage of the resonators and allowing the sound to really ring in each resonating space — your mouth, throat, and nasal passages. To make your tone resonate in each resonating space, you should visualize the tone going in a specific direction. My favorite visual is a cannon to aim the sound. You can aim your sound toward a bullseye on the wall or as a laser beam streaming across the room. Any visual can work as long as you aim the sound out of your body and forward.

Aim that tone forward as you explore all your resonating spaces. Knowing how to access all that resonance can help you fill an entire concert hall, rather than just your car, with great tone.

Exploring your resonators

When you sing, you want to discover how to activate all your resonators (mouth, throat, and nasal passages). At first, you may find it easier to feel vibrations on *ee* vowels, but with a bit of practice, you'll be matching all your vowels to this vibrant sound. Remember, you want all your vowel sounds to be equally resonant so that all your words can be heard at the back of the concert hall.

Resonance: From crying to crooning

Listening to popular music on the radio provides you with an opportunity to hear different types of resonance. Pop singers use much more *twang* — that sound that's similar to a cry or whine. The resonance isn't made with a wide-open throat and a low larynx, but it still can be a pleasant and enjoyable sound. Country singers use that same twang; they just croon a little more when they do it. Crooning is what Frank Sinatra did so well. You could almost call it lazy singing, because he wasn't worried about projecting to the back of the hall. He always had a microphone in front of him. Classical singers use a lower larynx and have to use plenty of brilliant resonating tones, because they don't have microphones on the stage. Now, some opera companies amplify the singers, but it's not common practice.

As you listen to your favorite singers, notice the difference in the sound and notice what you have to do with your own voice to imitate those sounds. What did you have to change to imitate their voice? You probably have to change the size of your mouth and throat, and sometimes, even change the position of your larynx. Have fun exploring these sounds as you discover the secrets of resonance. By experimenting with all the different resonators, you'll have a better chance of achieving a balanced resonant tone in your own singing voice. If you want some ideas of who to imitate, try imitating Loretta Lynn and Leontyne Price, Gracie Allen and Kathleen Turner, Steve Urkel (Jaleel White) and James Earl Jones, or Marlon Brando and John Wayne.

Ringing it out

Swallowing vowels moves the sound into reverse. To create resonant tones that resound around the room, roll the sound into drive. Find the buzzing *M* and roll from an *M* to singing an *ee* vowel. Notice if the *ee* buzzes in the same vicinity as the *M*. Take your chance to aim. When *M-ee* is easy, try *M-ooh*, *M-oh*, and *M-ah*. *M-ah* may be harder to feel, but see if you can sing *ah* keeping the same vibrations that you have found in *M-ee*. When that's easy, roll between consonants and vowels, singing words like *many* and *moment*. Maintain the same ring each time as you go to the vowel.

Eliminating Nasality

Your *soft palate* is the soft tissue on the roof of your mouth. Knowing where it is and how it moves can help you make resonant tones. A soft palate that lifts helps to create the ringing sound that you want. If the soft palate doesn't lift, the sound is nasal. Exercise your soft palate so that it lifts on command and so you avoid that nasal sound.

To check for a nasal sound, sing part of your favorite song and hold your nose. If the sound has a balanced, resonant sound, you can sing while holding your nose, and the sound won't change. On the other hand, if the sound does change, you likely have a nasal sound.

Getting the feel for soft palate work

Seeing your soft palate in action helps you visualize how it should work. But before you watch it work, you need to find out where it is in your mouth.

If you run your tongue along the back of your front teeth, then along the roof of your mouth, you can feel a ridge right after your gums, then you can feel the hardness of the hard palate and then the soft tissue at the back. That soft tissue is your soft palate.

In order to see your soft palate move,

1. Shine a flashlight in your mouth while looking in the mirror.
2. Yawn so that you can see the soft palate lift.
3. Say "Hung" or "Ugh" to see the tongue and soft palate touch.

If you aren't sure what your soft palate feels like when it moves, then I give you my permission to cut some zzzzzs and snore — just don't try this as an excuse for your nightly snoring habit. Because you know how your soft palate moves when you sing, snoring helps you feel it.

In order to feel the soft palate

- Pretend that you're snoring in your sleep. Snore with your mouth open and take in air through your nose.

- If this only gets your nose quivering, put your fingers on your nose and close off your nostrils. When you close your nostrils, try snoring again by breathing through your mouth.

   That quivering that you feel now is your soft palate moving.

As you practice the exercises in this section, bear in mind how it felt and looked to have your soft palate lift as well as to have your tongue touch your soft palate. These movements, when coordinated, keep your sound from being too nasal.

Coordinating your soft palate and tongue

After you know where your soft palate is as well as how it feels when it moves, you need to discover how to coordinate that movement of your soft palate with your tongue. Knowing how to move the soft palate is important for speaking and singing, because you want the soft palate to lift for a balanced resonant tone. If the soft palate doesn't lift, you'll make a sound that has too much resonance in your nose or a "nasal sound" as you may have heard someone say. To make a sound that has a balanced resonant tone, explore the exercises below to help you feel the movement of the tongue and soft palate in words. You can then take that same knowledge into your singing. When it's time to sing a consonant that requires the soft palate to move, move it down to meet the tongue for the consonant and then lift it back up.

In Chapter 9, you can explore consonants. To be prepared for some of the movements that you'll need to make in your mouth, you want to be able to move your tongue to touch your soft palate and then go back down and rest in your mouth. To feel how the back of your tongue raises to meet your soft palate and then moves back down, do the following

1. **Sing the word "Hung," holding out the _NG_ sound at the end.**

   You should be able to feel the buzzing or resonance of that consonant in your nasal passages. Because your tongue is touching your soft palate to make the _NG_, the air only has one escape route and that's through your nose. This escape route is just fine as long as you only allow the air to escape when you're pronouncing nasal consonants, such as _NG_, or when you're humming. When the soft palate lifts high again, the air escapes out of your mouth creating a more balanced resonant tone.

2. **Now sing "Hung-ah."**

   Feel the *NG* sound in your face or behind your nose (not *in* your nose) and then aim the sound of the *ah* to the same vicinity.

   After you release the consonant sound *NG* and move to the vowel sound *ah,* the air should come out of your mouth. Singing *hung-ah,* you can feel the resonance and then maintain that resonance as you extend the *ah.*

3. **Now say, "A cucumber."**

   Notice that your soft palate is nice and high on the word *A* and then the tongue lifts to meet the soft palate on the consonant *C.* The tongue comes back down for the vowel and then lifts again for the next *C.*

   You can feel the same movement if you say, "I got it" or "A ghost." This time around, you should be able to not only lift the tongue to meet the soft palate but also to feel the sensations of sound in your head as you hold out the vowel.

Moving air through the nose

Nasal resonance is different from a nasal sound. *Nasal resonance* is taking advantage of the sound resonating in the nasal passages. If all the sound resonates in your nasal passages, the sound is a nasal sound or too nasal. To help you understand the feeling of air moving through your nose, you can try the following exercise. Knowing what air feels like when it moves through your nose helps you to understand that the air shouldn't be moving out of your nose unless you're humming or for the split second it takes for you to make a nasal consonant *(M, N, NG).* To help you feel the sounds of nasal resonance and to feel the air moving out of your nose, try the following exercise.

1. Try humming a few bars of a song to feel the prolonged *M* that you feel buzzing around your lips.

2. Just for kicks, try humming (with your lips closed) and holding your nose. Didn't work did it? When you closed your mouth and held your nose, the air had no escape route.

3. Try humming again. Don't hold your nose and notice the flow of the air coming out of your nose.

4. After you open your mouth for a vowel, you want the air to come out of your mouth. If it doesn't, the sound is nasal.

Remember that you can have air coming out of your nose as you're singing nasal consonants, such as *M, N,* and *NG,* but not while you're singing a vowel sound. If you have air coming out of your nose while singing a vowel, you'll create an undesirable nasal sound, which doesn't take advantage of all the resonators.

Breathing: Nose versus mouth

What's the best way to take in air? Through your nose or your mouth? Taking in air through your nose or what's known as *nose breathing* allows the breath to drop low in your body and adds moisture from your nasal passages. This is a good thing, unless you have to take a fast breath for a quick entrance in your song. For those quick breaths, you need to take the air in through your mouth or through your nose and mouth at the same time. You get more air in and faster.

Debunking Common Misconceptions

Now that you understand what resonance is, finding out what it isn't is important, too. Myths and misconceptions about resonance abound and most have to do with what is or is not a resonator. If you buy into these myths, the tone of your singing voice may not be as good as it could be.

Resonating tone in your sinuses

Sometimes, a voice teacher says, "Let the tone resonate in your sinuses." That's a nice image, but sound doesn't resonate in the sinuses even though you may feel the vibrations in your face. You're feeling *sympathetic vibrations,* which is also known as *sympathetic resonance.* What the teacher is trying to get you to do is explore the vibrations of sound in your face or in the *mask,* as some teachers like to call it.

Your *mask* is the front of your face. Think of your bones and skin on your face as a mask sitting on top of another face. You may feel the sound vibrating like crazy as if you have some metal substance on the front of your face.

No need to correct someone who says, "Let the tone resonate in your sinuses." Just keep exploring sympathetic resonance, and everyone wins.

Placing every tone in the same location

The word *place* is misleading. You can visualize and feel, but you can't literally *place* a tone anywhere. *Place* is a common word used by voice teachers, and it's not all bad. What they really want is for you to explore the sensations and get the most resonant tone as is possible from your singing voice. They may say focus the sound to get the most resonance. Think about how we focus a flashlight to get a strong clear beam of light. Keep focusing your sound and know that focusing is often called *placing* or *placement*. Remember, these are images that can help you achieve the sound that you're trying to produce. The second confusing part is that not every tone is felt in the same location. Again, you can focus and try to feel sound in the same place. You probably feel head voice vibrations more in your head or on the top of your head, and you feel chest voice in your chest. Feeling the sounds of chest voice in your head is much harder, so "placing the tones in the exact same location" is tough. Work to find brilliance and focus to all tones and then remember that feeling no matter where it is.

Some time ago, I worked with a wonderful director who kept asking me to place the tone outside my lips. When he finally said, "That's right; that's the place," I didn't feel the sound anywhere near my lips. What I discovered is to find the correct sound, notice where I feel it, and what it feels like. Remember that every body is different. Where I feel a vibration, you may not. Make sure that you work for the quality of tone and that the vibration that you feel is a result of this.

Keeping your tongue completely flat

The tongue has to move to shape vowel sounds and consonant sounds, so it can't stay down all the time. Releasing tongue tension is different from keeping the tongue down. You can read about releasing tongue tension in Chapter 4. After releasing the tension, you then can move the tongue to shape vowel sounds and consonant sounds without pressing up or down. As you can read in Chapter 8, your tongue arches to make certain vowels. Sometimes, the arch is in the front of the tongue, and sometimes, it's in the back of the tongue. By trying to keep your tongue down at all times, you may end up muffling your vowels. Allowing your tongue to do its job when the time comes is easier.

Opening your mouth wide

Opening the mouth for singing is a good thing. Opening the space in the back of your mouth is excellent. Opening your mouth too far isn't good, however, because the sound spreads. For most people, opening the jaw too wide actually closes off the back space. To find the right space, place two fingers in your mouth vertically and see how that space changes the sound. You really can have too much of a good thing. Open your mouth to let the sound come out but don't show your tonsils, no matter how beautiful they are.

Don't worry about your soft palate

Your soft palate is the soft tissue on the roof of your mouth, and it is key for keeping the resonance from living in your nose. By lifting the soft palate, you can make all kinds of different sounds. If your soft palate knows what to do and is well versed in good singing habits, then you don't need to worry about your soft palate. I would suggest that you read the information about moving the soft palate in the "Eliminating Nasality" section, earlier in this chapter, and explore the sound as it moves. You can hear for yourself how important it is.

The more forward the sound, the better

It's true that if you swallow your vowels, you create a backward sound, which isn't so great. However, by thinking only of projecting your voice forward as much as possible, you create a brassy sound. Use that sound for a character voice (imagine Fran Drescher singing), but I wouldn't suggest that you try it for every song. This is another example of too much of a good thing. This little myth is similar to myth number one. You can't see sound unless you have some sort of equipment that measures the tone on a meter and graphs out the results. So you must rely on both sound and feeling.

Smiling to stay on pitch

The other counterpart of the smile-to-stay-on-pitch myth is raising your eyebrows to stay on pitch. Raising your eyebrows creates a lift that many people believe helps you stay on pitch. The problem is that this lift can cause unnecessary tension, and you look surprised all the time. The same is true about smiling. A smile is a beautiful thing, but it can also cause unnecessary tension in your face while singing.

You may also have explored pushing the lips out to focus a pitch. It changes the sound, but you can't always depend on adorable fish lips for ringing sounds. Find the bright resonant sound by exploring sympathetic vibrations, so your lips can round to shape the vowels. Read Chapter 4 for more information about matching pitch and Chapter 8 about vowels. If your pitch is good and your vowels are precise, you don't need to tighten anything to help the pitch.

Chapter 8

Shaping Your Vowels for Clarity

· ·

In This Chapter

▶ Knowing your back vowels from your front vowels

▶ Dropping your jaw and using your tongue and lips

▶ Singing and pronouncing distinct vowel sounds

· ·

*Y*our grade school teacher taught you that vowels are *A, E, I, O,* and *U.* However, the name of a vowel may be different than its pronunciation. For example, the name of the letter *A* sounds like *Ay,* although that same letter can have one of several different sounds, depending on the word it's in, such as *a*lw*a*ys, *a*fter, sof*a.* Those sneaky little vowels disguise themselves with different pronunciations in various words, 15 vowel sounds — not 5 — occur in American English. That may sound like a mouthful, but actually, you make all 15 vowel sounds every day without even thinking about it.

Because a vowel sound is made without any restriction on your breath, when you hold out a note, you sustain a vowel sound. Therefore, making clear, precise vowel sounds is important if you want to be understood. And in order to make those precise vowel sounds, you need to know how to shape the vowels quickly, using some sort of tongue shape or arch, lip shape, and opening of the jaw or mouth. If you fudge your vowels, "I miss pizza," may come out as, "A mus pit suh." So if you don't want Aunt Geraldine in the back row turning up her hearing aid until it squeals, check out the exercises in this chapter. I provide you with the information to shape most vowel sounds using your tongue and lips, to pronounce vowel sounds clearly in a sentence, and then to sing vowel sounds to make yourself clearly understood.

To make vowel sounds, you want to poise your lips in a certain position and arch your tongue in a specific way. But you should keep the tip of your tongue against your bottom front teeth for all vowel shapes. Think of this as home base — the tongue stays at home on all vowel sounds. The tip of the tongue moves to make consonants but always returns to home base after you finish the sound of the consonant to hold out the vowel as you sing a note.

Symbols used for pronunciation

In the front of your dictionary, you can find a chart of symbols used in the dictionary to help you pronounce the words correctly. Linguists have their own symbols that they use to notate the sounds of vowels and consonants called the International Phonetic Alphabet (IPA). The system was designed to give a common language to the pronunciation of sounds in any language. If a reader knows IPA, they can read a transcription of the words in IPA and sound like they know the language. Singers usually study IPA in diction classes. Without focusing on the translation, singers pronounce different languages using IPA symbols. You find that I spell out the vowel sound for you or use symbols found in *Webster's* dictionary, because that's more common to new singers or non-singers.

Getting Your Backside into Shape — Back Vowels, That Is

Now you get the chance to explore your *back vowels* — the vowels that are made with the back of your tongue arching or raising up near the roof of your mouth, while the tip of your tongue stays behind your bottom front teeth, and your lips are rounded. You may be familiar with these vowel sounds, such as *ooh, oh,* and *ah,* because of how you shape your lips. You do, however, need to make sure that the tip of your tongue stays against your teeth and that your lips are poised for action. Keep on reading, so you can discover how to quickly move from one vowel sound to the next with clarity and precision.

Exploring the shape of back vowels

In Table 8-1, you can read each vowel down each column out loud to feel and hear the same vowel sounds in several words and then read across the page to explore the differences. After you understand the sound and shape of each vowel, you should be able to isolate just the sound, without the word, which helps you move quickly from one vowel sound to the next when you sing.

If you read the words across the page from left to right in Table 8-1, you can feel your

- ✔ **Jaw** dropping the farthest for the vowel *ah.*

- ✔ **Lips** moving from rounded and slightly open for the *ooh* sound to relaxed and open to pronounce the *ah.*

- ✔ **Tongue** arching higher in the back of your tongue on the *ooh* vowel sound than on the *ah.*

Table 8-1		Exploring Back Vowels		
ooh	*OOh*	*oh*	*aw*	*ah*
woo	Foot	old	awe	father
moon	Took	obey	fraud	blah
two	Should	no	fought	bra
who	Put	over	talk	plaza

Most of these words are pronounced differently across the United States, but the sound of the vowel in *blah* should be the exact same sound for the words *bra* and *plaza*. These pronunciations are for standard American dialect — how American English is supposed to be pronounced. Singers can use their regional dialect when they sing folk music, country, and sometimes pop but not for classical music or musical theater.

Lipping around your back vowels

The sentences in the list that follows give you the chance to put all those shapes that you discovered in Table 8-1 into action, speaking through a series of similar vowel sounds. Try to recall the shape of each vowel, so you can easily differentiate between the vowel sounds when you sing.

- **ooh**

    Whom do you boot?

    Oops, noon hoops cooed Bruce.

    Whose pooch did Schubert smooch?

    Loose roots spooked Pooh.

- **OOh**

    The cook mistook your foot for soot.

    She took good sugar cookies.

    The bull stood in the crook of the brook.

    The rookie forsook pulled wool.

- **oh**

    Omit overt ovations.

    Olivia obeys Joanne.

    The motel located the oasis.

    Rotate the robust mosaic.

✔ *aw*

She s<u>aw</u> the fl<u>aw</u> in the l<u>aw</u>.

He <u>ough</u>t to have b<u>ough</u>t the <u>aw</u>ful s<u>aw</u>.

P<u>au</u>l, ch<u>al</u>k the w<u>al</u>k.

F<u>aw</u>ns gn<u>aw</u>ed the r<u>aw</u> str<u>aw</u>.

✔ *ah*

Put the c<u>a</u>lm b<u>a</u>lm on my p<u>a</u>lm.

F<u>a</u>ther made m<u>a</u>cho t<u>a</u>cos.

The s<u>a</u>ga at the sp<u>a</u> was a f<u>a</u>çade.

S<u>ua</u>ve dr<u>a</u>ma at c<u>a</u>sa L<u>a</u>s Vegas.

Singing the back vowels

Now it's time to get those lips making the right shapes in some musical patterns. Sing the pattern in Figure 8-1 to practice shaping the back vowels. (See Chapter 1 for some help with the musical notation in Figure 8-1.) Remember the shapes that you made when you were speaking through the words in Table 8-1? By making precise shapes with the vowel sounds, you can easily make yourself understood when you sing words. When the series of vowels becomes easy for you, look in Table 8-1 and find words that go with each of the vowel sounds and sing through them.

Figure 8-1:
Alternating vowels for precise lip shapes.

TRACK 9

ooh — OOh — oh — aw ——— ah

Mastering the Front Vowels

Your tongue arches in the front of your mouth to sing *front vowels*. Your tongue does most of the work shaping front vowel sounds, but make sure that both your lips and tongue are released and free of tension. The front vowels don't require as much lip action as the back vowels.

Exploring the shape of front vowels

The front vowels are much less open than the back vowels. That doesn't mean that your mouth lacks space, but these vowels aren't as wide open as the back vowels. It may sound odd, but it's true.

If I took a poll, the front vowel *ee* would win the favorite vowel contest. Because it's the favorite vowel, then you'll want to explore it too, to find out why so many singers are in love with *ee*. The reason that *ee* and his buddies in Table 8-2 are called front vowels is because the tongue arches in the front of your mouth to make these sounds. The tongue arches in the back for back vowels and in the front for front vowels. Keeping the tip of your tongue touching your bottom front teeth, say the vowel *ee*. Notice how your tongue arched in the front of your mouth, when you made the sound. You also felt the sides of your tongue go up. That's another difference between back and front vowels: When the tongue arches in the front, the sides of the tongue also raise and touch the upper teeth. As you speak through the vowels, you'll feel your

- ✔ **Jaw** drop slightly for the *ee* vowel and gradually move down more as you move from *ee* toward *a*.

- ✔ **Lips** are slightly open for the *ee* vowel and open more as your jaw drops as you move to the most open vowel *a*.

- ✔ **Tongue** arching in the front, the highest on the *ee* vowel and the lowest on the *a* vowel, and the tip of the tongue resting against your bottom front teeth.

Table 8-2		Exploring Front Vowels		
ee	*ih*	*ay*	*eh*	*a*
me	kiss	ate	bed	asked
eagle	myth	gain	head	passed
flee	wig	day	heaven	master
ski	busy	they	guess	danced

If you come across a word with two vowels in Table 8-2, the vowel sound that's being referred to is the one that comes first — in the first syllable.

Speaking the front vowels

Now it's time for you to put all the front vowels in sentences to practice speaking. Using these vowels gives you an opportunity to return to the correct arched position of your tongue after moving through the consonants. You can even use the sentences with front vowels that follow to sing the musical example found in Figure 8-2 after you're confident singing the individual vowels.

- **ee**

  We meet lean mean fiends.

  He greased Phoebe's knees.

  Greedy eels eat cream.

  Leave me peas teased, Eve.

- **ih**

  Hip chicks knit big mits.

  Cliff fixed its clipped wick.

  Tim's busy with his chips.

  Dig Phillip's little sister Lilly.

- **ay**

  Great Danes saves whale.

  They say Abe gained weight.

  Kate saves pale ale.

  James blames Dave's fame.

- **eh**

  Deb's pet pecked every peg.

  Ed shed wet red.

  Edge any hedge says Ned.

  Kelly's mellow fellow fell dead.

- **a**

  Lance can't glance last.

  Ask half after Fran.

  Vast masks pass fast.

  Prance aghast past grassy path.

The a*y* vowel is actually a diphthong or two vowel sounds together. I included it in the front vowel list, because the arch of the tongue is important for making the correct sound. As you make an *ay* sound, just know that it's a diphthong and you move through two vowel sounds.

Singing the front vowels

You want to make precise vowel sounds as you sing. You're forced to move quickly from one vowel sound to the other; you must quickly change the arch of your tongue to accommodate the different vowel sounds. You have to make the shape happen at the speed of the music. That's exactly what happens when you sing with a piano. You can take some liberties with the music, but mostly, you need to maintain a steady tempo. If you practice singing the vowels alone, you give yourself the chance to really get them solid before adding consonants in words.

You may not be able to tell the difference between each vowel sound as you're singing the pattern in Figure 8-2 in this chapter. So record yourself singing along with the CD and then listen to the tape. Pretend that you've never seen the pattern and try to distinguish which vowel you're singing. Notice which vowels aren't as distinguished as others, and you can make those a priority in your next practice session. If they aren't clear, go back and practice making the shape, saying the words with the vowels, and then singing again.

Work the vowel sequence in Figure 8-2 to get that tongue arched quickly to get the right vowel sound. If your tongue doesn't move fast enough, you may sing a different vowel. No problem. Just keep trying. When you're able to clearly distinguish between each vowel sound, insert some words into the pattern for variety and spice in your practice routine.

Figure 8-2:
Arching the
tongue
while
alternating
vowels.

TRACK 10

ee — ih — ay — eh ——— a

More than just *A, E, I, O,* and *U*

By now, you may be amazed to find that you have to reckon with singing 15 vowel sounds — not 5. Even more amazing are all the names given to vowels and their sounds these days: back vowels, front vowels, diphthongs, triphthongs, and so on. But to make things even more technical, vowels can also be *open* or *close*. (*Linguists* — people who study language as a career — don't say "closed," because you aren't supposed to completely close your lips.) Open vowels refer to vowel sounds that require you to open your mouth wider, such as *ah* or *aw*. Close vowels refer to vowel sounds, such as *ee* or *ooh,* because your mouth or lips aren't far open when you say those vowels. All these names for the 5 little vowels can be confusing or interesting, depending on your point of view. Just tuck this info away, so you can understand your director or voice teacher when he talks about vowels or wow your colleagues with your understanding of vowels the next time that you're at the water cooler.

Chapter 9

Exercising Consonants for Articulation

In This Chapter

▶ Singing consonants like a singer would

▶ Finding your consonant friends

▶ Shaping your mouth, tongue, and lips to fit the sound

▶ Giving your lips and tongue a consonant workout

I'm sure that you remember from grade school that consonants comprise the rest of the alphabet other than *A, E, I, O,* and *U,* but just knowing which letters are consonants isn't enough to sing 'em. You have to understand how to shape consonants with your tongue and lips. Understanding how to shape consonants helps you to sing them with clarity and precision.

Most people who mumble aren't working and shaping their mouths properly to make distinct consonant sounds. The same is true when you sing. You need to understand how to articulate consonants so that what you sing is clear to the audience. Struggling and forcing out the consonants makes you sound tense. So knowing how to move your lips and tongue as you sing consonant sounds makes all the difference.

Because the words of a song are the vehicle for telling your story, this chapter offers help so that you can spit out those consonants without crop-dusting the entire audience.

Your tongue is an independent mover and shaker. It doesn't need to move with your jaw. They're two totally different parts that should retain their independence when you sing consonants, because it's easier to keep the back space open for your high notes. Also, it looks much better when you sing a fast song if your jaw isn't bobbing for every single syllable.

The consonant *G* can be pronounced two ways as in the words *go* and *George.* I use the consonant *G* in this chapter to describe the pronunciation of the consonant *G* in the word *go.* I use the consonant *J* to describe the pronunciation for the consonant *G* in *George.*

Making Tip Consonants

Now it's time that you explored the *tip consonants*, which are shaped with the tip of your tongue. Most tip consonants are shaped with the tip of the tongue touching the gums or *alveolar ridge.* (By *shaped,* I mean that your mouth has to *shape* itself in a particular manner to pronounce the consonant.) If you slide your tongue along the roof of your mouth, you'll first feel your teeth, then a small section of gums, and then a ridge — the *alveolar ridge.* The only tip consonant sound not made on the gums or alveolar ridge is *TH,* which is shaped with the tip of the tongue touching the upper front teeth.

Keep reading to discover how to shape the tip consonants correctly as well as sing them. Practicing this gives you not only the precision that you need to sing but also the confidence that you're putting your best tongue forward while articulating the tip consonants.

Shaping tip consonants

For each of the words listed in Table 9-1 and Table 9-2, practice reading the words across the page to compare similar consonant sounds. Read down the column to solidify that particular consonant sound. Solidifying a consonant's sound as well as recognizing its differences from similar sounds helps you to quickly move from one sound to the next with precision while singing.

Working out with D, T, L, N, S and Z

To shape the tip consonant sounds in Table 9-1, the tip of your tongue touches the upper gums or alveolar ridge. While shaping these tip consonants, make sure that your

- ✔ **Tongue's** tip should be moving from your bottom front teeth to the gums or alveolar ridge behind your front teeth. The tip of your tongue flattens more for the *L* and *N* than for the *D* and *T.*

- ✔ **Lips** are released and free of tension. In Tables 9-1 and 9-2, as you move from the consonant to the vowel, your lips may be shaped for the vowel sound as the tongue tip touches the alveolar ridge.

Table 9-1			Practicing Tip Consonants		
D	*T*	*L*	*N*	*S*	*Z*
do	to	Lou	new	sip	zip
doe	toe	low	no	sap	zap
dab	tab	lab	nab	sing	zing

If you have problems with a lisp, make sure that your *S* is made with the tip of the tongue against the roof of your mouth (not your teeth) while the sides of your tongue are touching your teeth. If your *S* sounds too similar to a leaky tire, you need to release the grip on the tip of your tongue. Practice saying the word *pizza*. Hesitate on the first part of the *Z* (the *t* sound moves into *sah*). Release the air slowly to feel and hear the *S*. Take some time and hold out the *S* sound to feel the movement of the airflow.

Working it out with TH

In Table 9-2, you explore the other consonant sound made with the tip of the tongue — *TH*. Unlike the other tip consonants, the *TH* is made with the tongue tip touching the edge of the upper front teeth, rather than the gums or alveolar ridge.

Practice saying the words in Table 9-2. While shaping the *TH* in Table 9-2, take note that your

> ✔ **Tongue's** tip should be touching your bottom front teeth and then moving to touch your upper front teeth.

> ✔ **Lips** may move to shape the vowel sound following the TH.

Table 9-2	Practicing TH
Th	*Th*
this	theatre
the	thin
brother	tenth

Tipping for R

The consonant sound for the consonant *R* is the hardest of all the little stinkers to shape. An *R* can be confusing, because it sometimes stands alone as an individual sound, and sometimes, it's closely linked with a vowel. When you sing words that contain a consonant *R*, you may notice that your

> ✔ **Tongue's** tip rises up toward the roof of your mouth behind the alveolar ridge for this consonant.

> ✔ **Lips** shape for the vowel sound that follows the *R*.

In other languages, the consonant *R* is rolled or flipped. Flipping an *R* means to say the *R* like a *D,* and rolling an *R* means to touch the tip of your tongue on your gum ridge similar to a *D* and then blow air over it to make the tongue vibrate like the tongue trill in Chapter 6. Flipped or rolled *R*s aren't appropriate for American English. Try the following sentences to practice *R*.

- Row, row, row the boat.
- Right the wrong.
- Race red rover.
- Run rabbit, run.

Singing tip consonants

As you practice the pattern in Figure 9-1, speak through the syllable a couple of times just to get the feeling. Practice the five lines until each one is clear. Record yourself as you sing along and listen back to hear if your consonants were distinct.

Singing through the tip consonants in this way helps you feel how the right movement of your tongue makes each consonant easy to sing and easy to be understood. Watch yourself in the mirror to check the movement of your tongue.

TRACK 11

Figure 9-1:
Singing tip
consonants.

1.	loh	noh	loh	noh	loh
2.	dooh	tooh	dooh	tooh	dooh
3.	zah	sah	zah	sah	zah
4.	thy	thigh	thy	thigh	thy
5.	row	row	row	row	row

Making Soft Palate Consonants

If you slide your tongue along the roof of your mouth, you first feel your teeth and then a small section of gums, a ridge, a hard surface, and at the very back, a soft surface. That soft surface is your *soft palate,* where you shape the soft palate consonant sounds. To say the soft palate consonant sounds *K, G, NG,* and *Y,* you raise the back of your tongue to meet the soft palate. Just after your tongue touches your soft palate, the back of your tongue moves back down, and your soft palate raises back up. The movement happens quickly, and the back of the tongue remains flexible and free of tension during this movement. You'll notice that the *K* sound occurs in words even when you see the letter *C* as in the word cat.

Shaping soft palate consonants

To shape soft palate consonants, you need to keep the tip of your tongue against your teeth, lift the back of the tongue to touch the soft palate and shape your lips for the vowel sounds before and after the consonant. It's plenty to think about but follow these guidelines to find the right movement.

While shaping the soft palate consonants in Table 9-3, see to it that

- ✔ **The back of your tongue** rises to meet the roof of your mouth at your soft palate while the tip of your tongue continues touching your bottom front teeth.

- ✔ **Your lips** stay free of tension and ready to make the vowel sound that follows the consonant.

Table 9-3		Practicing Soft Palate Consonants	
K	*G*	*NG*	*Y*
keep	get	sing	yes
cup	gild	hung	yore
key	gore	bang	yum
caper	guppy	clang	you

If you struggle to sing a soft palate consonant as you sing, try this. For the first few practice sessions, make the consonant sound with the middle of your tongue arching to touch the back edge of the hard palate. By moving the consonant out of the very back of your throat, the sound won't get trapped in the back of your mouth. As you become more comfortable with keeping back space open while making soft palate consonants, you can touch the back of the tongue in the right spot on the soft palate.

Singing soft palate consonants

Singing the soft palate consonants, such as in Figure 9-2, gives you an opportunity to make the sounds of these consonants and practice keeping the back space open at the same time.

TRACK 12

Figure 9-2:
Singing soft
palate
consonants.

1. yah yah yah yah yah
2. kee goh kee goh kee
3. sing sing sing sing sing

Working Lip Consonants

Now that you have soft palate consonant sounds under your belt, you can
explore making consonants with your lips. Consonants that are made with
the lips use both lips for the consonants *P, B, M,* and *W* or the bottom lip
touching the top teeth for *F* and *V.* To make these consonant sounds, you
keep your teeth apart and close your lips. It's similar to having an egg in your
mouth and closing your lips.

Shaping lip consonants

Lip consonants are different than tip consonants, because it's the lips that
move instead of the tip of the tongue. The similarity is that the tip of the
tongue and the lips can move without moving your jaw. Figuring out how to
keep the space inside your mouth open as you close your lips helps you continue making those round tones as you articulate a consonant sound.

Shaping P, B, M, and W

While shaping the consonants in Table 9-4, you can feel your

- **Tongue** staying steady for all these consonants.

- **Lips** close as you make each consonant sound, but your teeth should
  be open.

Table 9-4	Practicing Lip Consonants		
P	**B**	**M**	**W**
pop	Bob	money	wear
pup	bubba	music	we
pope	bib	mother	witch
pimp	bulb	mimic	

Notice that if you go overboard pronouncing the ending in some consonants, such as *B,* you hear a shadow vowel of an *uh. Bob-uh* isn't what you want your audience to hear. You want them to know that Bob is the man you love and not Bob-uh!

Shaping F and V

While shaping the consonants in Table 9-5, your

- ✔ **Tongue** should stay touching your bottom front teeth.

- ✔ **Lips** should move up to touch your upper front teeth, but your teeth should be open.

Table 9-5	Practicing *F* and *V*
F	**V**
father	vapor
feather	vintage
Phillip	vittles

When singing the words *don't you, can't you,* and *could you* or any other combination that has a *D* next to a *Y,* make sure that you say, "Could you?" and "Don't you?" and not, "Could jew" or "Don't chew." You can get a laugh in a song in the wrong place if you chew too much on the wrong consonant combination.

Singing lip consonants

Singing the lip consonants (see Figure 9-3) gives you chance to make the sounds of the consonants and practice moving easily from a vowel to the consonant. Watch yourself in the mirror to make sure that you're keeping your jaw steady, your teeth open, and your lips moving.

TRACK 13

Figure 9-3:
Singing lip
consonants.

1.	pooh - boo	pooh - boo	pooh - boo	pooh - boo	pooh
2.	woh - moh	woh - moh	woh - moh	woh - moh	woh
3.	fah - vah	fah - vah	fah - vah	fah - vah	fah

Working Combination Consonants

Sometimes, two consonants are combined together to make a specific sound. Knowing how to articulate the sound makes it much easier to sing. These combinations of sounds listed in Table 9-6 are the few sounds that are made by closing the space in the front of your mouth when you're singing. They require special attention in practicing to be able to make the sound without totally closing down the space in the back of your mouth and changing the tone.

Shaping combination consonants

For these consonant pairs in Table 9-6, your

- **Tongue's** tip moves toward the gum ridge and makes the sides of your tongue touch the upper side teeth and gums at the side at the same time. You'll feel air blowing between the tip of your tongue and the gums. The tip of the tongue touches the alveolar ridge momentarily at the beginning of the *CH* and *J* sound.

- **Lips** should protrude slightly forward. The protrusion is slight and the movement happens quickly.

Table 9-6		Practicing *SH, ZH, J,* and *CH*	
SH	*ZH*	*J*	*CH*
show	visual	jump	chump
plush	pleasure	June	choose
shop	measure	age	chance

How do you say . . . ?

Students often ask about the correct pronunciation of words for singing and speaking. Follow these general rules. The *ed* at the end of a word is pronounced with a *D* sound if the *ed* is preceded by a *voiced sound* (vowel or consonant), such as in the words *headed, lingered,* and *roamed.* However, if the *ed* is preceded by an *unvoiced consonant,* it sounds like a *T* in such words as *picked, yanked, joked,* and *wrapped.*

Remember, *voiced consonant* sounds are produced by adding vocal sound. An example is the letter *M.* If you say the word *make,* you have to add sound to the letter *M* before you even get the vowel. *Unvoiced consonants* are produced by momentarily stopping the flow of air and making no sound. The consonant *T* is an example. If you say the word *to,* you don't make any sound until you get to the vowel.

Singing combination consonants

Sing through the sentences in Figure 9-4 following the words under each note. Sing through each one until you feel the fluid movement from consonant to vowel. Doing so enhances your ability to let your back space stay open as you momentarily close the space in the front.

Sing through the consonants in Figure 9-4 with a *legato* (smooth and connected) line and try not to anticipate the next consonant. Allow yourself time to extend the vowel before jumping to the next syllable and consonant.

Figure 9-4:
Combining
your
consonants.

TRACK 14

1. zhah_____ shah_____ zhah   shah   zhah
2. Joe _____ Choh_____ Joe   Choh   Joe

Part III
Developing Your Technique

The 5th Wave   By Rich Tennant

"What? I'm practicing my warbling."

In this part . . .

The exercises in this part are designed to give you an incredible vocal workout. Right after you work out that practice routine in Chapter 10, you get to explore even more exercises to develop your middle voice, chest voice, and head voice in Chapter 11. Your voice has many parts that can come together to make one seamless line from bottom to top. Just in case you need a good challenge and some harder exercises, head for Chapter 12. You won't get bored. The exercises work all the details that you heard about in Chapter 11 and challenge you to move to the next level.

Chapter 13 tells you what's unique about the male and female voice. I don't keep secrets, so the boys can read all about the girls. You can even sing along with all the exercises no matter what voice type or gender you are. See the information under each "On the CD" icon for tips on how to work on the exercises for male or female.

If you'd like to add a belt to your tune, see Chapter 14, and for locating the right instructor, head to Chapter 15. The issues of age — young and old — are discussed in Chapter 16 along with the various musical styles.

Chapter 10

Developing a Practice Routine

In This Chapter

▶ Running through the ropes of a routine

▶ Creating your own practice regimen

▶ Knowing when, where, and how to practice

▶ Choosing exercises that fit your needs

▶ Keeping track of your progress

*A*lmost everyone daydreams of singing on a big stage, being the star of the show, taking a bow after thundering applause, and thanking your agent as you accept the award for the world's most fabulous singer. Well, I just have one little question. How do you get to Carnegie Hall? Practice, practice, practice.

Singing is no different than any other art; you have to work at it on a regular basis to improve. Understanding how to schedule and monitor your practicing will ensure consistent progress. Knowing how to practice properly is key when it comes to making consistent progress toward that big dream of being the star attraction. A proper practice session consists of a physical warm-up, vocal exercises to improve tone, range, articulation, and breath, and then applying that work to songs. If you aren't sure how to practice your singing, this chapter is just for you, because I outline some of what I routinely suggest for my students and also apply to my own practice sessions. Call me odd, but I love to practice. Perhaps, after reading this chapter and realizing the benefits of practice, you will too.

Knuckling Down to a Practice Plan

Organizing your practice session greatly increases your chances of accomplishing something. If you only have 30 minutes to practice, you don't want to waste the first 20 minutes figuring out what you need to do. Plan it out.

Planning your practice time also keeps you from getting overwhelmed. I suggest many great exercises throughout the book for you to use to improve your technique. If you think about all the details of singing, you'll get discouraged. Pinpointing the goals for each practice session enables you to focus on two or three things in each session. If you really work those areas, you can add new exercises quickly. You don't have to plan out your time so much that you have no room for exploration. Read on to discover other elements to include in your practice session.

Every practice session should include the following elements:

- **A warm-up period:** In this part of your session, you warm up both your body (yes, your body) and your voice. Head to the section "Warming Up," later in this chapter, for details on what your warm-up should include and how long it should last.

- **The practice period:** After you warm up, you perform various exercises that you discover in the book and hear on the CD. Chapters 11 through 13 cover specific areas of the voice.

- **An update on how you're progressing:** To know whether you've made the progress you want, keep a chart, such as the one you find in the section, "Charting your practice" near the end of this chapter and listen to your tapes from previous practice sessions. See the "Taping yourself" section, later in this chapter.

TIP

"Hey! Will ya pipe down?"

Echoing sound is great for the singer but not so great for the neighbors. Apply these tips to cut down the noise:

- Put rugs on the floor to absorb sound (carpeting is great).

- Close the door or hang a thick blanket over the doorway to absorb sound.

- Talk with your neighbors or roommates and ask them about their schedule. They may hate to hear you sing at 8 a.m. but not mind at all around noon.

- Rent a practice room from a music store, recording studio, or church.

- Move the back of the piano away from the wall or tack a cloth on the back to deaden the sound.

- Use the soft pedal if you accompany yourself.

Getting Answers to Your Practicing Questions

It's okay if you still aren't sure what to do when you practice. Students frequently ask questions about practicing, so I'll answer them and get you practicing in no time. Knowing where to practice, when to practice, and what to use when you practice puts you on the right track for technique work.

Where should I practice?

The number one question is about location. You can practice anywhere that works for you. If your piano is in the TV room, consider moving it. You can choose which *it* I mean. The TV would be easier to move than the piano, but you may be outnumbered at home. Your practice space can be anywhere in your home where you can be alone and concentrate. Ideally, leave the space set up so that everything is ready each day for practicing. This practice space doesn't have to be the size of a football stadium. You simply need space to move around comfortably during the warm-up or when you create the scene for your song. Some of my students practice in stairwells, bathrooms (great acoustics in the bath!), and basements. Other students say their best practicing is in their car. Regardless of wherever else you do your practicing, just make sure that some of your time is devoted to standing up and practicing several times a week somewhere.

What's the best time to practice?

Schedule a specific time and duration for practicing each day. If the practice time is allotted on your calendar, you're more likely to practice. Decide if you're a morning person or an evening person. Many singers practice more efficiently at night because of their body clocks. You can also practice on your lunch hour or right before or after work. If your house gets plenty of traffic during the day, practicing in the evening when it's quiet may be more convenient. Or if your home is usually overwhelmed with familial comings and goings in the evening or early morning hours, then you may want to schedule a time in the middle of the day. To maximize your concentration, turn off the TV and turn on the answering machine during your daily practice time.

Have your practice space set and ready each day. If you have to search the entire place to find all your practice tools, you'll waste valuable singing time. Be organized, so you can enjoy your time being creative!

How long should I practice?

The length of the practice session depends on your level of expertise. Some-one who is new to singing can benefit from practicing 15 to 20 minutes a day. Gradually increase the practice time to 30 to 60 minutes per day and the warm-up portion appropriately. However, quality practice is better than quantity. Focusing for 20 minutes of creative practice is better than unfocused practice for an hour. The voice is like any other muscle group in your body. It becomes fatigued and needs rest. If your voice is tired after 20 minutes, rest for a time and sing again later.

If your voice hurts while you're practicing, then something isn't right. You may be pushing too hard to make the sound. Take a break and review the explanations with the exercises in the chapter to make sure that you're on the right track. Fatigue is normal and the muscles will feel warm and tired. But, stop practicing when the fatigue sets in, and the recovery won't take as long. As long as the voice is back to normal after a few hours of rest, then your practicing is on the right track. Improvement happens with fre-quent practice. You can't expect to practice once and be perfect. Oh, how I wish! Your goal for practicing is to make improvements in your sound. Longer endurance may happen, but it's not necessary for a beginner to practice for three or four hours a day. Set goals for each practice session for consistent progress.

What do I need besides my voice?

Of course, you need your voice in order to practice your singing. However, you need some other tools as well:

✔ **Keyboard:** Of course, you'd like to have one or two pianos, preferably a grand and a baby grand. Right? But beginning singers don't need a piano; they just need to hear their notes. So if you don't want to spend too much money so early in your singing career, why not start off with a small keyboard? Available in the electronic department of most depart-ment stores, a small battery-operated keyboard can serve your purpose. You can program some keyboards to remember the melody, so you don't have to pluck out the tune a second time to hear it. You just press a couple of buttons.

However, just about any new or used electronic keyboard works. A piano is fine, too, just as long as it's in tune. You don't have to know how to play the piano to sing, but if you'd like to get a better understanding of what keyboards and musical notation are all about, pick up a copy of *Piano For Dummies* by Blake Neely (Wiley).

- **Tape and tape recorder/player:** A tape player is super useful if you don't have a keyboard (or even if you do), because all you have to do is tape the music when it's played and then play it back over and over again during your practice time.

  Tape-recording your practice sessions is a great way to monitor your progress, too. Record yourself singing through the exercises and rewind to hear if you were right on pitch, whether the vowel really sounded like an *ah,* or maybe you're so perfect that you never need to practice again. If you want a sound that's a bit more sophisticated, buy a minidisc recorder. The sound quality is as good as a compact disk.

- **Pitch pipe:** This gizmo is what the leader of the choir or barbershop quartet whips out of his pocket and blows into to sound the starting pitch. It's usually round with the letter names of the notes on a dial that moves around to change pitches, and it's usually inexpensive. If you don't have a keyboard or a tape with your exercises handy, you can get a pitch pipe and play your starting pitch. You can also play a pitch occasionally to see if you're still on target.

- **Metronome:** This gadget monitors speed and maintains rhythm — not like a radar gun but more like a ticking sound that encourages you to stay at the same speed or tempo when you practice. Many singers slow down at the hard section of the song and don't realize it. While practicing, you can listen to the tick-tock sound of the metronome to stay right on the beat. Metronomes come in different sizes and shapes. Some of the newer metronomes are as small as a credit card.

  If you can't locate a metronome, look at the clock. The second hand on the clock is ticking 60 beats per minute. You can practice your song or vocal exercise keeping a steady pace with the ticking of the clock.

- **Mirror:** Mirrors are so helpful for practicing. Coif your hair perfectly and then watch your body! Notice your posture, the way your mouth moves to make each vowel or consonant, and what moves as you inhale and exhale and sing. By watching yourself in the mirror, you become much more aware of how you move your body as you sing.

- **Music and pencil:** As you listen back over the tape, take notes on your practice chart or on your music. Seeing the notes from your last practice session helps you remember your goals.

Warming Up

A good vocal warm-up gets your body limber and your voice ready to practice singing. The warm-up should last about ten minutes — long enough to get you focused on singing. You need to discover what works for you. Some people take longer to warm up than others. If I haven't been practicing for a few weeks, I sometimes need 15 minutes just to get my voice warmed up to practice. During those times that I'm singing quite a bit, I may only need a few minutes to get myself ready to practice.

Stretching to warm up your body

No matter how easy the day, start your practice session by stretching out. You want to get your entire body ready to sing, not just your singing muscles. For the breath to really move in your body, you need to be connected to your lower body. I suggest the following stretching routine that begins with your head and moves on down to your toes. For each segment, remember to continue breathing as you move.

1. Similar to the exercises in Chapter 2 regarding posture and releasing tension, shake out any tension in your entire body. Wiggle around until you feel the stiffness in your joints melting away.

2. Find your alignment. Gently drop your head forward toward your chest at a slow pace, inhale, and bring your head up. Repeat this several times allowing the head to drop farther each time. Please don't lose your alignment as your head moves.

3. Turn your head to the left and to the right. Roll your head around starting from the left side and rolling your chin near your chest to the right side. Please don't roll your head back unless you have worked with this kind of movement before. The vertebrae in your neck may not respond well to pressure from your head rolling backward.

4. Gently drop your left ear toward your left shoulder and pause. Inhale as you lift your head. Repeat several times and then repeat the sequence over your right shoulder.

5. Move all the muscles in your face. Tighten them and then release to feel the flow of energy in your face.

6. Move your tongue in and out. Stick it out as far as possible and then move it back in.

7. Lick your lips all the way around your mouth. Take your time as you lick to feel the stretching and movement of your tongue. If you went clockwise the first time, try counterclockwise.

8. Lift your shoulders up and then push them down.

9. Move your shoulders forward and then back.

10. Make circles with shoulders in one direction and then reverse. Keep your chest steady and open.

11. Swing one arm in circles. As you swing, wiggle your fingers and wrist to get the blood flowing all the way down your arm. Be careful; watch out for furniture. Repeat with the other arm.

12. Lift your left arm over your head and lean to the right. As you lean, feel the muscles between your ribs opening. Reverse and lift up your right arm and stretch your other side.

13. Swing those hips around to loosen that tension. Many women hold tension in their hips. You don't have to be tough now. Let 'em loose. Let the hips rock back to front as well as around in circles.

14. Stand up on your toes and then lower your feet back to the floor. Stand on one leg and shake out the other. Reverse to get the other leg in motion. Move up on your tiptoes and then drop back down to the floor and bend your knees.

15. Finally, take a nice deep breath and feel the energy flowing in your body.

Getting your blood pumping while warming up helps you to focus on your task at hand. If you're having trouble connecting your breath to your song, try being more physical in your warm-up or practice session. My favorite is "stationary" skiing. If the gym can have a stationary bike, I hereby invent an imaginary stationary skiing machine. Yes, skiing down the slopes with the poles in your hand propelling you along. Bend your knees and really connect with your lower body.

Another way to connect your body is to shoot basketball granny shots. Bend your knees, drop your arms between your legs, and throw the invisible ball up with two hands. This motion gets you connected to your lower body and really helps you connect energy to sing higher notes. If you shoot a regular free throw, you lift your body up to sing the note. I want you to think down to sing the notes. You can use any number of different physical movements.

Keep in mind that you want fluid motion. Any movements that cause you to jerk your body are going to jerk the singing voice also. Doin' the twist is better than jumping jacks.

Warming up your voice

If you were scheduled to run a race this afternoon, would you just show up and start running? I doubt it. You'd work for weeks or months to prepare your body for the big event, and just before the race, you'd warm up your body. That may sound odd for singing, but remember, your singing voice is made up of muscles just like any other part of your body. These muscles need a specific type of warm-up. Baseball players spend time stretching before the big game, and you need to stretch your singing voice before practicing.

Singing in any imaginable position

Experimenting with different postures allows you to feel your entire body as well as feel the movement of the breath. I recommend that you not always stand erect to sing. I suggest that you sometimes sit, squat, lie down, slump over, or create other positions that allow you to explore what's moving in your body as you breathe. Try singing in these various positions and then compare the feelings in your body with standing upright. Watch out for any tension that may creep into your body while experimenting. If you're momentarily confused when you finally do stand up, review the alignment exercises in Chapter 2.

What's the difference between practicing and warming up? A warm-up gets your body ready for practicing. The difference between the end of the warm-up and the start of the practice may be only slight. Think of the warm-up as the beginning of your practice session. Everything that you do in the warm-up leads you to the work that you do in your practice session.

Vocal warm-ups include making sounds to get your singing voice awake and ready to work out. Some good choices of warm-ups include:

- ✔ Humming a familiar tune or one that you make up (see Chapter 6)
- ✔ Sighing or vocal slides (see Chapter 4)
- ✔ Lip trills (see Chapter 3) or tongue trills (see Chapter 6)

The basic ingredients of a good warm-up work the body, blood, and breath: You get your body moving, your blood pumping, and your breath ready to move out and sing.

Exercising Your Voice

This is huge! This is big! Inquiring minds want to know what do you actually practice and how do you practice it? I thought you'd never ask. You can find many exercises throughout this book to help you develop your technique. By breaking down the practice session, you develop a routine that touches on all those areas.

Picking exercises that work for you

The exercises for posture in Chapter 2 offer you fun ways to create great posture. After reading Chapter 2, choose the exercises that appeal the most to you and write them in your practice chart. After working those exercises for a week, evaluate your progress. You may be ready to add more exercises for posture. Go back to Chapter 2 and find more exercises that work on another aspect of posture and add them to your practice chart for week two. You can apply this same process for each chapter. Find exercises to begin your technical journey and add new exercises weekly as you progress.

Picking exercises may seem more difficult than posture. The same principle is true for vocal exercises: While you can pick any exercise to practice, you may find it easier to start at the beginning of a chapter and look for the exercises that start at your level. If you've never had any lessons or any experience singing, then you're at the right place. Welcome! I wrote the chapters with your progression in mind. Readers who have some knowledge of singing may start at any point in the chapter that suits their level of expertise. If your singing training dates way back to high school or college, start at the beginning of the chapter and move at a faster pace to refresh your skills.

The big questions to ask when working on singing exercises are

- ✔ Have I read the instructions enough times that I can work through the exercise and focus on my task? Or do I have to keep looking at the book? Whip out that handy Cheat Sheet for help.

- ✔ Is the exercise just above your level of expertise without overwhelming you? If you've never had singing training, you may feel overwhelmed. However, feeling overwhelmed will be temporary, because you'll gradually understand the terminology, and the exercise will become second nature to you. If the exercise becomes easier after a week, you're on the right track.

- ✔ Reread the directions and instructions for the exercises often. After working an exercise for a week, you may find something that you forgot when you read the instructions again. I pile plenty of information in the exercises to keep you busy for quite some time. I don't want you to get bored!

- ✔ If an exercise is confusing, ask a friend to interpret it and/or practice it with you. By watching other singers, you discover a great deal about technique. Having to verbally explain an exercise to someone else really helps you to articulate your ideas.

✔ The biggest piece of advice I can offer about singing is that it requires discipline. It's really up to you to find the time to practice and improve your technique. You have many tools in this book to help you, but the tools need a user. Schedule the time, organize your session by choosing the exercises, and have a blast!

Breaking it down

In any given practice session, you need a warm-up to get your body and brain ready to focus and sing. Following the warm-up, work on each area of technique: posture, breath, articulation, vowels, resonance, and tone production, exercises that work your range, patterns that develop your ear, and combining acting and singing. Breaking it down into segments to work during each session allows you to grow in each of these areas without chucking your music out the window in frustration.

In addition to breaking it down, set goals for each practice session. I provide you with some sample goals for each day's practice:

Monday and Tuesday practice:

✔ Two breathing exercises that work on quick inhalation and long exhalation and then apply that work to your song

✔ Three vowels that you can work in exercises and then apply to your song

✔ Three consonants that you can work in combination with the vowels and then apply that work to your song

Wednesday and Thursday practice:

✔ Check in with the two breathing exercises. If one of those exercises is going well, add a third exercise.

✔ Sing through the exercises from Monday and Tuesday using the three vowels. If you aren't sure of the shape, review the explanation from the group of exercises in Chapter 8. If one of the vowels is going well, add a fourth vowel.

✔ Review the motion of the three consonants from Monday and Tuesday. Work that motion of the consonants until it's second nature. When those consonants are working well, add a fourth.

Friday and Saturday practice:

✔ Review all exercises from the past four days. Make a new checklist for adding exercises.

✔ Add to the bottom of the list new vowels or consonants to work this weekend.

TIP

Kids can say the darndest things

Don't let the comments of anyone discourage you from singing. Everyone is capable of singing well with practice. Have a family meeting to explain that tacky comments about your singing won't be tolerated. Inform them that what they think of as helpful joking is really unacceptable. Be tough! Take no prisoners! Train your friends and family to respect your practice time.

Practicing Correctly

Correct practicing means that you're making consistent improvement. You're applying the technical information that you gather in the book, and your voice feels good as you're singing. The folds of your vocal cords don't have pain receptors, so you can't assume that you'll feel pain if you do something wrong. If you do feel pain, you may be squeezing too hard, and the muscles surrounding your vocal cords feel constricted. Feeling tired after practicing is normal. You may have friends that can sing for hours and not feel tired. They may have spent many years singing to build up their endurance. If your voice gets tired after a reasonable amount of time singing, don't worry about it. After a month, if your voice still gets tired quickly, then you're not doing something right. For help, review the exercises for releasing tension in Chapter 2, breathing exercises in Chapter 3, and especially the onset of tone exercises in Chapter 6.

Charting your practice

Improvement happens with frequent practice. You can't expect to practice once and be perfect. If that were true, I would offer every student only one lesson. I could have saved plenty of my own money that I spent on lessons. Set goals for each practice session. Check out Figure 10-1, which illustrates a daily practice chart.

Taping yourself

Tape your practice session each day to monitor improvement. The first time that you listen to yourself on tape, you may not like it. That's a perfectly normal reaction. Performing artists spend big bucks in the recording studio, but they may not sound so perfect at home. The third time that you hear yourself on tape, you'll be used to the sound. Listen for the details, such as the precision of the vowel. Does it sound like an *ah* or *uh*? The two vowels are similar, but you need to be able to distinguish them in the exercise and in the text of the song. Record yourself saying *ah* and *uh* to feel and hear the difference. Then go back and listen to the tape.

If the camcorder is handy, videotape yourself on a regular basis to check out your body language. Information about body language is located in Chapter 2 and Chapter 19. Watch the tape three times in a row to get used to your sound on video. Think of it as a learning tool and not a critique of your outfit. You can even watch the tape without sound to really focus on your body movement.

Daily Practice Chart:

Date _____

Warm-up: stretches from Stretching to warm up your body in Chapter 10

Breathing: Panting, Sipping Straw, Blowing a Candle

Vowels/Tone: *a*h, oh

Consonants: TDL, Combined with vowels: T*a*h D*a*h L*a*h, Toh, Doh, Loh

Vocalizes/Range: Figure 11-1, 11-2, and 12-1

Acting Work/Songs/Story: worked on "Over the Rainbow" and answered the questions in Chapter 19

Length of Practice: 30 minutes today

Notes: Stretches are easier. Need to release tension in my neck. Panting was easy today but dropping breath quickly needs a little more work. Vowel shapes are easier--continue working on back vowels for precise sounds and shapes. Tip consonants were good today--work more on soft palate consonants tomorrow. Worked the text of my song and answered the acting questions in Chapter 19.

Notes to accomplish tomorrow: work dropping breath again, back vowels, tip consonants, range

---

Figure 10-1:
A sample daily practice chart.

Applying information and exercises

As you read about each of the exercises in the book, find a place on your practice chart for that exercise. Even if you think it's a wild exercise, give it a whirl. When you have tried the exercise for a week, then you can decide if it's too crazy. Most of the time, you can't see the benefit of an exercise until you've tried it a few times. Be brave! Try some funky exercises! Make some beautiful noise! You won't know what you're capable of until you move out of your comfort zone. Mastering some of the exercises takes some time, while other exercises only take a few days to master. The first time that you try an exercise, you may be tempted to just skim through the explanation, because you want to test it out. I totally understand. Make sure that you go back later and read the entire explanation and work through each step. The step you skip may be the most important one of the exercise.

For each big concept, I offer you several exercises. For those of you that are visual, I offer a visualization exercise. Kinesthetic types (those who learn through movement) can benefit from the movement description. Aural types (folks who learn best using their ears) will be told what to listen to as you practice the exercise. If you don't know which you prefer, try them all! Some people like to be organized and others want no boundaries on their technical process. I'm the organized type who likes to plan out each session.

Using the CD to practice exercises

This book's CD has so many wonderful exercises from which to choose. The exercises progress and gradually get harder. If you're a more advanced singer, skip to some of the later exercises. For beginners, I suggest that you start at the beginning of the book and work your way through each chapter. It may take a while, but you'll have plenty of fun along the way. Keep the CD handy in your practice space. The exercises are in order of difficulty.

The CD may seem boring, because it doesn't have many bells and whistles. The simplicity of the piano and voices allows you to completely focus on your technique. When your technique is really rocking, whip out the Karaoke machine and wow your friends. Until then, use the CD to steadily work on your technique.

Chapter 11

Discovering the Parts of Your Singing Voice

In This Chapter

▶ Bridging the gap between voices

▶ Using your chest voice for your lower pitches

▶ Discovering what your head voice feels like

▶ Switching into and out of the middle gracefully

*Y*ou have one singing voice that can do many things — three things to be exact. Your singing voice has three distinct parts: *chest voice, middle voice,* and *head voice,* which all combine to make one glorious voice. The notes in the middle part of your voice make up your middle voice; likewise, the notes in the lower part of your voice make up your chest voice, and the notes in the upper part of your voice make up your head voice.

To get a better idea of what each part of the voice is, you have to recognize how each area of the voice relates to another.

  ▶ **Middle voice:** This bridge between your chest voice and your head voice makes vibrations in your mouth and neck. Middle voice feels similar to head voice for many female singers and similar to chest voice for many male singers.

  ▶ **Chest voice:** The thicker, heavier sound made in the lower part of your voice; it makes vibrations in your chest while you sing.

  ▶ **Head voice:** The higher part of your singing voice makes vibrations in your head or skull as you sing.

Because differences exist between the female and male voices, not all patterns and exercises in this chapter apply equally to women and men. Some are easier for women than they are for men; on the other hand, some are easier for men than they are for women. Some even work different areas for women than they do for men. No matter what exercise you encounter, I provide clear information as to how it works for both women and men — practice all the exercises in this chapter no matter what voice it works. The ultimate goal is to strengthen all parts of your voice — middle, chest, and head — to work together as a team for beautiful sound.

Finding Your Middle Voice

Your middle voice is the bridge between your chest voice and head voice. You can explore your middle voice or even build one if yours is missing in action. Continue reading if you'd like to get an idea of what your middle voice feels like and when to use it.

Noting your middle voice range

The relationship of your middle voice to chest and head voice is the same, no matter who you are. But *how* your middle voice works, *when* it works, and the transitions you should watch for all depend on whether you're a woman or a man.

See Figure 11-1 for what the average female middle voice range looks like. In the beginning, your middle voice may be weak as you try to figure out how to reach these notes without transitioning to head or chest voice. Depending on the song, you can take your middle voice as low as you would like. If your voice gets too fuzzy or weak on the really low notes, you may need to make a transition into chest voice. The exercises in this chapter help you figure out how and when to make that transition. After you sense the vibrations in your mouth and throat, you can easily maintain your middle voice sound while you sing.

Figure 11-1:
Female middle voice range.

F above Middle C (F4) to the next F (F5)

See Figure 11-2 for what the average male middle voice range should look like. Your range isn't as large as the women's range; you may not notice a huge change when you enter this range. So understanding how your middle voice feels is important, especially when you transition from high notes or low notes. As you ascend in pitch, you may be tempted to take the really thick sound and feeling from the lower notes too high rather than transitioning to a sound and sensation that's closer to a higher male speaking voice. The middle voice is less thick than the lower notes and not light and spinning like higher notes, but it's a sound and sensation that's in between, vibrating in the middle of your body around your mouth and throat. If you try to push up a heavy sound from the bottom, it may take you longer to gain secure control over your high notes. You get an opportunity in this chapter to work out your voice, so you can easily maintain middle voice when necessary.

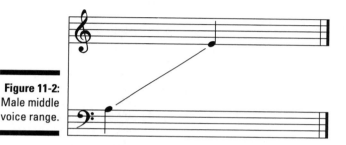

Figure 11-2: Male middle voice range.

A below Middle C (A3) to E above Middle C (E4)

Singing in middle voice

The following exercises give you a chance to work your middle voice by itself. Follow along with the CD and get a feel for where your middle voice should be as well as how it feels to sing in middle voice.

Figures 11-3 and 11-4 are designed specifically with your middle voice range in mind. The patterns in Figures 11-5 and 11-6 are specifically designed for the male middle voice range. Even though the patterns in Figures 11-5 and 11-6 are written down an octave, sing the patterns an octave higher than written to work your middle voice. (The distance between one note and the next note up or down of the same name is an *octave*. For example, the distance between two Cs is called an *octave*. If you start counting at the first *C* and count eight white notes up, you find another C.) Listen to the second note the piano plays. That's the note that you'll start on when you sing the pattern.

Middle voice for a male singer isn't nearly as wide a range as the middle voice for a female. The exercises in Figures 11-3 and 11-4 are designed with the female voice in mind. You're welcome to sing along with the exercises; just know that you're moving from middle voice to chest voice if you sing the pattern down one octave. Figures 11-5 and 11-6 are specifically designed with your middle voice range in mind. Listen to the first note the piano plays for the pattern. That's your starting note for the exercise.

On this track, listen to the singer sing the pattern in Figure 11-3. The sound you hear is her middle voice. Use the vowels listed underneath to help you find your middle voice sound. You can hear a male voice singing along also, so you know what to do when you join in on this pattern.

Figure 11-3:
Taking it
down.

TRACK 15

ah _____ *oh* _____ *ooh*

For this pattern, Figure 11-4, explore your middle voice by gradually working your way up to the top of your middle voice. The female voice demonstrates the sounds for you on the CD so you can hear the sound of a female middle voice. A male voice also sings along just so you guys know what to do if you join in.

This pattern starts low in your middle voice on purpose. Notice how the vibrations change slightly as you move higher in pitch. You'll sing the pattern to the top of your middle voice.

This pattern starts just below your middle voice but gradually works its way into middle voice. Listen to the male voice sing the pattern for you, so you'll know what the male voice sounds like as he demonstrates the sounds. Notice that the difference in feeling between the notes in chest voice and middle voice isn't big in the first few repetitions of this pattern. You'll feel a change, as the notes get higher in your middle voice.

Figure 11-4:
Descending
by step.

TRACK 16

ee _____ *ooh* _____

The pattern in Figure 11-5 specifically works the male middle voice range. Ladies, you can work your middle voice singing this pattern if you sing the pattern one octave higher than what's written in the figure. On the CD, you hear a male singer demonstrate the pattern using his middle voice. Notice that as he gets higher in pitch, he attempts to lighten the sound instead of making it bigger.

Listen to the piano play the second note, which is the note you'll use to start this pattern. This pattern also works your middle voice, but it's written out differently than Figures 11-1 and 11-2, so the men can understand where their middle voice starts.

Your starting note is the first note that the piano plays. The pattern gradually moves through your middle voice range so you can feel that the sound is higher than your speaking voice but not as high as the sounds you make in the highest part of your range.

Figure 11-5:
Gliding through the middle.

TRACK 17

1. moh ——————————————————
2. may ——————————————————

Listen as the male singer demonstrates the first repetition of the pattern in Figure 11-6 in his middle voice. The sound is lighter than the lower notes of your range but not as high or light as the higher notes. Use one of the four suggestions underneath the pattern to explore different vowel sounds in your middle voice.

This pattern is in your middle voice range if you sing the pattern one octave higher than what's written on the page. Use the vowels listed underneath the pattern, just like the guys.

Figure 11-6:
Moving along the four in middle voice.

TRACK 18

aw ——————————————————

This pattern sits right in your middle voice range. Notice how the male voice sounds as he starts the note solidly in his middle voice. You'll want to open the space in the back of your mouth and throat and take a solid breath before you begin the pattern.

Checking Out Your Chest Voice

Chest voice is that thicker, heavier sound in the lower part of your voice that makes vibrations in your chest when you're singing. You may have felt it take over a time or two — whether you wanted it to or not. The trick to singing in chest voice is knowing how and when to use it. If you need to find out how high to take your chest voice or even how to find your chest voice if you haven't been introduced, continue reading to discover how to have a strong but controlled chest voice.

Zeroing in on your chest voice range

Singing in chest voice can be such a powerful feeling. However, you have to be fair to your middle voice and not let chest voice take over too soon. Discover your range, so you'll know how soon is too soon to transition to chest voice.

See Figure 11-7 to see the average female chest voice range. Chest voice is often a strong part of the female voice. This area is often stronger than the middle voice, and you may want to strengthen your middle voice. You need to know your chest voice range, and you also need to know why not to take chest voice higher than the suggested boundaries. By taking chest voice too high, you can weaken your middle voice. Remember that you can always switch out of chest voice sooner, but preferably not later, than the range given.

Figure 11-7:
Chest voice
range for
women.

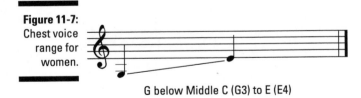

G below Middle C (G3) to E (E4)

Figure 11-8 shows the average range of chest voice for men. The male chest voice is your speaking voice territory. Because most men speak in chest voice, you often already have a strong chest voice. You can develop yours if you think its weak and so you can tell the difference between your chest voice and middle voice.

Distinguishing chest voice and belt

Chest voice and belt aren't the same. Chest voice is a thick, strong part of your lower range, and the chest voice sound is much heavier and deeper. The belt has a brassy sound, and it may sound like a healthy version of yelling. It may sound like it's dominated by chest voice sounds, but belting should have the ease of middle voice. A good belt is developed from the speaking voice. Most people who aren't fans of belting refer to it as yelling on pitch. But hey, belting

is what you all do at home around the dinner table when the discussion of politics gets heated, and it's also what you do when you call out for a taxi to stop.

If you're interested in belting, you can check out Chapter 14 for belting exercises. But don't rush to those exercises unless your middle voice is really strong, and you can distinguish between chest voice and middle voice.

Figure 11-8:
Chest voice range for men.

F about an octave and a half below Middle C
(or lower) to A♭ below Middle C (A♭3)

Feeling your chest voice

You may already know what's *supposed* to be your chest voice (if not see the section "Zeroing in on your chest voice range," earlier in this chapter), but you still aren't sure what it actually is. The best way to tell is by feeling it. To be sure that you know what your chest voice is and what it feels like, try out some of the following exercises, so you can feel those chest voice vibrations.

This pattern in Figure 11-9 gives you your first opportunity to find your chest voice. Listen to the singers on the CD to hear the sounds they make in chest voice. You'll notice that the sound is full and thick. Notice the sensations in your body and try to feel the vibrations as you sing.

The first couple of repetitions are low for you. Some women can sing quite low, so the pattern allows you the opportunity to find out how low you can sing in chest voice. With practice, you may find that the patterns gradually get easier and you gain some strength on lower notes. The second note that the piano plays is your starting note for this pattern.

This exercise is really low on purpose. Some men can sing low, and I wanted you to have the opportunity to find out if your voice can sing low notes. With time, you may find that the notes get stronger. Some tenors may not be able to sing this pattern because it's so low. You can try it several times, and if it's just too low, find other patterns in the chapter that aren't quite so low or sing up an octave for a few repetitions. Your starting note is the first note that the piano plays.

TRACK 19

Figure 11-9: Singing 4th.

The pattern in Figure 11-10 begins on *ah,* an open vowel, to help you start with a thicker, chest voice sound. You can stay in chest voice the entire time that you sing this pattern.

This pattern stays in your chest voice range. If your voice is high, you may find the first few repetitions of this pattern quite low. Try singing it to feel the vibrations of chest voice and to notice how the sounds and vibrations change as you move higher in pitch.

Gentlemen, sing the pattern in Figure 11-10 down an octave from what's written on the page. You can hear the male voice on the CD demonstrate for you. The pattern begins low and gradually moves higher in pitch. You can continue working on this pattern on your own and go higher in pitch. If you find the pattern too low for you, sing it as it's written on the page or wait until the pattern gets high enough for you.

TRACK 20

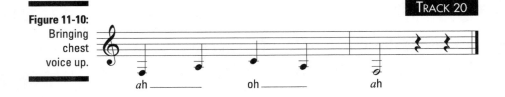

Figure 11-10: Bringing chest voice up.

Aiming High with Head Voice

The higher part of your singing voice is called *head voice,* because most people feel the vibrations in their head or skull while singing in head voice. Having a head voice for singing is necessary, so you can access those really high notes in the song. For women, the notes in the middle part of your voice may not feel that much different from the higher notes right now. As you move from the middle part of your voice to your head voice, you'll want to *lighten up the sound.* That means that you want to think of head voice as if it's lighter. Not lighter in sound necessarily, but lighter in the amount of effort or pressure in your throat. So you may feel like you open your mouth and the sound just comes flooding out.

Finding your head voice range

While women struggle with the transition between the chest voice and middle voice, the tough transition for men is moving into head voice. With some practice, men can successfully maneuver in this area of the voice.

See Figure 11-11 for the average female head voice range. Ladies, you may not feel much difference between your head voice and your middle voice until you get quite high in your head voice, because the vibrations gradually move up into your head as you go higher in pitch. You'll also feel a slight change as you descend. You may want to explore some of the patterns that leap around, so you can really feel how the vibrations change. Mezzos may have more of a struggle with head voice than sopranos. At the transition to head voice, you may find some notes are unreliable in the beginning. Keep practicing and you'll figure out how to work your head voice using the suggestions in this chapter.

Figure 11-11:
Female head voice range.

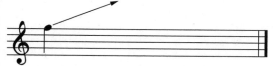

F about an octave and a half above Middle C
(F5) and up

FOR MEN

See Figure 11-12 for the average male head voice range. For men, working on head voice is important for a good balance when you sing. But I suggest that you work on your falsetto before attempting to push your head voice too high. If your voice feels strain as you work on the higher patterns, working your falsetto (see Chapter 13) until you can move in and out of it makes the exercises in this chapter more comfortable. You can also go back to the middle voice exercises until that part of your voice is really working easily. By understanding the feelings of middle voice, you can more easily understand when you're pushing too hard for head voice in ascending patterns.

Figure 11-12:
Male head
voice range.

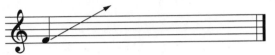

F above Middle C (F4) and up

Feeling head voice

Most singers feel the vibrations from singing in head voice in their head or skull. As you explore your head voice in this chapter, place your hand on the crown of your head, which is the top back part of your head. You can also put your hand on the back of your neck to feel the vibrations as you move up in pitch. As you ascend, you may feel the vibrations move from your neck or mouth to your head. When you get really high, you may feel the vibrations on the very top of your head. There's no one location that all singers can feel the vibrations, but you can explore how the vibrations change locations as you ascend in pitch. Also, be aware of the sensations in your mouth as you sing in head voice. You may feel sound on the roof of your mouth, on your hard palate, or even in the front of your face. All these vibration locations help you find the sensations of head voice.

A great way to feel head voice is to sing *close vowels.* Close vowels are those in which your mouth isn't as wide open when you sing. For example, *ah* is wider open than *ee,* so *ee* is a close vowel, and *ah* is an open vowel. (Check out Chapter 8 for more information on vowels.) The close vowels are helpful for singing in your head voice, because the sound is lighter than open vowels and creates vibrations that are easier to feel. That doesn't mean that you can't use open vowels like *ah* in head voice. It just means that you can explore the sensations of head voice more easily with close vowels and then take that same ease and feeling of vibrations into your open vowels.

Bobbing for pitches

A common misconception about singing is that you have to move your head up to sing high notes and put your head down to sing low notes. It may work for you in the beginning, but you may look funny bobbing your head when you start singing harder songs. Instead of bobbing your head, allow yourself some time to work on the exercises listed in each of the chapters, so the muscles inside your larynx can figure out how to do their job. If those muscles have never worked out before, they need a little time to figure out what to do when you sing high notes. Raising your head causes your vocal cords to become tense, because it prevents your thyroid cartilage in your larynx from tilting. The tilt is supposed to happen as you change pitch, but the tilting of the thyroid cartilage isn't the same as lifting your larynx. You want your larynx and your head to stay steady as the muscles inside your throat do their job.

When you sing the pattern shown in Figure 11-13, find the same spin to the tone, and feel the vibrations in your head. By aiming the vowels out in front of you, you're more likely to feel the vibrations in your head. Listen to the singers on the CD demonstrate head voice for you. As you try the pattern, find your alignment (see Chapter 2), take a breath (see Chapter 3), and open the space in the back of your mouth and throat while lifting your soft palate (Chapter 7). Using these steps for each pattern makes it easier to sing in head voice.

Figure 11-13:
Working
with close
vowels.

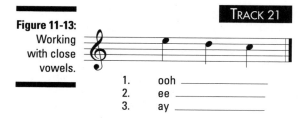

TRACK 21

1. ooh _____
2. ee _____
3. ay _____

Listen to the singers on the CD sing the pattern in Figure 11-14 for you. Notice that the sound is light and high as if the sound is spinning out of the mouth. If you open the space in your throat and mouth and apply proper breathing technique, head voice often feels like the sound is just flying out of your mouth. If the feeling is heavy and takes much effort, you're using too much weight or engaging the muscles that create chest voice.

Figure 11-14:
Spinning
out in head
voice.

```
1.  ooh ———
2.  ee  ———
3.  ay  ———
4.  oh  ———
```

Making a Smooth Transition

Middle voice is the bridge between head voice and chest voice, so you want to move easily in and out of middle voice. You may always *feel* a transition between the two registers, but the goal is to not *hear* a big change between the two. So you need to figure out where to make those transitions. Comparing the sound and feel of your middle voice to your chest voice and head voice is the easiest way to figure that out. To figure out those transitions and find out how you can transition smoothly and purposefully so that drastic changes don't occur in your sound, keep on reading.

It may be a little tricky in the beginning to get all the transitions to happen smoothly — keep trying and keep practicing.

Working around chest voice

Knowing when to make the middle voice transitions can be tricky. As you sing each descending or ascending pattern, notice how it feels — you should be able to feel your chest voice wanting to take over or give up to middle voice. Knowing what's too low for your middle voice and what's too high for your chest voice allows you to figure out where you need to make the transition from middle voice to chest voice. Practicing the exercises helps you make those transitions smoothly.

Descending from middle voice to chest voice

The following exercises work on your transition from middle voice into chest voice. Because you just found your middle voice, you may not be sure what the difference is in the feeling between chest voice and middle voice. The pattern in Figure 11-15 gives you the chance to explore the differences in sound, vibrations, and feeling.

The pattern in Figure 11-15 offers you a chance to move from middle voice to chest voice. The sensations are a bit different, and by moving down in scale, you have a chance to feel the changes as you move into chest voice.

The first repetition of this pattern should be sung in middle voice with a transition into chest voice on the bottom note. As the pattern gets lower in pitch, you may need to switch to chest voice sooner. No matter how low the pattern goes, always sing the top note in your middle voice.

Gentlemen, this pattern challenges you to sing from your middle voice to your chest voice. The first time you hear the pattern played, you'll sing the first two notes in your middle voice and then move to chest voice. As the pattern gets lower you can move into chest voice sooner. Notice the slight difference in feeling between the middle voice notes and the notes in chest voice.

Figure 11-15:
Smoothing
the
transitions.

Ascending from chest to middle voice

The exercise in this section moves from chest voice back up to middle voice. This may be harder for you in the beginning. Just like it's easier to gain weight than to lose it, working from middle voice to chest voice is often easier because that's about getting thicker and gaining weight. Working from chest voice to middle voice is about losing weight. Practice the middle voice patterns until you're confident of the sounds and feelings of middle voice. You can then move on to work this exercise, which moves from middle voice to chest voice. When you're really confident, try the exercise in this figure.

Remember what it felt like to make that transition from middle voice to chest voice? The feeling gradually got thicker as you went down the scale. The reverse is going to happen in the pattern in Figure 11-16. You need to gradually lighten up the sound as you ascend in pitch — the vowels listed help you make the move from a heavier chest voice sound and lighten up as you ascend into middle voice. If you find a lighter chest voice sound that moves easily from the bottom into middle voice, you have found the gold mine. If you aren't sure what it should sound like, listen to the singers a few times to hear the differences.

The first couple of repetitions starts in chest voice and move to middle voice on the top note. As the pattern gets higher with each repetition, you can transition to middle voice sooner. Try to sing the top notes lighter than the bottom.

The first two repetitions of the pattern are in chest voice. The third repetition moves from chest voice to middle voice on the top note. Allow the sound to lighten or use less pressure as you ascend.

Figure 11-16:
Creating a legato line in and out of chest voice.

TRACK 24

1. oh
2. ah

Working around head voice

Ascending to head voice means that you have to let go of the thick weight of chest voice or middle voice and lighten up the sound. You may have to go overboard at first try to get the sound to lighten up without squeezing in your throat. The best way to lighten up without the squeezing is by feeling the sound vibrating higher in your head. (See the "Feeling head voice" section, earlier in this chapter.)

Ascending from middle voice to head voice

Taking the middle voice too high means that the head voice doesn't get its fair share of the workout. It also means that your middle voice will grow stronger, and your head voice will grow weaker. The transitions in your voice also become more difficult if you try to push a middle voice sound too high. The transition notes won't be dependable, because you'll try to sing them heavy, and maintaining that heavy sound can be tricky. You can make a choice in a particular song when to change to head voice, but in the exercises, you want to keep the head voice strong by switching as early as possible.

Work the exercise in Figure 11-17 in this chapter to help you feel the transition from middle voice to head voice. Notice that the pattern has rests in it for you to detach the notes. Make sure you transition into head voice, not carrying up middle voice. Notice too, that the vowels are laid out, so your sound is thicker in the bottom and gradually lightens up as you ascend.

FOR WOMEN

Sing this pattern moving back and forth from middle voice to head voice. With each repetition, you can change to head voice sooner. As you descend in the pattern, notice how the middle voice feels heavier than head voice.

FOR MEN

This pattern starts in your chest voice, but you definitely move through your middle voice on your way up to head voice. As you ascend in pitch, you may be tempted to sing a full heavy sound. Instead, feel the vibrations changing as you ascend and allow the sound to lighten with less pressure in your throat on the higher notes.

Figure 11-17:
Working from middle voice up to head voice.

TRACK 25

ah _____ *oh* _____ *ooh* _____ *oh* _____ *ah*

Descending from head voice to middle voice

When moving from head voice to middle voice, the sound and sensations gradually thicken as you move down the scale. Taking head voice too low creates a light sound, and if the sound in the middle part of the voice is too light, it's harder to make yourself heard. Try the exercises in this section to smooth that transition from head voice to middle voice.

ON THE CD

In the pattern in Figure 11-18, you start on the high note of the pattern and work your way to the bottom. Find the spinning feeling of head voice on the first note, and gradually let the sound grow thicker as you descend. You may even feel the sound moving from your head to your mouth or your neck as you descend. That's just fine. The pattern starts slowly and gradually gets faster. Take your time. You may need to repeat the first few slower patterns to get accustomed to making the transition before you tackle the faster patterns.

FOR WOMEN

This pattern moves from head voice to middle voice. Some of the later repetitions move to your chest voice. If the first few repetitions are too high, join in whenever you can as the pattern descends.

As you descend in this pattern you land in chest voice. It's a great pattern for you to sing moving from your head voice down through your middle voice. If the top notes are too high for you right now, start in falsetto and move into head voice later. (See Chapter 13 for help with falsetto.)

TRACK 26

Figure 11-18:
Spinning
down.

1. oh _____ _ah_

2. ee _____ _ah_

Chapter 12

Raising the Roof on Your Range

In This Chapter

▶ Shifting gears with your voice

▶ Singing throughout your range

▶ Singing faster, livelier, and easier

▶ Running 'round your range: Pop

Singing throughout your range while making successful register transitions fine-tunes your vocal skills even further. *Range* is the highest and lowest pitch that a singer sings and all the notes in between. The *vocal registers* are chest voice, middle voice, and head voice; similar to shifting gears in a car, you switch between those registers as you sing through your range. (See Chapter 5 for more information on range and register.)

Because your goals should be to extend your range, make your highest and lowest notes stronger, and increase your singing agility, range for practicing and range for performing are two different things. For example, I practice singing high notes, but I may not sing all those notes in public. Instead, I stick to singing the strongest notes in my range in public, but I keep practicing to extend it and make my singing voice more *agile* — able to move quickly between notes.

In this chapter, you have an opportunity to extend your own practice range so that your notes grow stronger and your voice becomes more agile. You even work on some riffs to make your pop style really hot. As you listen to the CD, remember that you don't have to sing every exercise today. It may be better to work a few patterns until you're comfortable and then move on to some of the harder ones.

Tactics for Tackling Register Transitions

If you haven't had a chance yet, check out Chapters 11 through 13 for information about where to make transitions in your voice. Knowing where to make transitions makes it easier to figure out how to successfully sing a song. After you know the transition points, you can choose tactics, such as the following, to help you sing through the transitions when you practice:

- **Choose friendly vowels to sing.** Any vowel should be friendly, but some are friendlier than others in the beginning of your training. Close vowels, such as in the words *me, may,* and *to,* are often easier to sing than open vowels such as *ah.* (See Chapter 8 for more information on vowels.) The vowels that I've listed next to each exercise are the vowels that help you the most when you first sing the patterns. If you find that you're having trouble singing the pattern, go back to Chapter 8 and find some other vowels to help you sing through those transitions.

- **Close down the space in the front of your mouth.** As you make register transitions, closing down the space in the front your mouth prevents you from adding too much space and causing the tone to spread and sound unfocused as you explore how to make the transitions. After you know how to make the transitions successfully, you can choose the amount of space that works for you. For now, as you sing the notes right at the transition between registers, close your mouth a little while keeping the space in the back of your mouth and your throat open. (See Chapter 4 about opening the space in the back of your mouth and raising your soft palate.) It seems like I'm saying the opposite of open the space, but I'm not. I suggest that you close the space a small amount as you move through the transitions but only in the front of your mouth, not the back.

As you sing patterns throughout this chapter, use these tactics to help make those register transitions.

Working on Your Range

Figuring out how to sing in each of the registers in your voice is the first big step in singing. Then next big step is moving between the registers smoothly, and the final step is extending your range in both directions. Because most singers already have lower notes just from speaking lower in their range, singing exercises are often about singing high notes. You can explore singing lower notes by working on the exercises in Chapter 13 on chest voice. The exercises in Chapter 13 are low and give you an opportunity to develop lower notes if your voice is capable of extending downward. Because 99 percent of singers ask me for help on how to sing high notes, I offer you exercises that work your higher range and let you explore the lower range opportunities in other chapters in the book.

Taking your range higher

A great way to increase your range upward is by singing *staccato,* which means *short and detached.* By singing shorter, lighter notes, you can sing higher notes, because you're not using as much heavy weight. To sing staccato, you want to keep your larynx steady and watch the muscles in your neck. Your neck muscles should be still. If they flex or tighten, sing the staccato notes lighter and lower to figure out how to work the muscles inside your neck in your larynx. Allow the notes to be light and short and to connect to breath. If the sound is airy, too much air is escaping. Find a clear sound on a longer note and then gradually sing notes that get shorter and shorter to maintain that clarity.

Following the pattern in Figure 12-1, the singer demonstrates the pattern singing staccato. You may feel your abs move with the restart of the breath for each note. That's normal. You want your breath to connect to each note. Blowing too much air makes it harder to sing lightly. On the other hand, if you connect just the right amount of air, the notes bounce along the scale. Use the *ooh* vowel at first to keep the sound light and more head voice dominated. As your staccato gets easier, explore other vowels.

Figure 12-1: Staccato along the scale.

TRACK 27

1. ooh ooh ooh ooh ooh-ooh-ooh-ooh-ooh-ooh-ooh-ooh ooh
2. pah pah pah pah pah-pah-pah-pah-pah-pah-pah-pah pah

Figure 12-1 allowed you to slowly make staccato sounds on notes that move along the scale. Figure 12-2 gives you the opportunity to explore staccato sounds as you skip notes along the scale. As you ascend in pitch, allow the back space to open. It has to open fast, because you're moving quickly in the pattern. You can do it if you just think ahead.

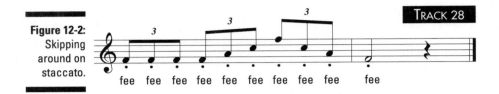

Figure 12-2:
Skipping
around on
staccato.

fee   fee   fee   fee   fee   fee   fee   fee   fee   fee

TIP

Break it down into steps: Open the space, send the breath, and then make the sound. Hopefully, it all happens at the same time, but break it down into steps if you're having trouble getting it all coordinated.

Varying the dynamics throughout your range

You've probably heard singers control their voice beautifully, whether they sang loudly or softly. As your flexibility increases in your upper register, you want to figure out how to vary the *dynamics* (volume). The exercise in Figure 12-3 is called a *messa di voce*, which means to *place the voice*. In a *messa di voce* exercise, the singer begins the note softly, gradually getting louder, and then growing soft again. By working on the *messa di voce,* you can become comfortable singing loudly or softly on any given note.

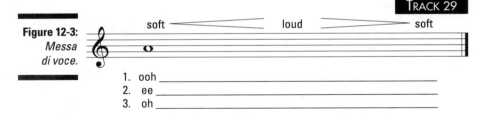

soft —————— loud —————— soft

Figure 12-3:
*Messa
di voce.*

1. ooh _____
2. ee _____
3. oh _____

ON THE CD

1. Listen as the singers demonstrate the *messa di voce* exercise in Figure 12-3. You can try this exercise starting on any note.

2. Start the note as soft as you can manage and then gradually get louder — *crescendo.* As you work this exercise, you may find that you can start the tone softer and grow even louder. This skill gradually gets stronger but sing only as soft or as loud as you can manage for today.

3. Maintain a steady flow of air as you grow louder and keep the air constant as you grow softer.

4. You can pretend that the note begins floating to help you to gradually grow softer. You want the sound to grow louder because of the increased airflow and not because you squeezed your throat.

   You may feel a bump or wiggle as you grow louder. Don't panic. The muscles need time to adjust to this new skill. Use a consistent flow of air to eliminate the wiggle.

Mixing it up: Combining registers for a comfortable sound

If you want some specific information about each register, you can check out the chapters that deal with each of the areas of your voice. Most of the patterns in those chapters are slow patterns and the notes are often right next to each other to give you a chance to really focus on every sound and sensation as you sing. After you have those specific areas down pat, you'll want the challenge of moving between registers to improve your technique even more. The patterns just ahead move faster, have larger intervals, and require you to quickly make smooth transitions between registers as you move up and down your range.

If the patterns are too high for you right now, wait until you're ready to sing them. Listen to them and get used to all the notes, so you're ready to sing them when your voice can handle the higher notes. Make sure you keep practicing, because you want to be able to sing the higher notes and not just avoid them. Remember, high notes are really fun to sing.

The pattern in Figure 12-4 may sound similar to others, but I added a few notes to get you moving around. For both men and women, this pattern moves between chest voice, middle voice, and head voice.

1. Because it's a longer pattern, work your breathing for a few minutes to find length, so you can last throughout the pattern.

2. As you leap up to the higher notes, keep your larynx steady and allow yourself to move in between registers. You want to sing in head voice on the higher notes.

   Later, when you're comfortable, leap up to an *ah* vowel without carrying too much weight into head voice.

Figure 12-4:
Mixing up
registers.

TRACK 30

1. *ah*_____ *oh*_____' *ah*_____ *oh*_____' *ah*_____ *oh*_____' *ah*
2. ee_____ oh_____' ee_____ oh_____' ee_____ oh_____' ee

The pattern in Figure 12-5 also starts on the top note, but it keeps returning to that top note. Always sing the higher notes in head voice. Remember to maintain a steady larynx as you ascend back up to the higher notes. You also need a steady airflow to make it all the way through the pattern. If you're having trouble singing all the way through the pattern, use your lip trill or tongue trill to work on your breath and then go back and sing the pattern on the vowels.

Figure 12-5:
Descending
down.

TRACK 31

1. ooh_____ oh_____ ooh_____ oh_____ ooh_____ oh_____
2. ee_____ oh_____ ee_____ oh_____ ee_____ oh_____

The pattern in Figure 12-6 ascends over an octave, which gives you a wonderful opportunity to move between chest voice, middle voice, and head voice. The pattern moves all the way up to High C. As you ascend, take care to make the transitions between the registers. If your voice feels sluggish or too heavy, make the transitions sooner. You can also drop down an octave if it's too high for your voice.

Figure 12-6:
Stepping
between
registers.

TRACK 32

ah _____ *oh* _____ *ooh* _____ *oh* _____ *ah*

Taking Your Agility to New Levels

Not every song you sing is slow, and you need to be comfortable singing both fast and slow songs. Singing fast scales develops *agility* — the ability to change notes quickly and easily. Agility is important no matter what kind of music you plan to sing. If your voice can move easily — easily *and* quickly — you're much more likely to enjoy singing faster songs, because you can sing them well.

Some voices are designed to sing fast. If your voice happens to only love slow songs, be disciplined and work through these agility patterns. Later on, you may be glad you did. Agility is especially important to sing classical music, because those composers loved to see plenty of black notes on the page, and pop songs are often upbeat and require the same agility. To advance your vocal agility, work through the rest of the exercises in this chapter.

Moving along the scale

The patterns in Figures 12-7 to 12-11 begin by moving quickly between just a few notes. The patterns get progressively harder, longer, and include more notes. Take your time getting used to all the notes. The tempo starts slowly and gradually speeds up. This gives you a chance to get yourself settled into the pattern before it starts moving too quickly. The exercises help you increase your agility because you get to sing faster notes and explore how to sing the notes faster without squeezing in your throat.

Notice that this pattern in Figure 12-8 moves up three notes and then back down. Release the sound after you go up the three notes, so you have to restart the sound on the way back down. Make sure that your breath is doing most of the work. Think of this as laughter on pitch. You may even use three notes when you laugh. Listen the next time that you get tickled to see if you're singing some of these patterns and don't even know it. This pattern uses middle voice and chest voice for male and female voice.

Figure 12-7:
Laughing
it up on
three notes.

TRACK 33

1. lah _____   lah _____
2. mah _____   mah _____
3. mee _____   mee _____

The pattern in Figure 12-8 moves along the five-note pattern and repeats a few of the notes along the way. Notice that the first two notes are repeated and so is the fourth and fifth note. This allows you to be flexible, not trying to control every note in the pattern. Make sure that you notice your breath connection, so the breath does the work of moving along the voice and not your jaw or your larynx.

Figure 12-8: Flexing out on five notes.

Picking up the pace

By practicing scales or patterns that move quickly, you can develop better agility. To improve your agility, practice the following exercise, which uses the pattern in Figure 12-9, to practice singing at a faster pace up and down a scale.

The pattern in Figure 12-9 is a full scale plus one extra note on the top. It's often called a *nine-tone scale* if you want to be technical. On the CD, the pattern starts slowly and gradually speeds up.

1. Try to feel the pivot points or accents on the fifth note and the top note. If you aim for these pivot notes, you can feel the pattern in two sections rather than one long run-on pattern.

2. Make sure your jaw stays still as you sing the pattern and your larynx doesn't bob up and down.

   Use a mirror and check the movement of both. Keep your fingers on your larynx if you can't see it in the mirror. Review Chapter 4 if you don't remember how to find your larynx.

Figure 12-9: Sliding up the scale.

4. If you have trouble getting all the notes, add a consonant, such as *L* or *D* to sing *lah* or *dah*. Using the consonant, you do and feel something as you sing each note, helping you land more confidently on each note.

5. Later, you can take away the consonant and sing just the vowels.

This is the same five-note pattern (see Figure 12-10) that you explored in other chapters, but I added a few notes. Try to hear that familiar five-note sequence and think of those notes as your pivot notes. You really have to let go of control to sing this pattern. Make sure that your jaw isn't bouncing for each note. Watch yourself in the mirror. If you find yourself trying to change the rhythm, sing half of the pattern each time it plays, so you can really focus on the first few notes to release the tension.

Figure 12-10:
Tripping
along the
scale.

TRACK 36

Skipping through the intervals

Most of the patterns that you've worked in the book have moved in stepwise motion. That means that the notes didn't jump around. However, not every song has notes that are right next to each other. You may have to hop all over the place, which requires agility; your voice can do that easily if you practice the following exercises.

The patterns in Figures 12-11 and 12-12 aren't easy. I want the CD to be beneficial to you for quite some time, so I added some hard patterns. It may take a few times listening to the CD to get used to these bouncing patterns. Just keep listening and humming along while following the patterns in the accompanying figures, until you get the pattern straight. After that, you can tackle the pattern using all the information and skills that you've been developing throughout the chapter.

As you sing patterns that hop around, keep your larynx steady. Remember to watch your Adam's apple if you can see it or put your finger on your throat. If you feel the larynx bobbing around, go back to some of the easier patterns from the beginning of the CD. When you can do those patterns with your larynx steady, come back to this section.

Check out that spunky syncopated rhythm in Figure 12-11! You've been singing mostly smooth eighth notes, but now, it's time to spice them up. Because the notes jump around so quickly, be positively sure that you're not bouncing your jaw or your larynx to change notes. Remember that the note changes inside your larynx and not because the jaw bops around.

TRACK 37

Figure 12-11:
Spicing
it up .

1. oh _____

2. ee _____

Notice that as the singer sings this pattern (see Figure 12-12), the sound is smooth, even though the pattern is bouncing around. Feel the momentum of your breath to keep the line moving but try not to let the notes jerk as you leap around on the intervals.

TRACK 38

Figure 12-12:
Bouncing
on thirds.

1. dah ____ dah ____ dah ____ dah ____ dah ____ dah ____ dah

2. mee ____ may ____ mee ____ may ____ mee ____ may ____ mee

3. mah ____ moh ____ mah ____ moh ____ mah ____ moh ____ mah

Improvising for a Better Pop Sound

When I listen to pop singers on the radio, it all sounds so easy. With all the instruments behind them, they can sound like a million bucks. At home, you probably don't have a professional sound engineer to record you every time you sing. You want to figure out how to make great pop sounds on a smaller budget. That means it needs to sound real by capturing the style of pop music without back-up singers. One of the key ingredients in a good pop sound is a flexible voice. Singers who can move their voices easily have a much easier time singing the riffs and licks in pop music. *Riffs* or *licks* are just short pieces of the music that move quickly in a specific pattern, often made up or improvised and commonly found in pop songs. Working on agility gives you a chance to get your voice moving, and now, you can explore some patterns that are found in pop music.

How do you get your voice to sound like a million bucks without an engineer? You figure out the style of pop music and add your fabulous technique that you've been developing. Pop music offers a freedom of movement and sound that's unlike classical music. When you sing classical, you sing what's on the page with musical precision. With pop music, however, you sing the lyrics with your own take on the music — called *improvising*. Most of the time, singers stay close to the melody, but the timing doesn't have to be as precise. Within the basic framework in the song, the singer adds notes that express their version of the song. With that in mind, I have notated some basic patterns that you can find in pop music. These patterns are about singing with a sense of freedom in the sound and rhythm. You still want healthy technique as you sing cool pop sounds. Try the exercises with Figures 12-13 and 12-14 to find your own pop style.

Mastering patterns in pop music

The patterns in Figures 12-13 and 12-14 are short, but they give you a chance to sing some basic riffs that you often hear in pop songs. As you sing the pattern, think about what makes a pop song sound pop. You hear the songs on the radio all the time. One of the characteristics of pop is freedom of sound: You can move along the melody line uninhibited. Try to find a free flow of the musical line as you sing.

As the singers demonstrate the pattern in Figure 12-13, they easily move without trying to sing a huge sound. You explored big sounds in the other chapters, but now you can explore a sound that's a little more casual.

Figure 12-13:
Checking
out pop riffs.

Try out this descending pop riff in Figure 12-14. Notice that it uses the same basic notes but in a different order. After you try out this one, experiment on your own to create an ascending riff. You can use notes from the other exercises in the book. Just make them funky to sound like pop music. You were precise in other exercises, but now, you can spice it up.

Figure 12-14: Descending pop riff.

yeah

Singing pop riffs with chords

The patterns that you just sang in Figure 12-13 and 12-14 help you to explore a pop sound. Because the patterns are often heard in pop songs, you can now sing those same patterns on your own with the chords that you hear. The first couple of times you try this, you may feel frustrated. Don't worry about it. Just keep trying. Each time that I try this with students who aren't used to singing pop music, they try to sing it *right*. Singing notes that don't blend with the chords is okay. Laugh it off and try again. You can even try singing along with a familiar song and adding a few notes yourself. You hear people do that all the time.

On Track 41, you hear a chord played and singers singing an improvised melody. They practiced the patterns listed in Figures 12-13 and 12-14 and then combined some of those musical ideas to create their own sequence of patterns. The singing is totally improvised. I simply played the chord and let them sing. After you listen to their improvisation, try it yourself. You can sing what they sang, or you can make up your own riff. After the singer demonstrates the riffs, the next few chords are for you to try to improvise by yourself. Be brave and make up something simple in the beginning. As you get better at it, you can make up longer patterns. As long as what you sing blends with the chord, then you're right on target.

On Track 42, you hear the background track to a pop song. You hear the singer improvise a melody and then call out for you to try it. You can make up your own melody using the riffs that you've explored. Listen to the track a few times to get the feel of it and then try your hand at improvising. The first few times, you'll feel lost, but you'll get better at it.

On Track 43, you hear the background track to another song. This time, the singer gets you started, but you get to sing the rest of it by yourself. Listen to the track a couple of times to get used to the sound. You then can make up your own pop tune with riffs.

Chapter 13

Guys and Dolls: What's Unique about Your Voice

In This Chapter
▶ Singing for guys 101
▶ Singing for gals 101

Most of the exercises throughout this book have specific instructions for men and women, because their ranges and register transitions are different. All exercises are great for either gender to practice, because they all work different parts of your voice. However, the difference between male and female singing voices doesn't stop at range and register transitions. In this chapter, you get to explore specific areas of your voice that apply just to your gender.

Doing It for the Boys

Dudes, you probably want to know what happened to your voice when you went creaking through puberty. Check out the info in the next section, "Singing through puberty," to answer your questions about why all that wiggling went on in your throat.

You'll also find out how to work a part of your voice that the girls don't have; falsetto is a unique part of your voice that you want to develop, because it helps your head voice get stronger. Sounds weird to say work on this to help that, but both parts help each other. The muscle groups, which create falsetto and head voice, get a good balanced workout if you work on both falsetto and head voice. You may not cotton to the sounds of falsetto in the beginning and you may be shy about letting someone else hear you singing in your falsetto. You may think these sounds seem too feminine. Just shut the door or find some quiet space, so you can concentrate and make some daring sounds. After you work your falsetto for a while, and it becomes stronger, you can see that it helps you develop a strong transition to get in and out of head voice.

Singing through puberty

As a young boy, you probably had a high speaking voice and your singing voice was also high and light. After puberty hit, everything started to change. The voice that you relied on started to betray you and crack and wiggle without much warning. Those cracking sounds were the result of changes in your body — specifically in your larynx — as you went through puberty.

Some males experience a change of voice in junior high and some as late as 15 or 16 years old. You may know of someone whose voice didn't change until much later, but the average change is before 15 years of age. Hopefully, your voice changed over the summer, and you returned to school in the fall with a deeper voice to impress the girl that you sat next to in math class or at least to impress your choir teacher to move you to another voice part. The male larynx continues to develop as late as the age of 20 or 21. Depending on your body and your rate of growth, you may continue to experience changes in your voice due to your body growth through your first year or two of college.

As your voice changed during puberty, your larynx grew larger and your Adam's apple appeared. During puberty, the male vocal folds can grow as much as 50 to 60 percent. As your vocal cords grew longer, your voice may have dropped an octave. This sudden growth spurt is the reason behind those cracking sounds that you experienced.

Figuring out falsetto

The male voice has three registers similar to the female voice: chest voice, middle voice, and head voice. The difference for the male singer is *falsetto* — the lighter part of your singing voice that sounds feminine. The notes in your falsetto are in the same range as your head voice, but the vocal cords are thin like a stretched-out rubber band. In the beginning of your training, falsetto may feel lighter or higher than your head voice. If you attempt to sing really high notes, you may even flip into falsetto. That's good for now.

Falsetto is an important area of your voice and needs to be developed to allow the head voice to grow stronger. Your head voice may be weak in the beginning of your singing training. You can explore sounds on high notes by singing in your falsetto and then later, when you have more strength, work on the same notes using your head voice. When the muscles that create head voice get stronger, you'll be able to sing the same notes in head voice that you originally could only sing precariously with your head voice or in falsetto. Experience the sounds that you can make with falsetto, and strengthen your falsetto. You may hear voice teachers referring to *falsetto* as your *head voice,* but I think using both terms is easier, so you know exactly what kind of sounds to make.

Discovering your falsetto

If you have ever imitated a woman, either by speaking or singing, you found your falsetto. Your falsetto may not be really strong, but giving it a good workout for singing is important. Even though you may not use your falsetto in every song, finding it is important so that you can use it in exercises to strengthen your head voice.

On Track 44, listen as the singer demonstrates falsetto sounds. Notice that the falsetto is light, unlike your speaking voice, and similar to your voice when you were younger. Now you try finding your falsetto by using the following steps:

1. The first thing to do with your falsetto is to slide around above Middle C. Most men can sing in falsetto from about the A below Middle C and up as high as they're comfortable.

2. Allow yourself the chance to just make sounds in your falsetto to get used to the feeling. You don't have to slide high in pitch but slide around enough so that you can check the position of your larynx as you ascend. See Chapter 4 for help finding your larynx.

3. As in other areas of your voice, the larynx should stay steady as you ascend in pitch. Take a breath and check the position of your larynx.

4. Allow the larynx to stay in the same position as you slide around in pitch and as you sing the patterns.

5. If your larynx moves up as you begin the first note, start on a lower pitch. Remember to open the space as you inhale, so your larynx can descend.

Experiencing your falsetto

After you find your falsetto (see the "Discovering your falsetto" section in this chapter), singing in it helps you get an idea of how singing in falsetto feels. After you know how singing in falsetto feels, you can strengthen it — as well as your head voice — by purposefully singing in your falsetto. Experience how it feels to sing in your falsetto. Try the exercises in Figures 13-1 and 13-2.

Sing through the pattern in Figure 13-1 to explore sounds in your falsetto. Listen to the male singer on the CD demonstrate in his falsetto. Check that your larynx isn't rising. (See Chapter 4 for help finding your larynx.) As you sing the pattern, open the space in the back of your mouth and throat.

Figure 13-1:
Checking
out your
falsetto.

TRACK 45

ooh

Sing the pattern (see Figure 13-2) in your falsetto using the vowels suggested. Allow the back space to open as you ascend in pitch and keep a steady flow of air moving as you sing.

Figure 13-2:
Getting the
hang of
falsetto.

TRACK 46

1. ooh _____
2. ee _____

Most beginners don't need to sing beyond the octave above Middle C in their falsetto range. You can certainly work it higher if you think you're a higher voice type to help you develop your High C and D. Work on your falsetto for at least three weeks or until it's easy for you to keep your larynx steady and make clear sounds. Then move on to the exercises in the "Descending from falsetto" section, coming up next in this chapter.

Descending from falsetto

The patterns listed in this section help you work from your falsetto down to your middle voice. This exercise may seem out of place, because you're focusing on your falsetto. However, the goal is to use the easy feeling of falsetto and get your notes in your middle voice to have that same *ease* or sound without pressure. After the notes in your middle voice are feeling easy, you want to find that same sensation of moving from falsetto to head voice with ease. The long-term benefit is that you'll be able to sing a song or musical pattern that moves from middle voice to head voice, and it'll be easy, because you know how to thin out your rubber band. The shift may be bumpy in the beginning, and that's good. As the transitions get smoother, you can make the shift easier without it being so bumpy. Go ahead and let it bump for now. By preventing the bump entirely, you don't allow yourself the chance to feel the difference between the two sounds. Eventually, you'll sing two notes, and they'll feel as if they're on the same plateau.

The exercises in Figures 13-3 and 13-4 in this chapter all give you the opportunity to sing through this transition.

Using the pattern in Figure 13-3, sing from your falsetto and flip down into your middle voice or chest voice on the last five repetitions of the pattern on the CD. Let the sound flip and make a noticeable change. You want to allow big changes when you move between the pitches in the beginning. The more that you work this transition, then the more confident you feel making a smooth transition later on. When this pattern is easy for you (usually after several weeks of practice), sing the pattern in Figure 13-4 and make a smooth transition to the bottom note.

TRACK 47

Figure 13-3:
Flipping out
of falsetto.

ooh   -   ah

In Figure 13-3, you flipped and bumped out of falsetto. In this pattern (see Figure 13-4), sing the first note in falsetto and slide down into your middle voice (or chest voice on the last three repetitions) on the vowels as written. You may feel confused in the beginning when you're making the transitions. Give yourself some time to explore a smooth transition as you descend in pitch. The more you practice, the more secure you feel moving down out of falsetto.

TRACK 48

Figure 13-4:
Gliding
down out
of falsetto.

ooh   -   oh   -   ah

Ascending into falsetto

Follow the directions for the exercises and explore the sensations of moving up into the lighter sound of falsetto from the heavier feelings of chest voice or middle voice. By exploring how to move up into falsetto, you're exploring the difference in feeling between singing lower notes and then singing in your falsetto. The benefit of this exercise is that with practice, you'll figure out how to make this same transition later and make a choice to sing the higher note in falsetto or your head voice. Your head voice will be stronger, because you'll know how to sing the notes without adding heavy pressure or thickness as if you were pulling a rubber band and it remained thick. Move on to this pattern in Figure 13-5, when you feel confident of your progress in the previous patterns.

Singing songs that use your falsetto

Even though it may seem that falsetto is just for exercises, you can find songs that allow you to use those sounds. This list of songs is from the musical theater repertoire. You can always check them out or find even more if you want an opportunity to use your newly found falsetto. Songs that use falsetto:

✔ "A Little Bit of Good" from *Chicago* by John Kander and Fred Ebb

✔ "Bring Him Home" from *Les Misérables* by Alain Boublil and Claude-Michel Schönberg

✔ "Maria" from *West Side Story* by Leonard Bernstein

✔ "Music of the Night" from *Phantom of the Opera* by Andrew Lloyd Webber

✔ "Buddy's Blues" from *Follies* by Stephen Sondheim

✔ "The Old Red Hills of Home" from *Parade* by Jason Robert Brown

✔ "Night of My Nights" from *Kismet* by George Forrest and Robert Wright

✔ "I Talk to the Trees" from *Paint Your Wagon* by Alan Jay Lerner and Frederick Loewe

✔ "Corner of the Sky," "Oh, My Dearest Love," and "With You" from *Pippin* by Stephen Schwartz

Following Figure 13-5, sing the first note in your middle voice or chest voice and then slide up into falsetto. Allow the slide back down to be smooth if possible. It's okay to really slide between the pitches for now. If you feel it bump as you make the transition, keep working and allow the bump to happen. Later on, you may find that the bump gets smoother as you become more accustomed to making this transition in and out of falsetto.

TRACK 49

Figure 13-5:
Sliding up
to falsetto.

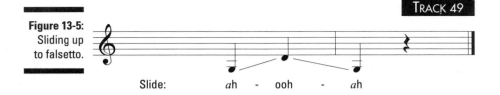

Slide: *ah* - *ooh* - *ah*

Mixing it up

As your falsetto gets stronger, it's time to mix it all up to help the notes that were once purely falsetto sounds to sound stronger, more like head voice. When you first began exploring head voice, you may have been pushing and pressing in your throat to get those notes to come out. Now that you know about falsetto and have had a chance to explore falsetto sounds, you can use that ease of falsetto and apply it to your head voice. In the male voice, when a combined effort of work between muscles creates head voice and chest voice, it's called a *mix* — a strong sound that's similar to your middle voice — it has the ease of falsetto but the strength of middle voice or head voice.

Mixed voice means finding a balance of the muscles that create head voice and chest voice. If the muscles that help you create chest voice are too active while you try to sing high notes, the sound becomes heavy and may even break. Allowing the muscles that create head voice or chest voice to engage at the appropriate time ensures smooth transitions from the top of your voice to the bottom.

Remember that you can sing the exact same notes two different ways. You can sing the F just above Middle C in your falsetto or in your head voice. Having the strength to make either choice gives you a chance to decide what kind of sound you want to make in each song. Just remember that the sound that's in between the falsetto sound and head voice is called a *mix*.

Listen while a male singer demonstrates the pattern in Figure 13-6, which moves from falsetto into a mix. Notice that as he descends, he drops into a sound that's not heavy. The sound is lighter, yet has fullness just like head voice. The feeling is of less pressure in the throat.

Figure 13-6:
Sliding
into a mix.

TRACK 50

ooh _____

Frying tones

Chest voice is that territory in the lower part of your voice, and *fry tones* are what you can experiment with to explore even lower notes of your range. Even though it sounds aggressive, fry tones are notes that are too low for you now, and you let them gurgle or fry a bit until they strengthen.

If you try to make a really low sound, your voice may not make a normal singing sound. It probably makes a soft scratchy sound that can lead to stronger, sustained low notes. By making that soft scratchy sound on the note just below the bottom note in your range, you can gain enough strength to sing a note one step lower than you normally sing. When that note becomes stronger, you may be able to add the note to your range in songs. It may take some time for the notes to grow stronger. It won't happen by working on fry tones just once. You also may only gain one or two notes on the lower end of your range.

On Track 51, listen to the male voice on this track demonstrate fry tones. The notes he's attempting to sing are low for him. By allowing the sound to settle low and *fry,* he's able to strengthen his vocal cords to thicken and discover how to sing lower notes. Women, you can make this sound if you're struggling to gain strength on your lower notes, but fry tones are more commonly used to help men sing lower.

Please remember that not every voice is meant to sing really low notes. If your voice hurts or feels very tired and scratchy after exploring fry tones, please take a break and rest. You may be attempting to sing notes that are too low for you right now. Explore fry tones that are just below your normal singing range and only for short periods of time.

You Go Girl!

Ladies, the female voice can make some really high sounds in an area above head voice called *whistle register.* If you're a really low female voice, your voice may not be able to make these sounds. That's just fine. For those of you who are comfortable singing quite high, you may find that you have notes above the female high C. By exploring your whistle register, you may be able to strengthen these notes enough that you can add them to your range for songs. The other cool thing that you can explore in this section is the female mix. The female mix is a sound that you can use when you want to make a thicker sound in the middle part of your voice. This sound is appropriate for most any songs other than songs from operas, called *arias.* Read on to explore your mix and your whistle register.

Ladies, you can backtrack and sing Figures 13-1 through 13-6 using your middle voice or chest voice.

Getting into the mix

Middle voice is different from *mix,* which is similar to a light chest voice or a stronger, thicker middle voice. Before jumping into this mix, please work your middle voice until it's quite strong. (See Chapter 11 for more on your middle voice.) Work on the speaking voice exercises, so you have command over the onset of tone and then tackle mix. (See Chapter 14 for more on your speaking voice.) You'll want to use a mix when you don't want to use a belt sound (see Chapter 14), or when you want to explore different sounds to express the text of your song. Some songs don't need a thick chest voice sound but rather a sound that's rich and full, like a mix. Sometimes, middle voice and head voice may not provide enough depth to the sound, so you can add more thickness by using a mix. A singer who frequently uses a mix is Barbra Streisand.

To find your mix, try the opposite of what you'd normally do to sing in middle voice. To sing from middle voice to head voice, you would gradually lighten up the sound as you ascend in pitch. To strengthen your mix, I want you to not lighten up the sound into head voice as you ascend.

Listen to the singer demonstrate the pattern in Figure 13-7 using a mix. Notice how she ascends in pitch and how the sound vibrates in the same place in her body. As you sing through the pattern, think of singing straight out. Allow the tone to move out in front of you and not rise higher in your head as you ascend in pitch. This will feel odd at first, but you'll gradually sense the sound getting wider as you ascend in pitch. You can also think of your chest opening wide as you move up in pitch. I pretend that I'm swimming into the tone. As you swim toward the tone, open your arms and your body to move into the sound.

Singing in a mix is a choice that you want to make. Make sure as you explore the mix that you continue to work on your middle voice transitions into head voice, so you can still make the sound gradually lighten as you ascend in pitch when you choose.

Figure 13-7:
Mixing it up.

TRACK 52

1. ee _____
2. ay _____
3. eh _____

Singing wicked high notes

Have you ever heard a woman sing notes that sounded higher than any note on the piano? Want to know how she did it? Well, she discovered how to sing really high in head voice into an area often called *whistle register* — turning over into a different register at the very top of her head voice range. You may feel that the sound is flipping over somewhere. If you allow the sound to flip over, you may find the whistle register. It's similar to what Mariah Carey did in her first few recordings. Not everyone can make those funky high sounds, but you can try if you want. Maybe you can use that sound on your first demo album.

Those wicked high notes that females sing have several different names: *flute register, bell register, flageolet,* and *whistle register.* I use the term *whistle,* because in the beginning, you feel that the sounds are squealing out of your body like a whistling teakettle.

First, you need to know about the feeling of whistle register. It feels out of control, really high, and small, and you may feel the sensations on the top of your head. These notes may not feel big and strong, like chest voice or even middle voice. If your voice is quite high anyway, try the exercise in Figure 13-8 in this chapter.

Laughing up high

You may discover during hilarious moments of laughter that you're in the same vicinity as High C. Allow yourself to have some fun and laugh like a child to discover those higher notes. Let the sound be light without trying to push it out and make it big. You may even find that some staccato or short detached laughter is in order to help you find those higher notes. Don't worry about exact pitches in the beginning when you're exploring these high sounds. Find a lighter, higher sensation and just explore. As the notes grow and become easier for you to sing, then you can try to sustain them. By exploring these high notes in whistle register, you may gain a little more strength and the sound may become similar to head voice or similar enough that you feel confident singing these notes in a song. For some heavier voices, you may find that the notes above High C are just too high for you right now. That's okay, because you have plenty of notes below High C to play with.

Listen to the pattern, illustrated in Figure 13-8, to hear the singer moving above High C to find whistle register. If you think this is a sound that your voice is ready to explore, give it a whirl. It's also fine to leave this exploration for a later time, too, when your voice is comfortable singing high. Find your alignment, prepare your breath, open the space in the back of your mouth (back space), and go for it.

Figure 13-8:
Soaring
above
High C.

TRACK 53

ooh

Chapter 14

Tuning Up Your Speaking Voice for Belting

In This Chapter

▶ Pitching to your speaking voice

▶ Resonating new sounds with your speaking voice

▶ Figuring out how to apply good singing technique

▶ Discovering how to belt

*B*y finding a really resonant speaking voice, you can fill an entire room with little effort. I didn't know how to use my speaking voice properly, and I became really tired after speaking for short periods of time. By discovering my optimum speaking pitch, applying the same breath that I use when I sing, and finding resonance in my speaking voice, I'm able to chatter all day without nearly as much effort and no strain.

By working the exercises in this chapter, you can discover your optimum speaking pitch, proper breathing, resonance, and range to make your speaking voice clear and commanding. After working on your speaking voice, you get the chance to finally try out some belting exercises. But check out the exercises after you've worked on your speaking voice. You need to have a healthy speaking voice that's ready for the high-energy work of belting.

Working the speaking voice helps you to feel the middle ground in your singing voice. Many people, especially women, speak low to sound tough. That's fine, but you can also speak in your middle voice and command attention.

Men usually speak in their chest voice. If you happen to have a high speaking voice, you may still be in chest voice. You're probably still in chest voice. You can still work the exercises in this chapter to get your speaking voice on track using breath.

No matter what sound you explore with your speaking voice, remember to apply your knowledge of breathing from Chapter 3. You may be tempted to squeeze your throat to make some of the tones, but that won't help in the long run. You would just have to release that tension later. Keep exploring tones with an open throat, consistent airflow, and an abundance of gusto.

Playing around with Pitch

To get the most benefit from the speaking voice exercises in this chapter, I want to work out your speaking voice in this way:

You'll explore the tones and pitch you currently use and make when you speak. You need to know what sounds you currently can make before you can explore other sounds and pitches with your speaking voice. After you know what your voice currently does, you'll explore chanting to find an optimum speaking pitch, but you'll take that same vibrant speaking tone from your optimum speaking pitch to other pitches. Your optimum speaking pitch is the pitch that resonates and sounds the best in your voice. Being able to make vibrant tones on a variety of pitches is important for you to be able to handle text that may need to be spoken in the middle of your song or just before your song starts. Those vibrant tones also make you sound great when you have to make a presentation at work or give a speech.

When you're confident that your speaking voice has more pizzazz, you'll work on high-energy speaking and resonance to prepare for belting, and then finally, explore belting. Because your speaking voice is so important to the health of your singing voice, the steps are detailed. To keep you speaking and singing well every day, try out all the exercises in the chapter but try them in the order that you see them to get the most benefit.

Talking to yourself

Before you explore the speaking voice exercises, record yourself speaking and listen to the tone. You can even listen to your message on your answering machine. Notice if your voice is low or high and if your tone is bright and forward or covered. You can also record yourself during a conversation discussing some happy event in your life. Your speaking voice may have more pitch variety with the excitement of your emotions. By playing back the recording of yourself, you can hear the tone of your speaking voice from an outside source. Just listening to yourself talk is a different sound than hearing your voice from a recording. When you hear your voice on a recording, you may recognize that the pitch of your speaking voice is much lower than you thought and realize that you need to explore your optimum speaking pitch.

Everyone has a central pitch that they return to when speaking. You can change your central speaking pitch to find one that helps you get the most ringing and resonant tone from your speaking voice. Find an optimum speaking pitch and explore chanting, so you can really focus on one note at a time and then choose which pitch sounds the best in your voice.

Chanting and speaking

To understand what I mean about resonant speaking voices, I want you to explore chanting, which is like speak-singing. By exploring, you'll understand the close relationship between a resonant tone for speaking and singing. To explore chanting, you'll sing some pitches, chant the same pitches, and then speak the same pitches.

1. Use the opening three notes to "Three Blind Mice." You may want to sing a bit of the song just to refresh your memory.

2. After you have the tune, sing the first three notes and notice the feeling in your throat. Make sure that your version of the song isn't in the basement, so to speak.

3. Speak the opening lines of "Three Blind Mice." Aim for a pitch that's in the vicinity of Middle C or a little higher for women and around an octave below Middle C for men. You can explore higher pitches if you think that you're speaking too low.

4. Go back to the "Three Blind Mice" tune and sing the first three notes; then chant the first three notes. Chanting means to speak-sing the pitches as you hear monks doing in monasteries.

5. After you have explored chanting, speak the first three words and see what pitches come out. The sensations of nasal resonance should be similar between your singing, chanting, and speaking all on the same pitches. Remember to connect your breath to the speaking voice just as you would for singing.

You can also choose to sing "Three Blind Mice" on higher pitches and then chant and speak into those pitches.

If you feel strain, you're probably using your full chest voice to create the tone. Try speaking again and use a tone more similar to your *middle voice* (a balance of muscle groups working together rather than just chest voice muscles) or find a pitch that's a little higher and doesn't use as much chest voice.

Gentlemen, if you feel pressure when you're speaking, it may be because you're not maintaining a consistent airflow as you're speaking. The feeling of pulling up weight from the bottom means chest voice is actively engaged. If the tone is too wispy and light, you're not connecting your body to the higher pitch. Your whole body should be ready to help you make the sound. You can pretend that you're about to leap up and dance like Patrick Swayze or Mikhail Baryshnikov to help you feel the commitment from your body. You can also explore the exercise in the section, "Using body energy to find clarity of tone," later in this chapter. Try again and open your throat, find your breath, and aim the tone right out in front of you.

Rapping for pitch exploration

For those of you that have been listening to classical music or country, today is your day to broaden your horizons. If you haven't heard a rap song lately (or ever), find a teenager and ask them how. Rap is a style of music where the performers use a cross between singing and speaking on pitches similar to what you did in the "Chanting and speaking" section, earlier in this chapter. Rap is speaking on specific pitches, which is exactly what you need to explore. Exploring the relationship between speaking and singing is important for finding a variety of pitches and resonant tones to your speaking voice.

On Track 54, listen as the singer raps this song exploring pitches with his speaking voice. He's using a variety of pitches and tones as if he's almost singing, but he is actually making a cross between speaking and singing. Now you try it. After a few tries, rap without the CD and listen to your speaking voice. Notice the pitches as well as the feeling of speak-singing on pitch. Exploring rap helps you find pitches that easily create a ringing tone and that will lead you to your exploration of your optimum speaking pitch.

> I'm out here just a rappin' about my speakin' voice.
>
> The pitch I gotta find to make the righta noise.
>
> If I'm too low, I grind, and that ain't right.
>
> The pitch, if it's too high, I sound like Minnie Mouse.
>
> Just the righta height, I sound so powerful.
>
> Take it to the limit and voice be right.

Finding your optimum speaking pitch

By exploring chanting earlier, you found that you can move from singing to chanting to speaking and apply your same breathing technique and tone production when speaking or singing. After exploring chanting, you can find the pitch that sounds the best in your voice, called the *optimum pitch*. Your optimum speaking pitch or the central speaking pitch that sounds the best in your voice is usually where you say, "Uh-huh." It's the pitch on *huh* that works the best for most people. If someone asks you a question and you answer without thinking about what you're doing, you probably make the tone on a pitch near your middle voice if you're a woman and chest voice if you're a man. This is a good thing. The tone of the optimum pitch is important and not just the pitch itself.

1. Say, "Uh-huh." Notice the second pitch that you sound for the *huh* of "Uh-huh." Say it a few times and move right into speaking. For example, say, "Uh-huh" and say your name immediately after the *huh*.

2. Notice the pitch when you said your name. Was it one of the pitches in "Uh-huh" or was it lower?

3. If it was lower, try again and say your name on the same pitch as the "Huh."

Your optimum speaking pitch helps you find prominent vibrations and easy carrying power to your speaking voice. You can then take that to other pitches. If you aren't sure what sounds best, ask a friend to listen or record yourself and listen back. It's okay to explore different pitches; that's the objective of the exercise.

Listen for the pitches that really buzz or really vibrate as you speak. The best speaking pitch is not the lowest or the highest note of your range. It's somewhere near your middle voice range for women and chest voice range for men.

Using body energy to find clarity of tone

Using body energy is really helpful to get a clear speaking or singing sound. By body energy, I mean that surge of energy in your body that helps you make the sound, such as when you're about to lift something heavy. You have to use air and exert energy to move your body. When this same kind of movement or energy is applied to singing, you can take advantage of that purposeful flow of air to create clear tones on a specific pitch. How do you get that to help you sing? One of my favorites in Chapter 10 is stationary skiing. By moving as if you were cross-country skiing, you get your lower body connected, and you feel as if your whole body is singing. So connecting this idea to speaking means to find your alignment from Chapter 2, find the breath from Chapter 3, find some energy from physical movement, and then make the sounds with your speaking voice. You find that your speaking voice can make plenty of noise just because of the breath and energy surging in your body.

✔ As you sing part of your favorite song, rock back and forth from one foot to the other to feel the surge or connection of energy for your whole body.

✔ You can also bounce in place just to get your legs in motion or engage an imaginary fencing partner.

✔ Using a *plié* from your ballet class is another way to engage your upper and lower body. *Plié* means *to bend.* In this case, you bend your knees as you gradually move toward the floor and then move back up.

✔ If you aren't keen on rowing or other physical exertion, you can also just hold onto something heavy as you sing. Don't go lifting the pool table but lift a heavy book as you sing. Notice that as you lift the book the tone of your voice responds to the energy moving, which probably made the tone clear. Keep your breath moving as you experiment with lifting things.

You want the breath to keep moving. It's possible to really squeeze and make clear tones, but you know what tension feels like by now and know that it won't help you in the long run.

To pump up the volume and make a louder tone, use a faster flow of air and add more energy. To gradually get louder *(crescendo)* as you speak or sing, gradually speed up the flow of air and exert more energy. See Chapter 3 about breathing for singing. Practice speaking through some dialogue from a song or a monologue and start the tone softly and then gradually get louder to practice this consistent energy flow idea.

Defining Healthy Belting

Belting is such an exciting sound for a singer. Belting is the high-energy sound that singers make in pop, musical theater, and rock music. It's similar to yelling on pitch but with more of a singing tone than yelling. Famous belters include Ethel Merman, Bette Midler, and Kate Smith.

Because your speaking voice is so closely related to belting, using the speaking voice to develop a belting sound allows you to use a balance of muscles to create the sound rather than just full chest voice.

Belting is also controversial among singers and voice teachers. The most common statement that you'll hear is that belting is dangerous and can ruin your voice, but any type of bad technique can hurt your voice, including a bad technique for belting. However, healthy belting is possible if you take the time to really work on your speaking voice to prepare you for the high-energy sounds, which will prevent you from having to use a heavy, full chest voice to make the belting sounds.

Belting is similar to a strong mix for a female, rather than a full, heavy chest voice. Save the heavy chest voice sounds for the bottom of your voice. Belting can be detrimental to your singing voice if you don't take the time to gain strength in your middle voice (see Chapter 11) and work on your speaking voice to prepare your voice for the high-energy sounds that you'll need to make.

In the beginning, when you're working on belting, you may think the sound is too intense. That probably means you're doing something right. The feeling shouldn't be too tight, but the sound may be intense due to the increased amount of vibrations around your face from nasal resonance. Keep reading to experiment with resonating qualities and understand nasal resonance. (See Chapter 7 for more on resonance.)

If you're not a fan of belting, you can pass this section up and head straight to Chapter 16 where you can find information about other styles of singing. For those of you who really want a chance to explore belting, please work on the speaking voice exercises and then come back to explore the belting exercises.

The steps to making a healthy belt require that you find some high-energy speaking sounds before using your singing voice. You'll have a harder time figuring out how to correctly make the sounds if you jump right to the belting on the CD. If you're an advanced singer and have some experience with belting, you can explore the exercises at a faster pace.

For a beginner, I strongly suggest that you work on your singing voice in another chapter, such as Chapter 11, and then return to this chapter. When you begin this chapter, you'll need to really focus on your progress in each exercise before moving on to the next. Most beginner singers need up to a year or more to work on their singing voice and then another six months to a year to belt successfully.

When you do return to these exercises to begin belting, take some time to practice some singing exercises to get your voice warmed up before you begin the belting exercises. You'll have an easier time making the sounds if your voice is warmed up.

When you figure out how to belt, move back and forth between your different styles of singing, so you don't get stuck. Singers often like to belt so much that they neglect the rest of their voice. The top part of your voice still needs a good workout to stay in shape, so you're able to move back and forth between your other styles of singing.

You can sing any pattern you like using a belting sound. As long as you're within the right range for belting, you can use any pattern or exercise that works for you. I find that working the speaking voice is the most helpful for any singer. After the speaking voice is working well, singers can use a variety of patterns to continue making the sounds.

Knowing your limits as a beginner belter

Belting is like any other singing skill; it takes time to master it. If you're just beginning to belt, make it part of your daily routine but not the only part of your daily routine. You wouldn't go to the gym on the first day you bought the membership and spend the entire day on the treadmill. Take it easy and give yourself time to build up the muscle strength to make the sounds in a healthy way. If you find yourself pushing or are tired at the end of a work session, go back and check your technique. If all the things on your checklist are in good working order, shorten the amount of time that you work on belting at your next practice session. Continue to also work on your speaking voice to keep it in good shape. Continue to work on all areas of your voice after you discover belting. You want to keep your technique balanced and have strength in all areas of your voice.

Noting the difference between the sexes

Not only is belting different between women and men, but it's also different for different voice types. Keep reading, so you can discover the differences for yourself, so you can know how to develop a healthy belting technique, custom-designed for your voice.

Belting is going to be easier for the lighter sopranos than for mezzos. That doesn't mean that you mezzos shouldn't try it, but you may have to work a little harder to figure it out. Your cords are already fatter, so making them thicker for belting takes a little coordination. A healthy belt for the female voice means using a consistent flow of air, nasal resonance, and a strong speaking voice sound that sustains into sung tones. When the belt is right, belters say it feels like middle voice but sounds like chest voice.

Belting for the male voice can be fun. It's not a huge technical feat for you to change the sound enough to create this style of singing. To create a belting sound, you need to find a forward resonating sound and a fullness of tone as you ascend in pitch. The fullness of tone can happen from using nasal resonance or, if you can handle it, letting the sound stay quite thick until you turn over into head voice. Because this sound is so much harder for the female, there is only one example of a male voice belting. You'll find more time devoted to the male voice and falsetto in Chapter 13 if you're feeling left out.

Most men allow the sound to roll back as they ascend in pitch. This is a perfectly normal action to take when singing classical music. When the sound moves back, it's called *cover*. This means the sound moves back (or uses more resonance in your throat) and the vowels slightly modify. To make a distinction between your classical sound and belting sound, you want to keep the sound rolling forward or use more nasal resonance. All resonators are used for singing, but for belting, the prominent resonance comes from the nasal resonator.

Coordinating breath and energy

When you're making belting sounds, you must maintain a consistent flow of air. If your air isn't flowing quickly, you may find yourself squeezing or tightening to make the sounds. You must also increase energy flow as you make more intense belting sounds. The flow of energy needed to create belting sounds may be greater than the amount of energy needed in your chest voice or middle voice. Move around the room to connect your whole body to your singing as you did earlier in the chapter in the "Using body energy to find clarity of tone" section. To take coordinated breath and energy to the next level for belting, pump up the volume.

Preparing for Belting

To feel the vibrations necessary for belting, you need to explore some tones that aren't very pretty. Belting is not about making pretty tones. Belting sounds like yelling on pitch. I don't think of yelling as a bad sound. It's a normal sound that people make in heated discussions or during moments of excitement. To take the first step toward singing and belting, explore the many vibrations in your face, so you move closer toward making the necessary high-energy tones for belting.

Being bratty to feel resonance

I want you to imitate a little kid who is about to rat on his big brother or sister. You know that taunting, singsong sound, *nya-nya-nya-nya-nya*. Be a brat for a few minutes and find that tattletale sound and feel the vibrations as you make the sound. If you didn't feel the sensation in your face, try again and be even more of a brat. Let the bratty sound buzz in your face and not happen because of squeezing in your throat. When the sound is right, you'll feel vibrations in your face or just behind your face. You want the sound to be buzzing behind or beside your nose but not in your nose. If you think it's too nasal, hold your nose and make the sound. The sound stops if it's "in your nose," but it will continue buzzing if it's just buzzing behind your nose. If the vibration is in your head or face, you're on the right track. The vibrations will not be in one single area; you may feel your whole face, especially your cheeks, vibrating. Some people like to call the area behind their face "the mask." If that's a term you're familiar with, you're trying to create tones that generate plenty of vibration in the mask.

On Track 55, you can hear a female singer demonstrate the *nyah* sound for you. The sound should really buzz in your face behind your nose. Not in your nose as in nasal, but behind your nose to take advantage of nasal resonance. After you find the *nyah* sound, speak some text from a belting song in this same manner. As you make these sounds, keep plenty of breath moving, so you don't push in your throat. The sound may not be your favorite in the beginning, but you may grow to like it.

Being confused about belting in the beginning is normal. Many singers aren't sure if they like the sound right away. Knowing that the first sounds aren't the finished product, continue to explore the sounds. As your skill develops, you can play with the tone to find a quality that you can live with. Remember that the first few songs that you sing to practice belting need to be spunky, feisty characters. You have to have a reason for making those brassy sounds, or it won't work as easily.

Calling out to a friend

Making high-energy speaking sounds, such as calling out to a friend or making demands to an imaginary foe, helps you find nasal resonance and coordinate breath and energy.

Let's pretend that your friend is across a noisy room and try to get his attention by calling out, "Hey." Use your knowledge of breath and energy to connect to this sound. If your imaginary friend didn't respond, then call out "Hey" again on a different pitch. Remember that it's okay to explore different pitches with your speaking voice. You can also call out phrases, such as "Give me that back!" or "Back off!" or "Never!" or even sell them something. Many of the vendors at the ballpark are belting, and they don't even know it. Try selling some apples, oranges, or popcorn to an imaginary crowd. Use your knowledge of resonance from Chapter 7 to get the tone vibrating in your face to find nasal resonance.

On Track 56, the speaking quality that you need to work this exercise feels nasal. It doesn't *sound* nasal, but it may *feel* nasal. This is perfectly legal belting. The wide-open, dark, resonant sounds are good for your classical music. This twang sound that's spoken is perfect for helping your belt. For those of you who've never heard the type of speech that I'm about to describe, get out the CD and listen to the example before attempting this exercise.

Increasing your speaking range

The next step in your quest of a belt is to practice speaking with a tone that uses strong nasal resonance and high energy on various pitches. Please don't try this exercise until you explore the exercise under "Finding your optimum speaking pitch" section, earlier in this chapter. By knowing your optimum speaking pitch and exploring that sound and feeling, you'll be more prepared for this exercise, because you'll understand the pitch in your speaking voice.

1. First, try being monotone. Find your optimum speaking pitch and practice reading a recipe or an article from the newspaper in a monotone on the optimum pitch. That means saying every word on one pitch and not varying as you do when you normally speak.

2. When the monotone is quite easy, vary your reading by alternating between two adjacent pitches. Use only two pitches for now, so you can feel the sound, connect the breath, and feel the sensations in your body and face.

3. When you're feeling confident, move up to a slightly higher pitch. If you have a piano or a pitch pipe, you can find your optimum pitch by playing a note on the piano until you find the note that matches your speaking pitch.

4. Each time you're confident of the pitch you're speaking, play the next higher note and use that as the central speaking pitch when you repeat the recipe.

After you get to the F just above Middle C, you'll feel like you can't speak any higher. You can. Find a middle voice sound, not chest voice, and continue speaking. After you've tried the exercise and explored a few pitches, listen to the corresponding track on the CD.

On Track 57, you can hear a female singer demonstrating the sound of speaking with her optimum speaking pitch and then moving higher in pitch while maintaining the fullness of tone she had on her optimum speaking pitch. She starts near Middle C and gradually works her way up the scale. Notice that as she moves up the scale, her speaking voice stays strong. The first few times you try this exercise, you may only feel comfortable going up a few steps. When those few steps are solid in your voice, try moving up a few more steps. The singer demonstrating on the CD is an advanced belter who has worked on this exercise for quite some time and is confident moving quite high with her speaking voice.

Trying out a belt

If you have been working on the speaking voice exercises in this chapter and feel confident about your progress, please continue and try belting with the singers on the CD. You'll hear one track with a male belter and four tracks with a female belter. The male belter demonstrates the sounds of a male singer belting high in his range. The first female singer demonstrates the difference between a pitch in chest voice and then she belts the same pitch. The next three tracks are a progression of songs for belters. The first one is a beginner belt song. For those of you who are new to belting and who just want to get your feet wet, start with the first one. The next song is a little more advanced and requires that your speaking technique is strong. You can start on this pattern if you have some experience belting but are a little rusty.

I strongly suggest that you work these two songs until you can successfully sing them without strain and use the proper technique of breath and tone. The third pattern is much more advanced, because the range is higher and the notes are sustained longer. When these three short songs are comfortable for you, I suggest you look in Appendix A for the list of suggested belt songs and try one out.

On Track 58, listen to the singer demonstrate the difference between a belted sound and a chest voice sound. By working on her speaking voice, she was able to develop her belt without engaging her full chest voice.

On Track 59, you can hear a male voice belting. The male singer says, "Listen to me wail!" so you can hear the sounds of a high male voice belt. Notice that the notes are in the head voice range, yet the sound is different than the other sounds you hear the male voice singers make on the CD.

Practice the speaking voice exercises in the "Playing around with Pitch" section, earlier in this chapter, before you try to sing along with the three tracks of belt songs that follow. You'll have much more long-term success if you allow yourself to work slowly and make consistent progress. The belting exercises aren't easy, but you can do them with practice.

On Track 60, the singer on this track sings a short beginner belt song. The song has a narrow range and stays in the same vicinity. Work on this song until you're comfortable singing it before moving on to the next track just ahead.

On Track 61, the singer sings a short belt song that allows you an opportunity to take your belting skills a little farther. Listen to the track a few times to get used to the sound. Be sure you're warmed up before you try singing this pattern.

On Track 62, the singer sings a short belt song for advanced belters. This is a more advanced belt song, because the range is wider, the notes stay higher, and you have larger leaps. You're required to move from lower in your voice, near your chest voice range, leaping up to higher notes using a belt. Continue working on the exercises in this chapter for belt strength and endurance. If you feel fatigue after singing this song, go back to the first belt song and practice it until you feel your technique is solid.

Chapter 15

Finding the Right Voice Teacher for You

In This Chapter

▶ Deciding what you want from lessons

▶ Understanding common policies of voice teachers

▶ Interviewing a potential teacher with specific questions

*F*inding the person who's just the right voice teacher for you can be tricky. The different types of instructors that are available may be confusing. You may have no idea how to select a voice teacher or what to expect. You may have no idea what to expect from the lesson itself. No matter what your level of understanding may be, this chapter gives you insight and advice so that you can know how to select a voice teacher. This chapter also lets you know what to expect from the voice teacher, the lesson, and yourself.

Yes! — A Voice Teacher Is Right for You

The fact that there are different types of singing instructors — *vocal coaches, pianists,* and *voice teachers* — as well as stark differences between them — is enough to make you second-guess your decision to take voice lessons. However, the decision-making is simple after you read this section. Check out the differences between instructors, and you discover why a voice teacher is the right choice for you.

A *vocal coach* plays the piano well, provides you with some basic tips on technique, and supports the work of your voice teacher. She also usually works with singers who have a working knowledge of singing. Beginners are better off sticking with a voice teacher. A *pianist* plays the piano for you to practice singing, but he doesn't offer advice. The *voice teacher,* however, is the technique specialist. Although the coach may have knowledge of technique, the voice teacher is the pro and expert. Although the pianist may play the piano better, the voice teacher makes up for it in knowledge and advice on your vocal technique.

Vocal coaches and pianists are all viable options if you just want to work on repertoire without focusing as much on the nitty-gritty details of technique. A voice teacher provides you with the best all-around advice on technique, and she specializes not only in working on technique, but also in applying that technique to your repertoire. So, no matter what your level of singing, if you want to improve through lessons, a voice teacher is your best solution.

Searching for the Best Voice Teacher

Okay, so you realize the benefits to working with a voice teacher over other types of instructors. Now, you need to start doing your homework to find the one who best suits your needs. I provide you with some ways to find a voice teacher, as well as some questions to ask both yourself and the prospective teacher before you even step into the studio.

Finding a prospective voice teacher

You can track down a voice teacher in many ways. The following list makes finding a good one simple, even if you aren't Nancy Drew or one of the Hardy Boys.

- **Get recommendations from friends who take voice lessons.** Keeping in mind that no teacher is perfect, ask your friend what he or she likes and doesn't like about the teacher. Compare his or her preferences with your own.

- **Ask for suggestions at the local music store.** The store may even have someone on staff who can work with you. If not, they're probably familiar with at least a few local voice teachers.

- **Look for ads in the local newspaper or trade paper.** Before you give the person a call, have your list of questions ready. If you feel uneasy during the conversation, just say that you want to think about it.

- **Call the music school at the college nearest you.** Many graduate students make great voice teachers. They're often in the heat of the training and want to share all the juicy information that they've gleaned. They may not have years of teaching under their belt, but that may work very well for you. The two of you can explore singing together.

✔ **Search online.** You can also find voice teachers online at different Web sites, such as `nats.org` (the National Association of Teachers of Singing, Inc.). If you live in a rural area or just aren't having any luck finding a voice teacher, the Internet has several sites that can help you.

If possible, you want to try to get input from students, current or former ones, about a particular teacher before you contact him. Although no teacher is perfect for everyone, if you hear one bad review after another, take the warning that this teacher probably isn't the best choice.

Identifying what you want

You can't get far choosing a voice teacher if you can't identify what you want out of your lessons. You may have questions for the prospective voice teacher, but he may also have some for you. To be prepared, consider the following questions before you begin chatting with prospective teachers.

✔ **What exactly do you want from lessons?** If you want to improve your technique, sing higher notes, hold out phrases longer, or make yourself understood, discuss these goals with your prospective voice teacher. Your prospective voice teacher can tell you what she focuses on and how a lesson may be structured around your goals, and you can see if that fits your wants and needs.

✔ **Are you doing this for fun or are you interested in a career or exploring some major singing?** If you're looking for a singing career, your teacher may move you at a faster pace through your lessons and make more demands on your practicing; on the other hand, your prospective teacher may assign different kinds of songs or not worry so much about the business aspects of singing if you're just taking lessons for fun. No matter whether you want a singing career or a better sound on the karaoke stage, you want the lessons and experience to be fun. So discuss with your prospective voice teacher how she would structure a lesson around your interest level. You may be interested in being pushed a bit harder, even if you're singing just for fun, and you want to be sure that she's willing to adjust the pace to meet your needs.

✔ **How much time do you want to spend practicing?** If you're really busy and can only spend one hour per week practicing, discuss this availability with your prospective voice teacher. Find out whether she's flexible enough to provide lessons every other week to give you enough time to practice between lessons.

✔ **What do you want to sing?** Check out Chapter 17 if you aren't sure what your options are. After you know what you want to sing, talk it over with the teacher to see if she teaches that style of music. Some teachers only teach classical music and prefer that their students not sing pop music or jazz. Working on classical music has great benefits but that may be the wrong choice for you if you have your heart set on rockin' around the clock.

Interviewing a prospective teacher

Regardless of whether you've identified what you want from a voice teacher, finding out basic information about the prospective voice teacher, such as his qualifications and costs, is equally important in order to get the best teacher.

Really good voice teachers are probably busy and quite booked with students. They may not have time to answer all your questions. If that's the case, you may want to try a few lessons and find out the answers during that time. Either way can work quite well.

If you call a teacher and start quizzing her as if she's being audited, you may not get a good response. Treat the questions in this section as suggestions to steer the conversation in order to get the answers you need. After all this questioning, if you get a good feeling about the teacher over the phone, give it a try.

Finding out about a prospective teacher's background

Consider getting answers to the following questions about a prospective voice teacher's background:

✔ **How many years have you been teaching?** You want to find out if this person has been teaching more than just a few years. Some brand-new teachers are really great, because they've recently had so many lessons themselves. Meanwhile, a more-experienced teacher may know how to address the type of vocal problems that you want to focus on and may be a better choice for you. He may also have years of experience explaining how to do something and may have a variety of ways to explain the technique, so you're sure to understand. If the prospective teacher has been around for a while, you're also more likely to find some current or former students who can tell you about her strengths. A newer teacher probably charges less than someone with more experience and may have more options for lesson times or may be more open to working on contemporary music, such as pop or rock.

If you have some serious vocal health problems, such as nodes or severe acid reflux (see Chapter 24), I recommend finding an experienced teacher. She may have more experience with rehabilitating voices.

Avoid teachers who promise remarkable results in a very short period of time, claim to be the expert of a particular teaching method, offer only a few exercises that are supposed to fix all vocal problems, promise you wondrous results if you just study with them, and promise that only they can give you the information that you need.

✔ **Where did you study, or where did you get your singing education?** You want a voice teacher who's had years of performance experience or years of lessons or training in a degree program that focuses on the voice. The teacher doesn't have to have a degree from an Ivy League school to be a good teacher. He just needs to know a great deal about singing and how to pass on the knowledge of singing to his students.

If you're interested in singing classical music or choral music in other languages, find out whether this teacher has knowledge of foreign languages during your conversation with him. You may find this answer by asking what kind of songs the students sing.

Choir directors and piano teachers commonly also teach voice. As long as this person knows quite a bit about how the voice works and how to help when something goes wrong, it's worth a try. If you do take lessons from the choir director, find out how much of her training was about individual singing. Many degree programs allow choral directors to graduate without any knowledge of how the voice actually works. They spend many hours coaching choirs to make lovely sounds, but how to make those sounds is very important for voice lessons.

✔ **Do you perform? If so, where?** If you have an opportunity to hear a voice teacher sing, by all means go. You may discover a lot about his personality that you may not get to see during a lesson. The teacher may be very businesslike in the lessons and seeing him sing a comic song can help you realize that he can help you with interpretation of your songs as well as how to improve your technique.

✔ **Do you work with many different voice types or just students with voices similar to your own?** Do you teach different styles of music, and do you understand belting and how to teach it for musical theater? For those of you who need help with specific types of voices, such as a countertenor (see Chapter 5), or who want specific kinds of help with styles of singing, such as jazz, pop, or belting, you want to make sure that the prospective teacher can work with your voice type or the particular style of singing that you're interested in pursuing. See Chapter 14 for more information on belting.

✔ **Do you play the piano or do you have a pianist play?** Keep in mind that you're seeking out a voice teacher, not a pianist. Most voice teachers don't play the piano that well. They spent their days training the voice and may have skipped the piano lessons. However, you want to ask this question, because many voice teachers who don't play the piano well hire a pianist to accompany their students. You need to find out if the cost for this extra person is already figured into the cost of your lesson. Most times, it is. If it's not, however, you need to decide if you're willing to take on the added expense.

If the teacher doesn't play and doesn't have a pianist available, find out what kind of system she has for working on music. Many teachers use accompaniment recordings for the students to sing along with. Your teacher also may have a keyboard with songs already programmed into it. If this system doesn't work for you, ask if you can hire a pianist to come in occasionally to play through your songs. Or you may want to find a rehearsal pianist to record them for you so that you can take a tape to your lessons to sing along with.

✔ **Where do you conduct your lessons?** The teacher may hold lessons in her home, at a studio, at a school, or even at your home.

If the teacher is willing to come to your home, that certainly may be your most convenient option. However, keep in mind that you may have to pay more for this convenience. (See the next section in this chapter, "Figuring the costs.")

✔ **Where do your students perform?** Hopefully, the teacher puts on at least one studio recital each year. This way, you have at least one opportunity to strut your stuff each year. The teacher may also tell you how many students are performing in local productions or other local venues. Asking this question gives you an idea of how familiar the teacher is with local performing venues, and you'll have some idea about the variety of students within the studio.

✔ **What kind of music do your students sing?** You want to find out if the teacher is interested in the same kind of music that you enjoy. If she only assigns songs and doesn't allow the student to choose, think about how you feel about her preferred style of music before you commit.

Figuring up the costs

Let's face it — lessons cost money. But you don't want to get stuck adding up costs at the last minute only to find out that you can't afford them. Ask your prospective voice teacher the following questions to get a grasp on how much money you're gonna have to fork over:

✔ **What do you charge for lessons?** The cost of voice lessons varies depending on location. The price of voice lessons in New York City or San Francisco may be $100 to $250 for an hour-long lesson, but you may only pay $35 to $50 for an hour's instruction in a small town in the Midwest. You may also want to ask the teacher whether you can opt for a half-hour lesson (or an hour lesson every other week), if that fits your budget better.

The fame of the voice teacher can also affect the cost. Voice teachers who've had successful performance careers or famous students charge more than teachers just starting out. The famous teacher may be able to help you with contacts in the business as your technique advances, but high prices don't guarantee better results or a better teacher. You'll have to try some lessons to know if it works for you.

If you're a beginner, you're better off taking a half-hour lesson anyway. Your muscles are just figuring out what to do, and your voice and brain may be quite tired after a half-hour of work. When your skills improve, you can increase the time.

The price of lessons doesn't guarantee the best or worst teacher. You may find a young teacher just starting out who has terrific rates but doesn't know anything yet about teaching. The famous teacher who charges more than your rent may not be the right teacher for you, either, if you resent having to shell out the dough for lessons. Shop around and ask plenty of questions.

✔ **What's your cancellation policy?** You don't want to be surprised when you call in sick, and the teacher requires you to pay for the missed lesson. Most teachers require that you give 24-hours notice if you plan to cancel a lesson. Other teachers require that you make up a lesson within a certain period of time to prevent being penalized. Teachers who have very full studios may not even offer a cancellation policy. If you miss a lesson, you pay for it regardless of the reason behind the cancellation. Be sure to ask so that you know going into it whether getting sick can cost you big bucks.

✔ **What's your payment policy?** If you agree to set a specific lesson time each week with a teacher, the teacher may require that you pay in advance. This policy is common with teachers who have large studios. Other teachers may allow you to set up a lesson whenever you find enough money. Ask about scheduling during your initial conversation so that you don't encounter any surprises.

You also want to ask about the method of payment. If your teacher requires cash, you need to make sure that you hit the ATM before lessons. Checks are usually acceptable, but teachers rarely accept credit cards because of the hassle of paying a percentage to the credit-card company and having to get approval for each transaction. If you pay in advance, keep track of the number of lessons. Most teachers are good about keeping up with lessons, but you want to know when that next payment is due.

For those of you who must pay cash, you can ask the teacher for a receipt. If singing becomes your primary source of income, you can deduct the cost of lessons from your taxes. When that happens, pick up a copy of *Breaking Into Acting For Dummies* by Larry Garrison and Wallace Wang (Wiley) to read about what's tax deductible.

Knowing What to Expect from the Teacher

A voice lesson is usually a time when you're alone with one person, so you want to feel comfortable with that person and also feel positive about the work you're doing on your voice. In order to evaluate how well you work with your teacher, you need to know what you can expect from her. This section gives you an idea of what type of interaction to expect with your teacher in your lessons.

Feeling good when you leave the lesson

Feeling good about your lesson is a two-way road. The purpose of a lesson is to gain more information about singing, so you want your teacher to focus on the work. However, you need to able to shoulder her criticism well.

During a voice lesson, you should be doing plenty of singing, and your teacher should be giving you feedback on the sounds that you're making and offering suggestions on ways to improve those sounds.

Constructive criticism is about your singing technique and isn't directed at you personally. If you feel your teacher isn't giving you positive feedback, ask him.

Focusing on the work helps you see the teacher's constructive criticism as a means to help you get to the next level. If you expect your teacher to do nothing more than gush over your talents, you're going to be sorely disappointed. Any teacher worth her salt won't shy away from telling you what you're doing wrong (or from telling you what you're doing right). Even if you find a teacher who does nothing but praise you, you're wasting your time because that type of lesson won't help you improve.

To feel confident at each lesson, you need to make sure that you know what to practice. During your lesson, your teacher should suggest exercises for you to practice to help you improve your technique. She should then help you apply those concepts to songs that you're singing. If you aren't sure about what to practice, you can ask your teacher to clarify which exercises to focus on for the next lesson.

Being good friends with your voice teacher isn't really all that important, but you should feel confident about the work you do in each lesson.

Working with imagery and other tools

Because you can't see your voice, you have to have some tools to help you make changes. One way to obtain these tools is to make sure that your lesson involves work with a variety of techniques such as imagery.

As your lessons develop your singing voice, the teacher may use images to help you understand how to make the best sounds. The teacher may ask you to notice the sensations as you sing, give you something to visualize as you sing, or give you something to listen for. All three approaches can work beautifully for you as you work on your voice. You may also find that one approach works best for you. Knowing which one works best for you is good, because you can translate what your teacher says into your own language. For instance, if your teacher describes something to you and explains the anatomy of why that worked, you may remember what it felt like when you made the best sounds. If you enjoy working with images, you can find a way to visualize the sound to enhance your experience.

Don't fret if a teacher wants to explain physically what's happening. You may not want to know in the beginning, but later on, you may be glad that you understand why a particular image works.

Applying tried-and-true singing methods

Teaching people to sing is an old profession. If you encounter a teacher who claims to have a "never-before-revealed, life-altering system of teaching," be wary. You want a teacher who bases his teaching on facts and not just experiments. Your voice may be very different from your teacher's voice. That's not a problem if your teacher has been teaching for at least five years. He should've encountered different vocal problems and figured out a way to work with them.

If you discuss lessons with a prospective teacher and she doesn't have a "system" of teaching, that's okay. Many great teachers combine all the information that they've encountered into their own method.

You may need three to six months to really grasp the concepts in voice lessons and hear changes in your voice. You should hear changes within the first month, but the big concepts and tough technical exercises may take a while to gel. Enjoy each lesson with the understanding that you're on a journey that you can't make in one day.

Knowing What to Expect from Yourself

Yes, you do have to take some responsibility for creating your own singing success. Although knowing what to expect from your teacher is important, understanding what you should be doing in and out of your lessons is just as important.

Developing your own practice process

You may have a weekly lesson with your voice teacher, but you have to practice between lessons in order to apply the techniques discussed each week. Practice leads to improvement. (For more details about practicing, check out Chapter 10.)

The best way to create a practice routine that works for you is to record any lessons and practice sessions and to keep notes in a journal. You want to record the lesson so that you can listen to it to hear the changes you make during that time. Taking notes as you listen to the tape helps you figure out how you made those changes so that you can make them again on your own.

The concept and purpose of an exercise is more important than the exercise itself. For example, you can find many ways to work on breath, but the principle of moving breath is more important than one exercise. So when your teacher assigns you an exercise, make sure that you understand what it's for and how to use it. Simply doing an exercise won't help you improve if you don't know what to do or what to listen for.

At the end of each voice lesson, I suggest that singers recap what they're to practice before the next lesson. If you recap the big concepts that you intend to focus on, you and your teacher both have a list of goals. Your goal is to do the work, and your teacher's goal is to listen to you sing at the next lesson to determine if you need to continue in the same direction or expand your work.

Avoiding overworking your flaws

In your lesson, you want to focus on the entire voice and find a good balance of skills in all areas. By spending too much time on the "flaw," you may get discouraged and not feel like you can do anything. Find a balance for your practice session and your lesson, so you work on things you do well and on things you don't do well. I hope the list of things you don't do so well grows shorter with each practice session.

If you find that your teacher is focusing so much on your flaws that you're becoming discouraged, ask your teacher for feedback on the things that you're doing well. A teacher understands what it's like to be frustrated because she's been in the same boat. Don't be shy about asking for positive reinforcement in lessons. Your teacher may assume that you know what you're doing well and may not be telling you as often. By calling this to her attention, she can offer you some needed words of encouragement.

If you've never had a voice lesson, you may be nervous during your first lesson. The teacher knows that the first lesson is a little bit scary and may encourage you to be brave and try to make some new sounds. Admit that you're nervous and know that feeling this way is perfectly normal. Nervousness is just your body's way of dealing with the unknown.

Performing in recitals

Many teachers have yearly studio recitals to give their students an opportunity to sing for family and friends. You want a chance to test out your new skills and show off your hard work, so take advantage of these opportunities and strut your stuff.

If singing in a recital scares you, read Chapter 20 about performance anxiety. You may find that singing in the recitals gives you a chance to let go of your anxiety and find a way to enjoy being in the spotlight.

It's fun seeing yourself on videotape or listening to an audio recording of your voice — one of the perks of studio recitals. Looking at old tapes is great to realize what progress you've made. This new sense of confidence may lead you to some auditions or even to performing in other venues, such as choirs, church solos, or even the community theater.

Making Your First Lesson a Success

Now that you've chosen a voice teacher and know what to expect from the lesson, check out the following list to get a few tips on how to make your first lesson go smoothly.

- ✔ Before your first lesson, you want to ask the teacher if you need to bring your tape recorder. He may have one that you can use at the studio. If not, you want to bring one.
- ✔ Bring along a bottle of water to keep your throat moist during all the singing.

Don't set the water on the piano unless your teacher tells you that it's okay. Pianos are expensive, and spilling your water into the baby grand makes a really bad (and expensive) lasting impression.

✔ If the lesson is in a school or other location without supplies, you may also want to bring along a small mirror. Check out the list of supplies that you may need for practicing or lessons in Chapter 10.

✔ Also ask how many copies of the music you should bring. Some instructors want you to bring an extra copy of the song for them or the pianist. Finding this out in advance is easier than having to look over someone's shoulder at the piano.

Chapter 16

Training for Singing

In This Chapter

▶ Training for different musical styles

▶ Beginning your drills at any age

▶ Determining whether to train with a choir

*T*he training requirements for singers can be confusing. Every singer needs a basic healthy technique, but knowing what to do with that technique depends on what kind of music you want to sing. In this chapter, you find out what it takes to sing your favorite style of music, when to begin that training, and whether singing in the choir offers the right kind of training for you.

Defining Training Requirements

No matter what type of music you want to sing, you need a healthy technique to have a long life of singing. If you're interested in singing a specific type of music, but you're not sure what it takes to sing those songs, check out what kind of sound you should be shooting for. (I also provide a list of talented singers.)

Opting for opera

If you're interested in training to sing opera, you have plenty of territory to cover. The demands of training for opera usually require a long process of lessons or study, which isn't necessarily bad. Studying singing for a lengthy period isn't a punishment. It provides you with the opportunity to master your voice. For many singers, the long process of studying also means starting early in life. Review the following list to see what you may experience as you train for opera.

- **Sound:** Singing opera requires you to sing long phrases, sing loud enough to be heard over an orchestra in large halls, and sing material that is musically demanding. In pop, the singer makes all kinds of sounds that may be funky and not so pretty, but that's part of the style. The rock singer may present a stage show with spectacle where the singing is just part of the show. For opera, the performance is about the sounds the singer makes and the sounds are consistent and not varied like they would be in jazz, musical theater, and rock.

- **Healthy technique:** Singing opera means making beautiful sounds and the focus of the performance is on the singing technique. The technique for singing opera is about a *legit* technique, which means the sound is round, and the space in your mouth and throat should be wide open. Endurance for long operas is an issue for singers. You want to practice enough, so you can sing well for the length of the opera, which can be two to four hours.

- **At the audition:** In the operatic world, you want to know your exact voice type. Within the opera world, knowing your specific voice type or voice category, which is also called a *fach* (pronounced "fahk"), and sticking to it is important. See Chapter 5 for more details about the different types of voices and voice categories. In musical theater, you can sing a variety of roles, and you're expected to do so with ease, but in the classical world, you want to excel within your voice category. Listing only *arias* (songs from an opera) within a specific vocal category on your audition form or resume is a good idea. By listing arias from several different categories, you give the impression that you have yet to determine your voice type, or worse, that you don't know what you're doing.

- **Language:** Not only do you have the wonderful opportunity to sing in English, but you may also end up singing in Italian, French, German, or even Russian. You don't have to be fluent in all these languages, but you want to be familiar enough with them to easily sing and sound like you're fluent in them. You can work with a teacher or coach when training for each aria or opera, or you can take classes (called *diction classes*) to help you see the words and pronounce them correctly. You also want to be able to translate what your scene partner says so that you know if he just said "I love you" or "I love those satin slippers." You can't react appropriately if you have no idea what your scene partner just said.

- **Naming names:** Some familiar names in the opera world are Annie Sofie von Otter (mezzo with warm, round, tones), Bryn Terfel (baritone, fine diction, good actor), James Morris (bass, deep, rich, dark sounds), Renee Fleming (soprano, luscious tone, flexible voice).

Making your mark in musical theater

Unlike the opera, the musical-theater production is about the story first and the singing is somewhere down on the list of priorities. It's wonderful when a musical-theater performer sings well, but you won't be cast just because you sing well. They cast you because you look the part, can dance or move well, can act and then sing. You also need to know how to make a variety of sounds as a musical-theater singer. Read on to find out some of the requirements.

✔ **Sound:** With musical-theater repertoire, you want the sound to be chatty, conversational, and not over-sung. The simplicity of the voice allows the singer a chance to portray the text, which is at the top of the list.

✔ **Healthy technique:** A healthy musical-theater technique means you can make the beautiful open, round sounds called *legit* (open space and round sound), similar to the opera singer, but you also can belt. Belting means to make sounds like Ethel Merman. The sound is brassier, more forward, sometimes nasal, and sounds similar to a high chest voice. You make this sound by working to combine the sounds of your speaking voice and singing voice. See Chapter 14 for help with your belt.

✔ **At the audition:** In musical theater, you also need to switch your style of singing. Right after you sing your lovely, legit selection, such as "I Could Have Danced All Night," you may be asked for your belt song (an example of a belt song is "Tomorrow" from *Annie*). Bouncing back and forth between the styles is expected, and you have to practice both until they're comfy. You may find some musical-theater performers that are not belters, but you'll be better off if you know how to do both.

At the musical-theater audition, you're expected to portray the story and take the listener on a journey. The journey may only last 16 bars, but you have to take them for a ride no matter how short the trip. You can check out Chapter 21 for information on making cuts to your musical-theater song and how to prepare it for an audition.

✔ **Naming names:** Joel Grey (conversational, high belt), Mary Martin (legit sound and belter), Robert Goulet (rich round almost operatic sound), Gwen Verdon (great dancer, makes many different sounds with her voice to create her character).

Crooning as a country singer

Country music is the kind of music that has the good ol' boy songs about whiskey and women as well as the newer songs that have an updated attitude. The artists put on quite a show at their performances and use a variety of sounds when they sing. You can read about some of the sounds that you hear from a country singer. The biggest common denominator about country music is that it's about telling a story, telling about how you feel, and making sounds that are similar to your speaking voice.

- **Sound:** Country music is slowly and surely becoming more and more similar to pop music. For now, you can assume that country music is about sounding like a real person and telling a story with simplicity in the voice. More often than not, you get to sing with a microphone, so you don't need to carry the hall like classical singers. Country music also has more twang than what you hear in the opera house. Country singers create the song from their speaking voice — they think of singing as an extension of speaking. For this reason, they don't need wide, open spaces (in their mouth and throat) and round, rich tones. You may have this ability, but you don't need to use it when you sing country. Some examples of singers who use these styles are Shania Twain and LeAnn Rimes (sound similar to pop); the sounds of twang are the specialty of Loretta Lynn and Tammy Wynette; those singers who speak right into their singing include Hank Williams and Garth Brooks.

- **Healthy technique:** When singing country music, you want to take a breath and use it without squeezing your throat. You also don't want to sound cultured when it comes to vowels. (See Chapter 8 for more on pronouncing vowels.) Figuring out how to create healthy belt (see Chapter 14) is also a good idea. Many singers use a beltlike quality when singing their songs. Knowing the difference between a belt and chest voice (see Chapter 11) helps you keep your voice in balance.

- **At the audition:** Country singers often audition for an act at the local saloon, music hall, or performance space where they can draw a crowd. For this kind of audition, the singer needs to have a group of songs ready to show that he can hold the audience's attention for at least a half-hour set. Unlike the opera or musical-theater venue, where the show is usually already written and you audition for a part in that show, the country singer makes up the show. He often writes the music or performs groups of songs that have a particular theme to keep an audience clapping and singing along. When you land the gig, the audience behaves differently also. At the opera, the audience sits and listens and then politely applauds where appropriate. A country music loving audience can hoot, holler, and stomp their feet with pleasure.

- **Naming names:** Trisha Yearwood (strong legit sound as well as belt, good storyteller, emotions, and voice create interesting sounds), Clint Black (twang and cry of country), Reba McEntire (belts easily, good storyteller, some twang), Johnny Cash (great storyteller, speaks similar to how he sings).

Performing pop and rock

The lines in the music industry are starting to blur. Rock music is connected more with pop. The styles are similar vocally but the variety in the kinds of sounds is wide. You can remember the early pop songs that were about her boyfriend coming back with the doo-wop sound in the background. Pop singers today are expected to sing or lip sync at their performances while they dance in their spandex. Rock singers have the heavy guitars backing them up, making a variety of sounds from screams to moans. They, too, need to know how to keep their singing voices healthy for their demanding music.

- **Sound:** Because you have a microphone, you don't need the same kind of intensity and clarity when singing pop or rock as you do when singing opera. Having a fuzzy tone is okay, as long as that's your choice. Your microphone can help the sound carry if your tone isn't clear and focused. Because the lines and phrases may not be as long and drawn out in this repertoire, you also don't need the intensity of long, legato lines, as do opera singers. The latest technology in sound systems can instantly correct the wayward pitch of a singer. Newer karaoke machines use this technology and so do some pop singers.

  Choosing to delay the onset of the vibrato is also perfectly legal. You can sing with a straight tone and then allow the vibrato to happen later or at the end of the phrase. As you ascend in pitch, you can allow the sound to flip into another register or yodel. You can also allow the sound to get lighter as you ascend instead of growing stronger as you may in opera or musical theater. Using a mix or a stronger middle-voice sound (see Chapter 11) is a choice that female singers make and guys can choose whether to use falsetto (see Chapter 13) or head voice. You may not need a wide space in your mouth and throat as you would with other styles of music, such as classical. The space may be more closed. Examples of female pop/rock singers who use a mix are Karen Carpenter and Carly Simon; belters include Celine Dion, Bonnie Raitt, Ann Wilson, and Aretha Franklin.

- **Healthy technique:** When singing pop or rock music, you want a basic, solid, healthy technique, but your abilities need to blossom when it comes time to strut your stuff onstage. Pop singers are expected to dance and sing, so you need to be in shape or be famous enough that you can say no. Because the sounds rock singers make are often scratchy and close to screaming (Meatloaf), rock singers need to be aware of how to keep making those funky sounds that fans adore without causing damage. Screaming too much for too long in concerts can tax the voice and cause fatigue, strain, and tone changes. To prevent damage, singers can use resonance to create sounds that they normally make by screaming. See Chapter 7 for an explanation of resonance and Chapter 14 for suggestions on working with resonance in the speaking voice and belt.

✔ **At the audition:** When you audition, you want to tell a story just like you do when you're singing any kind of song. When you perform, you may have to dance, sing, and lip-sync all at the same time. Pop singers are often cast by their look and producers hope the voice can last. Many new musicals are closer to pop and rock music, so musical-theater singers are also now studying this style of singing. Finding pop and rock songs that don't require exciting back-up bands is tricky. Find songs that work well with piano or write your own. Most pop and rock singers have to create a demo recording, so producers can hear what they sound like when their voice is mixed on a professional quality CD. It's expensive but often a necessary part of the business.

Jazzing it up

Familiar jazz songs that you may know are sometimes arrangements of songs from other styles of music. When jazz singers create an arrangement of a musical-theater standard, they usually change the notes and rhythms from the original music. Jazz singers create their style with rhythmic flexibility, and the singer and pianist don't always have to be together note for note (called *back phrasing*). Read on for more about jazz.

✔ **Sound:** The world of jazz is similar to the other contemporary fields in that the singers have to make a variety of sounds. The sounds in jazz are often more about using the voice like a musical instrument as opposed to making big vocal sounds like you hear at the opera. The singer often sings syllables or rhythmic sounds in place of words.

✔ **Healthy technique:** Jazz singers need to have a good ear, because their music is often improvised and changes with each nightly performance. The singer also has to know how to *scat,* which is using doo-wop kind of syllables, while singing a variety of notes that may or may not be written out on a page of music. The jazz singer needs a great sense of rhythm, because the musical instruments are often playing background music, and the singer offers his own melody line.

✔ **Clubbing it:** Jazz singers don't have to do the same kind of audition routine that opera or musical theater singers do. They do have to audition for a band or group unless they plan to play the piano themselves or just work with a pianist for a nightclub or cabaret act. An audition for a band means the singer sings some songs along with the band members, so they can get a sense of what the voice sounds like and how well that singer blends in with them. Like country singers, jazz singers may often be in dark, smoky clubs singing and need to make sure to keep their body and voice healthy. See Chapter 24 for information on the effects of second-hand smoke.

✔ **Naming names:** Some jazz singers that apply great jazz technique include the famous scat queen herself, Ella Fitzgerald; the man who uses his voice like an instrument, Bobby McFerrin; and the laid-back sultry sounds of Diana Krall.

Training to Sing at Any Age

If you can speak, you can sing — and you can enjoy singing no matter what your age. I had students in their 80s take classes, and they loved it. So, it's never too late to start. And as long as you're ready for the work it takes to develop a healthy technique, you're never too young to begin singing. However, in order to develop and foster a healthy singing technique, understanding how your voice may change with age is essential. Keep reading to find out the best way to train young singers (under the age of 12) and teenagers and get some insight into a few voice changes that you may encounter at the different stages in life.

Recognizing differences between young singers and teens

Music preference may be the most obvious difference you encounter between a young singer and a teenager, but other differences exist, as well. Both young singers and teenagers can have fun with singing as long as you keep the following differences in mind:

✔ **Range:** Young singers have a limited range; they need songs that have a narrow range and focus on subjects that they enjoy. Teenagers need music that's a little more hip and cool yet still not incredibly taxing vocally, because their voices are still developing. For teenage males who've recently experienced some voice changes, lower sounds may be entirely new and temporarily unreliable. The young singer probably has a range less than 8 notes and a teenager should have the range of between 8 to 16 notes.

✔ **Training:** Most young singers can benefit from being in a choir or joining a group singing class just to explore music. If your youngster joins a choir or group singing class, make sure that the class is focused on sounds appropriate for his or her age. Really young singers often can't make much sound when they sing until they discover more about breath control (see Chapter 3) and resonance (see Chapter 7). However, plenty of sound is usually the first thing a novice director asks for. If your child ends up pushing or is really tired after rehearsals, explore other choirs or classes that are more appropriate for his or her level.

Many young singers want to sound just like the latest pop star. They don't really realize that the pop star has all kinds of equipment and sound engineers helping make the sounds. The more you can expose the young singer to singers their own age, the better. Take them to elementary school music concerts or junior-high concerts so that they can hear their peers sing and know what voices their age sound like.

Some teenagers with mature voices are ready for lessons and training. As long as the teacher is quite good with adolescents, lessons can be good. If the teacher doesn't allow the students to choose any songs, or if the students aren't allowed to pick anything fun to sing, they may lose interest. Keep an eye on your teenager to make sure that his or her progress is consistent. You don't have to know a lot about singing to help your child. Keep asking questions, like you do about any other subject you aren't familiar with, and listen to your child talk about her like or dislike of the songs (not wanting to practice is a good sign they don't like the music), and her enthusiasm for the next lesson.

Some teenagers are more ready to take direction and constructive criticism than other teenagers are. If your child's ego is still a bit delicate, you want to hire a teacher that is going to make positive changes in his voice with humor and enthusiasm.

Developing long-term technique in teenagers

Most teenagers only want to know what they can do today to sound fabulous. They may not know the long-term benefits of healthy technique, and they may not have enough patience to listen. However, taking advantage of healthy technique and training their ears for singing is important for maintaining long-term technique.

Pushing the voice too far, too fast doesn't help in the long term. This concept is important for both parents and teachers to know. By pushing the voice, I mean making big sounds, such as the chest voice dominated sounds like belting at a young age. Working on chatty sounds is fine at a young age, but making pressed or pushed sounds may make it more difficult later to undo the unhealthy sound.

Having a healthy technique means singing within your range. An adult may have a very wide range, but a 13-year-old may only have an octave (see Chapter 1), which is about eight notes. Range develops with time, and pushing the singer higher won't benefit him in the long run. When the voice is ready, the singer can make huge sounds for the rest of his life. Make sure that your young teenager is aware of the advantages of using breath and resonance to help him find reasonable sounds. Let him know that he can shoot for the big guns later on.

Something any singer, especially young singers, can work on to help their long-term musical life is developing their ear. Matching pitch is a skill you can read about in Chapter 4. If the youngster can match pitch but also sing a series of pitches after hearing them for the first time, he is more likely to quickly conquer new songs. Ear training can also benefit singers that end up in the choir. Singing the top soprano part may be easy because it's on the top, but those middle parts can be quite tricky to hear. If the youngster already has exposure to intervals and chords, the middle part — or any part — can be a snap.

Understanding that voices change with age

All voices change with age whether you sing or not — that's why, on the phone, you can easily tell whether you're speaking with a younger or older person. The following list describes a few types of voice changes that may affect singing and offers tips on how to work around them.

- ✔ **Puberty:** Letting young men who are going through puberty sing is okay. But because you really can't predict what their voice is going to do, puberty isn't a good time for them to make a big debut. Being in an all-male choir at that age can give the singer comfort, because he knows that the rest of the guys are going through the same thing. Allow his voice to wriggle and crack, and know that it is going to become much more steady in time. The female voice also changes during puberty but the change isn't as extreme.

- ✔ **Menopause:** After menopause, women may experience a little more stiffness in their singing. This stiffness is due to the loss of the elasticity in their muscles after the slow down of estrogen production. Estrogen replacement can help to stall the changes after menopause. Menopausal women may also be able to keep their voices flexible with regular workouts. Continuing to practice specific exercises for the different areas of the voice increases the chance of maintaining stamina in each particular area.

✔ **Aging:** One common occurrence with aging is the wobble. You may have heard older singers' voices wobble when they sing. The wobble is a result of a lack of muscle toning, specifically in the singing muscles. Working out your singing muscles on a regular basis can help keep that wobble at bay. Getting lax with your breath is another common factor that may contribute to a wobble in your singing. If your breath backs off, your voice is more likely to flounder or wobble. A steady flow of air helps keep the rate of the vibrato steady. You can also continue working on exercises that move back and forth from straight tone to vibrato, to help maintain your ability to support the vibrato. Vibrato and a wobble aren't the same. *Vibrato* is the normal undulation of pitch when you sing. You may feel the slight shaking feeling in your throat as the vibrato happens, and that's normal. Wobble is when the vibrato rate is very slow as compared to normal vibrato, which is about five to eight pulses per second. See Chapter 6 for exercises that help explore vibrato.

Training with a Choir

As an individual singer, you want to stand out and be unique. You want your voice to carry the hall or resound so that every person in the audience hears you. Because having a loud voice is desirable in solo singing, you may want to focus your attention on projecting your voice. However, when singing with a choir, you may find the director holding his hand in front of your face to get you to sing quieter and blend in with others.

In this section, I discuss the benefits of training with a choir. I also tell you about the differences between singing as a soloist and singing in the choir. If you decide that training with a choir is up your alley, I give you tips on how to select a great choral director. (If you do decide to sing as a soloist rather than train with a choir, check out Chapter 15 to find the right voice teacher for you.)

Enjoying the benefits of singing in the choir

Many people thoroughly enjoy being in a choir. You get a chance to sing different kinds of music, and you get to be around others who share your interest in music. (Sometimes singing at home can be lonely.) Making music with a group of people may give you just the balance you need between practicing alone at home and singing with a group.

The following list details some of the benefits you gain from singing with a choir.

- ✔ **You discover how to listen carefully.** When singing in a choir, you have to listen so that your voice blends with the voice of the person next to you, as well as with the sounds of the particular type of song you're singing. If the music requires a specific style of singing, you have to work to make sure that you're making the appropriate sound with healthy technique.

- ✔ **You discover how to monitor your sound based on how it feels.** If you can't hear your voice standing out, you have to rely on the feeling to determine whether your technique is still in good shape. Monitoring how your sound feels is a good idea, because each room is different, and you can't rely on the sound bouncing back to you. Sometimes choral singers put their hand to their ear to hear their voice. You can try this using this technique to help direct the sound of your voice back to your ears. Just make sure that the person next to you doesn't think that you're trying to block out the sound of their voice.

- ✔ **You get an opportunity to work on your ear.** Picking out your part when the other voices of the choir are surrounding you is a good work-out for your ear. Simply hearing and being able to hear your note in the middle of many other notes are two different skills. Solo singers may not have someone else singing different notes in their ear. The choral singer may be mixed up with other voices singing other parts and have to rely on her ability to read music or really listen for her note in a chord. Picking out your part while other choir members are singing around you may take a while to develop.

- ✔ **You get a chance to work on your social skills.** In choirs, you often find people that like similar music or are inspired by beautiful music. You may feel right at home and normal by being around people with similar interests, which can give your sense of belonging a big boost. You also get opportunities to discuss which song you like the best and defend your answer by talking "shop" or singer talk. That may be a really fun outlet for you if your family would rather talk about sports than music.

- ✔ **You get to travel with the choir.** You may have to raise money to go on trips, but traveling with fellow musicians who enjoy making music in beautiful concert halls can make it worth your while. Teenagers and young singers often enjoy traveling with the choir, because they get to travel around doing what they enjoy: singing with their peers.

- ✔ **You get to work on reducing your performance anxiety by singing with a group.** Onstage with your peers, you may find that your anxieties about performing dissolve. If you feel comfortable within a group, you may be able to transfer that comfort level into your solo singing. If you suffer from anxiety about singing in public, slowly work your way from singing in the choir to auditioning for one of the solos with the choir. Many choral pieces have small sections for soloists. By auditioning for the small solo part, you may be able to take a step forward toward releasing that anxiety. Furthermore, you have the support system of the entire choir. Just talking about your performance anxiety with other choir members and asking them how they cope with their performance anxiety can help alleviate your own anxieties.

The challenge and joy of singing in a group may be just the lift you need at the end of a long week of work. Singing is a wonderful release and opportunity to express your thoughts and feelings through music and singing. Joining a choir may give you that regular opportunity to enjoy singing if you just don't have the time to practice on your own.

Singing in the choir versus going solo

Depending on how you want to explore your own singing voice, singing with a choir may or may not be for you. Because the choral singer has different needs, before you join a choir, you may want to explore the differences between training with a choir and going solo:

✔ **You may frequently be asked to sing without vibrato when singing with a choir; whereas, going solo, you often sing with vibrato.** If you can make the change in the sound without pressure, singing without vibrato won't be a problem. The sound without vibrato can be free and loose and supported. (See Chapter 6 for an exercise that helps you to move between straight tone and vibrato.)

✔ **You need to find a part that works for your voice and works for the choir director; whereas, going solo, you can sing songs within your range.** The notes may stay pretty high or low when you sing certain parts in the choir. If you're a low female voice, you may even be asked to sing with the tenors. You can agree to sing tenor once in a while, but the part was designed for the male voice and not the female voice. If you feel tired after singing the top soprano part, you may want to ask if you can switch to a lower soprano part.

✔ **You may be asked to sing quite loudly in the choir if few people are on your part.** Use this opportunity to rely on your knowledge of resonance so that you don't push too hard. If you find yourself tired after singing loudly, you need to take it easy for a while during the rehearsal so you can rest up a bit, or talk with the choir director about how your voice feels after rehearsal. Singing alone means you can work at any volume and not worry about having to lead others with your voice.

✔ **You may also be asked to stand for long periods of time when singing in a choir; while rehearsing by yourself, you can rest whenever you need to and give your legs a break.** Having to stand for a rehearsal can provide a good opportunity to practice standing with your weight evenly distributed on both legs. If you find this tiring, explore your options with the director.

✔ **You may have a problem with choreography when moving back and forth from choir to soloist.** Show choirs provide great opportunities for big groups to sing together while doing movements that are planned in advance. Soloists, on the other hand, need to tell the story and let the story dictate how their body moves rather than plan out the moves ahead of time.

✔ **You need to be aware of your facial expressions when moving back and forth from choir to soloist.** Sometimes, choir directors tell you to raise your eyebrows or smile to keep the pitch steady. You can do this as long as you know that when you sing alone, you need to put your eyebrows back down. You can keep the pitch steady by keeping your breath consistent and by making sure that your vowels are precise. Keeping your breath moving at a steady rate and singing precise vowel sounds is easier than trying to change each pitch up or down. The smile can also be deadly to a soloist. The problem is that smiles don't work for sad songs when you're a soloist. The smile also can cause tension inside your mouth when you try to open the *back space* (the space in the back of your mouth and throat). Find enjoyment in singing from the joy inside your body and let it reflect on your face without the tension of a frozen smile.

Picking the perfect fit

Finding a choir that meets your needs means not only finding the right choir but also finding the right choir director. You want to find your best choral fit and determine the right questions to ask your potential choir director. Auditioning for a choir means to sing a song you know and to sing a song you don't know (called *sightsinging*) so the director can assess your ability to read music.

Locating a choir

Choirs, like singers, come in different shapes, sizes, and styles. You need to know what kinds of choirs are out there to know what may suit your needs. The following is a list of the kinds of choirs you may encounter in your area.

✔ **Barbershop quartet and Sweet Adelines (the female equivalent of the Barbershop quartet).** Both groups often sing show tunes or pop tunes with very tight harmony. The singers often use choreography and wear similar outfits. You have to audition to join this type of choir.

✔ **Church choirs** come in all shapes and sizes. Depending on the denomination of the church, parish, or synagogue, you find different kinds of music. Some churches use more gospel music and others prefer singing more traditional church hymn music. Some church choirs require an audition and others allow anyone to join as long as you can match pitch. See Chapter 4 about figuring out how to match pitch.

✔ **Professional choirs** comprise singers that are making all or part of their living by singing choral music. These singers are often quite good at reading music and know a great deal about different styles of choral music. You have to audition to join a professional choir.

✔ **Show choirs** are the choirs often in high schools where students sing with choreography. The songs are usually more contemporary. Show choirs usually have an audition process to join.

Singing in choirs in the public school system often gives adolescents the opportunity to sing with different types of choirs. Many schools often have a male chorus, female chorus, concert choir, jazz choir, or other type of chorus that allows students to sing in various groups. Jazz choirs use close harmony, require a good ear to hear your note in thick musical chords, and a good sense of rhythm.

Finding a choir director

Finding a good choir director is like finding a good voice teacher. (See Chapter 15 for more information on finding the right voice teacher.) You have to know where to look, you have to ask many questions, and you have to keep your ears open. If you happen to live in a metropolitan area, you probably can pick and choose what kind of choir and which choir director you prefer. If you're from a small community, you just may have to like it or lump it. You have to give the director a chance, because first impressions aren't always fair. The choral director may be so inspired by singing that he seems to have a language all his own. By joining the choir, you may find that you like this kind of language and love singing in a group.

After you find a potential choir director, discuss your singing goals and try to get a picture of his background and style. In order to steer the decision in the right direction, you need to bear in mind that a good choir director

✔ **Waves his arms in such a way that you know what to do.** Choral directors have a variety of ways to conduct. Some wave their arms around and others use very small movements with their hands or batons. Either way can work just fine as long as you get in-sync with the waving and know what to do with your voice.

✔ **Understands music theory or the nuts and bolts of how the music is put together.** You want a director that knows enough about music that she can lead your choir to make beautiful sounds appropriate to the style of music. The director may be a pianist or organist, who can work out just fine. Having fancy degrees in music isn't necessary as long as the director understands how to work with singers and reads the music on the page well enough to help you sing it.

✔ **Knows basic history of music and the different singing styles.** The choir director needs to know enough about the music to find the correct style. If she doesn't make singing an enjoyable process, it doesn't matter how much she knows. Being able to inspire a group of singers is an art and a good choral director can enlighten you about singing and music and make it fun all at the same time.

✔ **Has good rehearsal skills.** Choral directors have different ways of running a rehearsal. Some directors start rehearsals on time and others start when everyone is present and ready. Some also have a great warm-up and others expect you to get yourself ready to sing. The choir director should have a system of how the choir works and polishes music. If you've never been in a choir and don't know what a rehearsal is like, you may find a local choir that allows you to watch them practice.

If your choir director doesn't routinely warm you up before the rehearsal, you want to find time to do that on your own. Singing that highest part means you need to warm up your voice up, so it's ready to make those sounds. If you just jump right into singing the highest line, you may find that you become fatigued quickly during rehearsal.

✔ **Is familiar with how the voice works and how the heart responds.** I've been in choirs where the director knew plenty about the voice but didn't know how to inspire a group. Some directors enjoy sarcasm and use it as a teaching tool. If you enjoy sarcasm, a director who uses it may work just fine for you. Other directors use different levels of energy and tones of voice to inspire singers. A good choral director respects her singers and understands that they need to be inspired to make their best sounds.

You may love the director, but she may not fit all the criteria in the previous list — if so, that's just fine. The most important factor is that your voice stays healthy. Most choir directors have no training in singing. They spend many hours making beautiful music with groups, but they may not be aware of the technical aspects of how the voice works. However, directors need to understand how the voice works so that they can keep the singers healthy. I would rather have a director who keeps the singers healthy than a director that knows six languages fluently. The director can look up the pronunciation of the language before the rehearsal, but he needs to have good ears and know how to work out problems in the heat of the moment to properly evaluate voices and keep them healthy.

Part IV

Singing in Performance

The 5th Wave   By Rich Tennant

"Here's a little technique I use to help people reach the high notes."

In this part . . .

Plenty of information is jam-packed into this one part. You can pick and choose which chapter you read first. If you're just itching to choose some songs, check out Chapter 17 and then head to Appendix A for a list of songs that you don't want to miss. Choosing just the right song can make those new singing skills rattle the rafters. Your fans won't have to ask if it's live or if it's Memorex, because it's you showing off your singing chops.

If you're on a tight schedule, read Chapter 18 for a step-by-step process to get a new song under your belt quickly. Taking a new song apart to discover all the details that make it a cool song takes less time than trying to get all the details in your ear in one session.

One of the great joys of singing is using acting skills. (See Chapter 19.) You not only can sound great with your dependable technique, but also you can look good and give your audience a reason to watch you sing.

For those of you who are interested in the bright lights of Broadway or a musical theater audition in your hometown, Chapter 20 offers advice on overcoming stage fright, and Chapter 21 has tips and lists of what you need to know to have a great audition. It's time to take your technique out of the practice room.

Chapter 17

Selecting Your Music Material

In This Chapter

▶ Defining beginning and intermediate songs

▶ Exploring some familiar songs

▶ Finding songs online or in music stores

In this chapter, you find out how to choose an appropriate song and where to find the music. I show you how to choose the right style, key, song at your level, and how to show off your strengths. Knowing whether to buy the original score, a *fake book* (a book with only the melody line, chord symbols, and words), or sheet music makes your shopping experience so much easier. You may even prefer to shop at one of the online music stores that allow you to download the music right to your computer. How cool is that!

Choosing the Song

Starting a new song can be so much fun. Digging into the phrasing, the story, and the vocal challenges of a new song can provide hours of entertaining work. But how to choose the song can stump many singers. Keep reading for some tips on how to choose just the right song for you.

Finding songs at your level

Your level of expertise and technical ability at this moment in time is the primary determination for finding music to sing. Choosing a song that's too hard for you may only frustrate you. You may choose more difficult selections farther along in your singing career. Selecting material that's too easy for you may be really fun to sing but won't help advance your singing technique. Choosing songs at your level requires you to balance your current abilities with what you want to accomplish. To advance your singing technique, you want to choose songs that are just a little bit above your comfort zone. Selecting a song to sing for a performance is different than selecting songs to practice and to develop technique. Songs for a performance should highlight your current level of ability at the time of the performance. The song you choose to perform may be a song that was once a little difficult for you, but you practiced long enough to master the technical challenges.

You can figure out your level of expertise by asking yourself these questions.

- **What's your range?** If your range is about eight notes, then a beginner song would work well for you. An intermediate song has a range less than two *octaves* (an *octave* is eight white notes on the piano and two octaves is 16 white notes apart, or to go up an octave from a black key, just find the next black key in the same pair of two or three black notes), and an advanced song may have a range wider than two octaves. For more on musical notation, see Chapter 1.

- **How comfortable are you singing big leaps in a melody?** Many beginner songs move in *stepwise motion,* which means the notes in the melody are right next to each other. An example that you may know is "Mary Had a Little Lamb." Yes, it's a nursery rhyme, but if you sing it, you notice that most of the notes are right next to each other and that's called stepwise motion. Intermediate songs have bigger leaps of skipping five or six notes and advanced songs can have leaps up to eight notes or an octave. Wider *intervals* (the distance between two notes) challenge your ear. You need to spend some time working the larger intervals in a song to make sure that your throat stays open (see Chapter 4), breath is flowing consistently (see Chapter 3), and your larynx stays steady (see Chapter 4). Singing wider intervals also makes you listen more. If you figure out the wider intervals, you're more likely to repeat that sound when you see the same interval in your next song.

- **What's the highest note you can sing successfully?** If your highest note is F5 or the top line on the treble clef staff (see Chapter 1 for an explanation about staff and F5), a beginner would want to choose a song that has the majority of notes below D5 or E5 and maybe only one F5. An intermediate singer with the same range would want to choose a song that has one or two opportunities to sing that F5. An advanced singer (knowing his voice type) should know his voice well enough to determine how many times he can sing that F5 with ease. A soprano may sing her highest note four to five times in an advanced song, but a mezzo may only want one or two repetitions of her highest note. The same is true for a tenor and a baritone or bass. The tenor can handle more repetitions of those high notes than a baritone or bass. (For more on voice types, see Chapter 5.)

- **What causes you to get tired as you're practicing?** Many singers get tired when they sing a song where most of the notes stay at the top of their range. Even if the song doesn't have many repetitions of your highest note, if the majority of the notes sit near that top note, you may get tired. Think of it as lifting weights. You can lift a weight several times, but how long can you hold it up? By staying near the top part of your range, you're holding up the weight or having to use quite a bit of body energy to maintain that physical exertion. If the high notes come at rapid-fire pace, that may be just the thing to get you singing the notes without worrying about it. It can also be quite a challenge. The more you practice and get to know your singing voice, the better you'll be at answering this question.

✔ **What is the song's speed?** A song's speed may cause you to spit out words at the speed of lightening. If you've been working on articulation (see Chapters 8 and 9), you can spit out those words easily without getting tense from the constant movement of your *articulators* (tongue and lips). Beginner songs are often slower, so you can articulate and really notice the movement of your lips and tongue as you work on articulation exercises in the book. Intermediate songs may move at a faster pace and have tougher combinations of sounds. Advanced songs may be quite fast and require you to make your words understood as your melody bounces along the page.

✔ **How confident are you singing with a piano or other musical accompaniment?** A beginner song usually has the melody line played by the piano and in an obvious way. An intermediate song may have the melody line in the piano part, but the chords may be thicker and your melody may be harder to pick out. An advanced song may have an accompaniment that is totally different than the melody written for the singer.

✔ **How comfortable are you at combing multiple details when singing a song?** When you look at a song or hear it for the first time, you probably need to hear it a few times to get a feel for it. However, if you have to listen for a few weeks to get the notes right, the song is too hard for you right now. By breaking down the details when you figure out a song (see Chapter 21), you're more likely to get all the details of the song working faster. If your ear picks up a tune pretty fast, you may assume that you can take on harder songs. Give yourself some time to work on songs to work a variety of technical details, such as breathing, articulation, and storytelling, before you jump to more advanced songs.

✔ **How familiar are you with acting and singing at the same time?** Actors on television or stage make it look so easy, but acting and singing at the same time is a skill to make the song sound good and look good at the same time. Beginner songs are often for either gender and have easier stories to tell. Intermediate songs often contain more detailed lyrics, and advanced songs often are written for a specific gender with a through-line in the story. See Chapter 19 about acting and singing.

✔ **How comfortable are you with rhythms?** Some singers can pick up rhythms very quickly and others struggle to hear the difference between sounds. Beginner songs often have more simple rhythms to allow the singer to focus on one or two types of rhythms. Intermediate songs have a wider variety of rhythmic combinations, and advanced songs may have complex rhythms. For more help with rhythms, you can check out *Guitar For Dummies* by Mark Phillips and Jon Chappell or *Piano For Dummies* by Blake Neely (both by Wiley). By knowing a little bit about rhythms, you can look at the song and know whether the piece is complicated musically.

Starting at the beginning

A song has a combination of ingredients. A beginner song may have a simple melody, narrow range, but have a spunky pace. It's still a beginner song even if the pace is faster or you have to count *rests* (places in the song where you don't sing) before you start singing again. The more you look at songs on the page, the easier your decision is if this song is an appropriate level for you.

Beginning songs have simple rhythms, a narrow range, an accompaniment part that plays the singer's melody, a melody line and accompaniment that are the same, and have simple articulation opportunities.

Examples of a beginner's song include "The Sound of Music" and "Edelweiss" from *The Sound of Music*. "The Sound of Music" has rhythms that are fairly easy to count, and the range isn't too extreme. "Edelweiss" also has easy rhythms, a narrow range, and smooth lines to help you work on phrasing.

Just in case you don't know the songs from *The Sound of Music*, I give you some other songs in different styles that may be more familiar to you: the folk ballad "Greensleeves," the Old Scottish Air "Auld Lang Syne," the traditional air "Drink to Me Only With Thine Eyes" by Ben Jonson, "In The Gloaming" by Mete Orred and Annie F. Harrison, the spiritual "He's Got the Whole World in His Hands," "Paper Roses" by Janice Torre and Fred Spielman, "You Light Up My Life" by Joe Brooks, and "Love Me Tender" by Elvis Presley and Vera Matson.

I'll take mine medium-well, please

Intermediate songs have harder rhythms that test you just a little bit beyond your current level. If you're an intermediate-level singer, you can opt for a wider range, a few high notes to test your top notes, more difficult intervals that challenge your ear, and opportunities to explore more detailed articulation. The piano accompaniment may not follow the melody note for note.

Some intermediate songs that you may know include "Over the Rainbow" from *The Wizard of Oz* and "My Favorite Things" from *The Sound of Music*. "Over the Rainbow" is an intermediate song, because the rhythms are a little more complex and varied than a beginner song, such as "Edelweiss," and the leaps are much wider than songs that move in stepwise motion. "My Favorite Things" moves quickly with more variety and more complex rhythms than

"The Sound of Music" from the same show, and the articulation of text has to be much faster. By taking some time to work on slower songs, such as "Edelweiss," to get your articulation fluid, a song like "My Favorite Things" offers you the challenge of articulating faster after you've already had some experience.

If you missed both movies, *The Sound of Music* and *The Wizard of Oz,* the following is a list of familiar songs that you may recognize that are also intermediate level songs. Even though you know them, notice the details as you sing through them: "Crazy" by Willie Nelson, "Another Somebody Done Somebody Wrong Song" by Larry Butler and Chips Moman, "I Honestly Love You" by Peter Allen and Jeff Barry, "You Needed Me" by Randy Goodrum, and "O sole mio!" by E. di Capua (tenor).

An advance in your song salary

An *advanced* song is a song that really tests your skills. The melody that you sing may be completely different from the accompaniment and have intervals that don't always blend with the piano music. You may be confronted with long notes that require breath control, several high notes that demand skill in execution, a detailed story that requires you to make the journey of the text as you use your technical skill, text that enables you to portray the height of the story, and an opportunity to portray the specific style appropriate for the song, such as high belt, classical legit, or the twang of a country song. I discuss training for different styles of singing in Chapter 16. See Chapter 14 for more on belting. You know your voice well by the time you're an advanced singer, so I didn't include songs for advanced singers in Appendix A. A list of advanced songs that you may know include "Looks Like We Made It" by Richard Kerr and Will Jennings, "Vision of Love" by Mariah Carey and Ben Margulies, "Habañera" from the opera *Carmen* by Bizet (mezzo), "I Know That My Redeemer Liveth" from *The Messiah* by Handel (soprano), and "Se vuol ballare, Signor contino" from *The Marriage of Figaro* (*Le Nozze di Figaro*) by Mozart (bass).

Appendix A has a list of songs divided into levels for beginner- and intermediate-level singers in different styles of music.

Determining the appropriate key for you

You hear a great song on the radio and rush out to get the sheet music so that you can sing it at home. The trick is to read music well enough to know whether the song's notes are within your range. You don't have to know everything about what's on the page but enough so that you know the difference between the right key for you and the wrong key.

When a singer says, "I need this song in a higher key," what he means is that he wants the notes of the song higher, so it's in his range. After looking at the song, you may also determine that you want the notes to be lower or that the song needs to be in a lower key. A song's key just means that the song is written with one note as the *central note* or tonic. That central note is the name of the key. If Middle C is the central note, then you'd return to Middle C on a regular basis in the song. You don't have to know all about reading music, but you need to know if you want the song four steps higher or two steps higher. Wanting the song in a higher key means you want the song to sit higher in your range.

Sometimes singers ask, "What is my key?" when they actually mean, "What is my range?" Not every song that has Middle C as the tonic or central note has the same range. You want to be able to describe your range (see Chapter 11) and to know if you need the song in a higher key.

Selecting a suitable song style

You may love to listen to operatic arias but aren't yet able to sing one. Your voice may be suited to belting out show tunes, even though your car radio is set to the country music station. If you're choosing a song to sing for fun and for your own listening pleasure, then settle on a song in a style you like but that also challenges you to use your knowledge of technique. You can choose some songs to sing for fun and some that make you work a little harder on your technique.

Chapter 17 helps you choose a musical theater song that works for you. Other styles of music require similar thoughts. If you're going the classical route, make sure that the music is appropriate for your voice type. If you're a mezzo-soprano, opt for arias written for that voice. Many arias written for the mezzo voice have the same range as arias written for sopranos, even though most of the notes in the soprano aria may be higher than those written for a mezzo-soprano. Read Chapter 5 for information about voice types and how to determine yours.

For pop, folk, country, or other styles of singing, see Chapter 16 for more information about singing different musical styles. Is the copy of the song within your range or do you need it in a higher or lower key? Can you project the low notes if the song is quite low for you? Does the song on the radio have a huge back-up band that made the song spectacular? Do you like the song just as well if you don't have a band? Is the song on the country station and the pop radio station? If it is, you just have to decide which style suits you and allow yourself to use that particular sound.

Singing to your strengths

You want to emphasize your particular singing talents whether you sing at your cousin's wedding, at a family gathering, an audition, church, or karaoke at a local pub.

Perhaps your strength is a lovely tone to your voice. In that case, choose a nice ballad that enhances your tone. If acting is your forte, choose a great story song with a conflict that you work through as you sing the song. Examples of good story songs include:

- ✔ "Poor Wayfaring Stranger" Folk Ballad (female)
- ✔ "Will He Like Me" from *She Loves Me* by Sheldon Harnick and Jerry Bock (female)
- ✔ "I Can't Make You Love Me" by Mike Reid and Allen Shamblin (female)
- ✔ "Long Cool Woman In A Black Dress" by Allan Clarke, Roger Cook, and Roger Greenaway (male)
- ✔ "She Wants To Marry a Cowboy" by James Williams (male)
- ✔ "Black Is the Color of My True Love's Hair" by John Jacob Niles (male)

What other skills and strengths can you emphasize? If your strength is:

- ✔ **A strong head voice,** sing a song that has some high notes, such as "Oh, Holy Night" by D.S. Dwight and Adolphe Adam in the high key.
- ✔ **An ability to sing notes quickly and easily,** sing "Rejoice" (female) from *Messiah* by Handel.
- ✔ **Switching quickly between registers,** sing "The Lonely Goatherd" (female) from *The Sound of Music* by Richard Rodgers and Oscar Hammerstein.
- ✔ **A strong low voice,** sing "Ol' Man River"(male) from *Showboat* by Jerome Kern.
- ✔ **A strong range from top to bottom,** you can sing "Crying" (male) by Roy Orbison and Joe Melson because Orbison's recorded version has some high notes.
- ✔ **Your great sense of humor,** poke fun at yourself and sing "Great Balls of Fire" (male) by Otis Blackwell and Jack Hammer.

Shopping for the Hard Copy

When you finally know what you want, you have to go shopping to get it. Choosing music may be the harder of the tasks. You have the choice of walking into a store and looking at the music or letting your fingers do the buying online or over the phone. You may be able to check out sheet music at your local library and purchase it later if you like it.

Finding retail outlets

Just in case you don't care for all the hype about shopping online and want to hold the music in your hand before you make a decision to buy, look in the Yellow Pages for your local music store listed under *music* or *musical instruments.* You can call the store to ask if it carries vocal music before you hop in the car. If the store doesn't carry your song, it may offer to order it for you. Ask the clerk if you have to purchase it if you decide you don't like the key or that particular arrangement of the song.

Some stores allow you to browse online or call them up and ask for advice. Most large bookstores now carry music. You may find a Barnes and Noble in your area (call 1-800-TheBook) or Borders (1-888-81-Books). If the store doesn't have your music, they can order it for you or you can call the customer service department and order it.

Several music distributors have online catalogs that you can browse through and some offer help online or phone help. The list that follows contains some of the more useful Web sites and their specialties.

- **Hal Leonard** is the world's largest publisher of printed music. You can browse through the company catalog online at www.halleonard.com or write Hal Leonard Corporation, P.O. Box 13189, Milwaukee, WI 53213. You can't buy music directly from them, but you can get your local store to order it for you or follow links at the Web site to find a retailer.

- If you're looking for classical music that's a little tricky to find or for some help finding your song, check out **Classical Vocal Reprints** at www.classicalvocalrep.com. The Web site only has about 4,000 titles listed, but the owner carries more than 100,000 in his store. The owner, Glendower Jones, is happy to help you in your quest to find that favorite classical or musical theater song. Call him up for some advice at 800-298-7474 in the United States, or 718-601-1959 or fax 718-601-1969.

- You can browse through a huge catalog of songs at the **TIS** Web site at tismusic.com, order online, or call them at 800-421-8132 or locally at 812-355-3005 to purchase it.

- **Amazon.com** also sell songbooks and sheet music. You can't get individual answers to your questions if you need to call, but you can easily browse through the collection of music to find your song in sheet music form or in a song collection book.

Downloading sheet music

Online sheet music stores are popping up like crazy. You can search a Web site for a specific song and may even be able to choose the key you want it in. You may have to download software from the site to read the song, but this option is worth exploring especially if your only time to shop is in the middle of the night. You can use your favorite search engine and type in *sheet music* or try the Web sites that follow:

- ✔ www.broadwaymidi.com allows you to listen to songs. Students find it helpful to listen to the song before buying a copy. Be careful when you try to master a song by listening to it from a recording. The artist may or may not be singing what's written on the page. Try to listen only to get a sense of the style. You have to figure out how to make it your own. You don't want to sound just like the artist. The world wants to hear your version and not a rerun.

- ✔ www.musicnotes.com allows you to see page one of the music and use its software to hear samples of the music.

- ✔ www.sheetmusicdirect.com where you can download free software to hear, view, and transpose the music before printing and purchasing.

- ✔ www.sheetmusicnow.com lets you view a sample of a classical song before purchasing.

Web sites that offer cheaper prices may be offering you the music from a fake book, which doesn't include the piano part. A *fake book* has just the melody, chord symbols, and the words. If you choose this copy, your accompanist has to make up the accompaniment. Some accompanists are really good at this and others aren't.

Flipping through compilation books

As you shop online, you have the choice to buy the song in a single sheet of music or in a *compilation book,* which contains a collection of songs, usually adhering to a theme, such as movie theme songs, love songs, pop hits of a certain decade, or a particular artist's songs. You have to decide if you want to pay a little extra to have a few more songs or just get the song in the exact key you want for a smaller fee when you purchase one song in sheet music.

As you look through a compilation book, check the key of the songs that you like to make sure that they're in your range. Songs are often printed in keys that are easy to play on the piano, which doesn't mean the best key for your singing voice. Know your range and your comfort zone for singing before you shop. If you buy the book online, you won't know which key each song is printed in. You may have to explore the book in a music store or a bookstore that sells songbooks to decide if the collection is for you.

Checking out music at your local library

The library is a great place to search for music. It's free, and you can check out the book to try out the song at home at your own pace. If you find it's not in the right key, you have saved yourself a few dollars and some frustration. You can even take the music to a pianist to play through it for you if your music-reading skills are still pretty new. If you decide that you like the song, jot down the name of the songbook as well as the name of the publisher and edition of that publication. Some books are republished and songs are added. Ask before you purchase, so you aren't disappointed.

If you own the original sheet music, making a photocopy of the song for your own use is legal. For more information about making sure you're making a legal copy of your music, visit www.copyright.gov or use your favorite search engine and type in *copyright music.*

At musical-theater auditions, taking along a photocopy of the song is okay. At most classical auditions, taking an original is customary. You may be able to use a photocopy for the audition, but at competitions involving classical music, you're required to own the original. The reason? Songwriters deserve to make a living by selling their music.

Chapter 18

Mastering the Musical Elements

In This Chapter

▶ Separating out the words from the melody

▶ Figuring out the music as it's written on the page

▶ Finding ways to use your vocal technique

▶ Knowing when to take a breath

Mastering a new song is tough. In this chapter, you discover how to take the song apart and study it step by step. I even work through a song with you, so you can banish whatever doubts you may have as to whether you can master a new song by yourself the next time.

Tackling a Song in Steps

Getting a new song is so much fun. The new melody and new words makes you want to just burst out singing.

Many singers try to conquer all the details of a brand-new song in one session. But picking up an unfamiliar song and getting the words, rhythms, and melody right at the same time may take more than one session. The process goes much quicker if you take some time and scan the song, break it down into manageable pieces, and then conquer it one piece at a time.

By *scanning*, I mean checking the musical details, such as

✔ **Direction of the melody:** A melody can move up or down in stepwise motion, meaning the notes are right next to each other or just one step away from each other, or in leaps called intervals. The more you look at your music the more you can get used to seeing the notes on the page and knowing what the distance between those two notes sounds like.

✔ **How the rhythm and the words work together:** The melody may have one note for every word or you may have to sing two or three notes for every word.

- ✔ **Repeating sections:** Sometimes music is written with no repeats of anything at all and sometimes you have sections that repeat. Look at the music for signs to indicate what you're supposed to repeat.

- ✔ **Speed:** Tempo or speed markings are usually at the very beginning of the piece. Sometimes the words describing the tempo are in Italian. Some of the more common terms to describe tempo are in Table 18-2 in this chapter.

- ✔ **Volume variations:** In music, volume is called *dynamics* and common terms and symbols that indicate the volume of a song are in Table 18-2.

If you give yourself time to absorb these details one at a time, you can master the song much quicker than if you try to cram it all into your head. Read on to find out how to create steps in your discovery process.

When working on classical music, follow what's written on the page. In pop music and jazz, singers have plenty of flexibility and don't have to sing exactly what's on the page. You have more artistic freedom to make changes.

Memorizing the lyrics as text

Look at the lyrics as a monolog or a story. Write or type out the words, including the punctuation, so you can examine the lyrics apart from the melody and take a look at the big picture. If the song has words that you don't know, look them up. Notice the punctuation, because you can breathe at the punctuation marks in a song. (See the "Paying attention to punctuation" section, later in this chapter.)

Read the lyrics out loud, so you can hear the inflection of the words. As you read the lyrics, look for the *operative words* — the words that you emphasize in normal, natural, everyday speech. Keep reading the text aloud until it sounds conversational.

If you forget the words, speak through the text quickly until you no longer stumble on the words. You can also use key words in phrases to help you remember what comes next. Find some system to help you remember the order of each phrase's key word. Do the key words happen to be in alphabetical order? Just knowing if the list is in alphabetical order or has some characteristic in common, you can easily remember key words to help you get to the next phrase.

Sometimes, when you read poetry or lyrics for the first time, they may not make complete sense. The more you read it, the more that you're able to understand the meaning behind the words.

After you really have a grasp on the words, memorize them. You may find that it only takes a short time to memorize the words.

Tapping out the rhythm

Even if you don't read music well, you can tap out the rhythms. Just look at the rhythms on the page and try to tap out that rhythm without worrying about words or speed. The first time that you try, it may be difficult, but you get better each time. After some practice, you get accustomed to certain rhythm patterns and can quickly master them.

Lucky for you, only a few rhythms need to be worked out in the sample song, "Simple Things." The rhythm in this song is a great example of what I mean by beginner song. (Chapter 17 has more information about beginner, intermediate, and advanced songs.) I chose a beginner song for you to explore so you can feel totally confident about figuring out rhythms.

For more help on reading rhythms, pick up a copy of *Piano For Dummies* by Blake Neely (Wiley).

After you tap out the rhythm of your new song, try speaking the words in rhythm. Speaking the words in rhythm can help you solidify some of the rhythms and divisions of syllables.

Reading the time signature

To figure out a song's rhythms, you have to know a little about reading music. At the very beginning of a song, you can find some numbers that look like a fraction. This fraction, or *time signature*, tells the singer how to divide up the beats in between each of the bar lines. As you look at the music, notice the single vertical line between the words *simple* and *feeling* at the beginning of the song. That line is called a *bar line*. In that bar or measure, the time signature indicates that you'll find four beats. The way I know that is because the top number of the time signature, 4/4, indicates how many beats you find in each bar and the bottom note indicates what kind of note gets one beat. (4/4 is also notated as C, which means *common time*.) Because the top number is four, each measure has four beats. The bottom note is also four, which means the quarter note gets one beat. See Table 18-1 for more types of notes and how many beats each note gets in 4/4.

Knowing how long to hold notes

In "Simple Things," you find three kinds of rhythms in the song: eighth notes, quarter notes, and half notes. The duration of notes is similar to math. Table 18-1 in this chapter shows the various types of notes and tells you how many beats each gets when the bottom number of the time signature is four and when the bottom number is eight.

Simple Things

Words and Music by
Martha Sullivan

Figure 18-1:
Sample
song —
Simple
Things.

Sun - shine at dawn, a clear blue sky, and friends with hearts so strong;
Mus - ic to dance to, songs to try, this life where we be -
long.
D. S. al Fine
ritard.
p
mp
mf
f
Ped.

Table 18-1		Musical Notes and Timing	
Note	*Name*	*Number of Beats in X/4 Time*	*Number of Beats in X/8 Time*
𝅝	Whole	4	8
𝅗𝅥	Half	2	4
𝅘𝅥	Quarter	1	2
𝅘𝅥𝅮	Eighth	1/2	1
𝅘𝅥𝅯	Sixteenth	1/4	1/2

The first two notes in "Simple Things" (see Figure 18-1) are eighth notes, and because quarter notes get one beat, eighth notes get half a beat each. When you see a note with a dot next to a note, you hold the note for the full dura-tion of the note plus half of the original value. For example, the quarter note with the dot next to it at the word *are,* means you hold the note for one beat plus another half for a total of one and one-half beats.

On Track 63, the singer taps out the rhythm of "Simple Things" and says, "Tah" for each note. Listen to the track several times until you can distin-guish between eighth notes and quarter notes.

Even though listening to a recording to get a song in your ear is easy, try not to do that. You may want to hear your favorite artist singing the hit song you've chosen to sing, but the fact is that most recordings differ from the music as it's written. If you want to hear and sing a song for fun, however, by all means get out the recording and sing along.

Singing out the melody (without the words)

Sing the melody without the words. This may seem like strange advice, but singing the melody without the distraction of worrying about whether you're getting the words right helps you to fix the melody in your mind and also focus on your breathing technique (see Chapter 3), back space (see Chapter 6), and legato line (see Chapter 6). You add the words after you have the melody down pat.

On Track 64, you hear a singer singing the melody line on a single vowel. You can sing along while watching the melody line of the song in Figure 18-1. You know the rhythm, so add the melody to the familiar rhythm.

Putting words and music together

Are you ready for the last round? It's time to put all the puzzle pieces together. Because you already know the words, rhythm, and melody, singing the words with the melody is a breeze.

On Track 65, listen to all the parts put together. The first time through, the singer sings the song with you. The second time through, you get to sing by yourself.

Notice how long the musical introduction lasts, so you're prepared when you sing by yourself.

This same step-by-step process can lead you to great discoveries of new songs. Take your time when you find a new song and get all the steps down. With each new song, you get faster and faster. Pretty soon, you can get a song down in no time. Have fun singing along.

Reading Musical Notation

Written music uses all sorts of signs, symbols, and foreign words (usually Italian) and abbreviations to indicate

- ✔ **Dynamics:** Degree of loudness and softness
- ✔ **Symbols:** Signs that tell you whether to repeat a part or skip a section and symbols and signs to indicate specific sounds
- ✔ **Tempo:** Speed

To sing a song as the composer intended, you need to understand these notations. Table 18-2 runs through the basic notations.

Table 18-2	Musical Notations	
Dynamics	*Tempo*	*Order*
cres. (crescendo): Gradually increasing volume	**a tempo:** Resume the original tempo	**breath mark:** An apostrophe or comma above the vocal line
decresc. (decrescendo): Gradually decreasing volume	**accel. (accellerando):** To accelerate	**refrain:** A repeated section of music
dim. (diminuendo) : Gradually decreasing volume	**rit. (ritardando):** Gradually decreasing tempo	**coda:** A tail; a short passage ending a musical composition
ff (fortissimo): Really loud	**rall. (rallentando):** Gradually decreasing tempo	**D.S. (dal segno):** Go to the sign; from the sign
f (forte): Loud	**adagio:** Slowly	**D.C. (da capo):** Go back to the beginning; from the beginning
mf (mezzo-forte): Medium loud	**andante:** Walking speed	**fermata:** Hold
p (piano): Soft	**animato:** Animated, lively	**fine:** The end; sing to the end or to the word *fine*
mp (mezzo-piano): Medium soft	**allegro:** Fast, rapid	**tr. (trill) :** To rapidly alternate between two pitches
pp (pianissimo): Very soft	**ad lib. (ad libitum):** At the pleasure of the performer; the tempo may be varied	**caesura** (or Railroad tracks): To pause

Dynamics	Tempo	Order
sotto voce: In an undertone; sung quietly	**rubato:** Stolen time; accelerating and slowing down the tempo to create a flexible pulse	━ **tenuto:** Held, sustained to the full value
subito: Suddenly; *subito piano* means suddenly softer	**colla voce:** Follow the voice	**8va (ottava):** Indicates passage should be played an octave higher than written
dolce: Sweetly	**più mosso:** Faster	• **staccato:** Detached and shortened in duration
	poco: A little; *poco rit.* means to gradually slow down a little	**D.S. al coda:** to the coda
		repeat sign: Indicates to repeat the section within the repeat sign

Using Vocal Technique in Your New Song

When you begin a new song, the first thing you probably want to do is sing it over and over. That's fine as long as you take some time to apply some work on your singing technique. You can sing along with the exercises on the CD, which helps you advance your singing technique, and then you can apply that information to songs. By breaking down your work on a song, you can work on technique and a song at the same time.

Making the song your own

Preparing a song for an audition means that you need to understand how to read the sheet music a little. After you know what's written, you can work on making the song your own.

For example, if you listen to a famous singer, you may sing the song exactly the same way. At an audition, however, the music director wants to hear *you* rather than a carbon copy of someone famous. Find out what's on the page and then make it yours by

✔ Varying dynamics

✔ Plotting out tempo changes

✔ Looking for *operative words* — words that you emphasize in natural speech

✔ Choosing some acting objectives from Chapter 19

The composer has put some really great ideas into the music that he wrote if you just know how to find them.

Giving voice to vowels

Working on single vowels in the exercises on the CD is a great way to make sure you know how to make distinct vowel sounds. When you know the sounds of each vowel (see Chapter 8), you can take the same work and apply it to your song. By taking the time to focus on which vowel sounds you make in each word, you can make sure your technique in singing vowels gets better with each practice.

Singling out one vowel

As you explore the melody of a new song, sing it on one single vowel to find a *legato* (smooth and connected) line and work on your breath moving smoothly through long phrases. You can apply this idea as you sing along to the CD with the singer singing the melody of "Simple Things" on a single vowel. See "Singing out the melody (without the words)," earlier in this chapter to find the correct CD track to sing along with.

Streaming through the vowels

You can also sing the song on a *stream of vowels*. The stream of vowels in a song is the vowel sounds in the words minus the consonant sounds. When you can successfully speak through the vowels in one continuous stream of sound, apply that stream of vowels to the melody, singing straight through the song without pausing between each vowel sound. This helps you really listen to each vowel to make it distinct.

To sing the first five words — *Sometimes a simple feeling comes* — of "Simple Things," you need to sing through the vowel sounds. (See Chapter 8 for more information about vowel sounds.) By taking the time to focus on the vowel sounds, you can make sure your sounds are crystal clear and distinct. Adding the consonants back in allows you to make those specific vowel sounds followed by very clear consonant sounds.

Look at the words of "Simple Things" in Figure 18-1. Speak through the text without the consonants. After you get used to pronouncing the stream of vowels without the consonants, sing that stream of vowel sounds with the melody. When you feel confident that your vowels are top notch, put the consonants back in. You may be surprised at how clear your vowels are now that you've given them your undivided attention.

Backing into phrases

Another good way to improve your technique is to work the phrases backward. No, I'm not telling you to sing the song backwards, just to work from the last phrase you find difficult, and gradually add the preceding phrases as you master the hard one.

Take the last few measures of a song and sing those measures over and over until your phrasing is really solid. When you can do that easily, take the preceding few measures and make another grouping. So say your text is: "The loud cows aroused the sows. The sound of the hounds resounded all around."

1. You can practice the last phrase, "resounded all around."

2. When that's working well, work through "The sound of the hounds resounded all around."

3. When that phrase is smooth as glass, add the preceding phrase, "aroused the sows."

4. Then work through the whole enchilada, "The loud cows aroused the sows. The sound of the hounds resounded all around."

The phrasing and breath flow should be more obvious now. You can apply this same idea to "Simple Things." By working some of the phrases from the last few words, you can gradually work your breath control to make it through the entire phrase. In "Simple Things," you can work the phrase "These are the simple things that I would celebrate in song," by starting at "I would celebrate in song." When you can successfully sing "I would celebrate in song," then go back and add "simple things." After that much of the phrase is easy to manage, go back and sing the entire phrase "These are the simple things I would celebrate in song" and see if you can tell the difference in your breath control.

Breathing heavy — fogging up the windows

You probably already figured out that you have to pay attention to your breathing when you sing. In fact, proper breath control can make the difference between singing successfully and failing. Keep reading if you want to know how and when to breathe properly in order to sing properly.

Knowing how to breathe when you sing is a great skill. Taking your breathing to the next level in a song means breathing with the intent to say something when you sing. So, for each phrase that you sing, you need to plan the amount of breath that you need to complete that phrase or that thought. That sounds like a big concept, but it's what you do everyday in your conversations. As you're deciding what to say next in a conversation, take in air and then express those thoughts.

Try taking a breath and saying, "I have some bad news." That breath was probably slow and deliberate, because you knew something unpleasant was about to follow. Take a breath and say, "I won the entire jackpot in the lottery." Wow! That breath is certainly different than your bad-news rendition. When you sing songs, you want to know clearly what you're trying to say that you take the breath for each line with the intention of expressing a specific thought but not allow the emotions to negatively affect your breathing.

Knowing where to breathe is also helpful. In a song you can breathe in the following locations. Breathe

- Anytime you see a rest in the music.
- Anywhere you see punctuation, such as a comma or period.
- Anywhere that makes sense with the musical phrase and the lyrics.

Marking the places where you intend to breathe gives you an opportunity to try out that breath and see if it works for you. The breathing parts may seem logical, but then when you try out the breath, you may not feel confident. Just choose another place and try again. The more you practice singing through songs and plotting out the breaths, the better you'll get at figuring it out.

Read through "Simple Things" again and notice the punctuation. You can breathe in a lot of places because the song has quite a few commas.

Paying attention to punctuation

The punctuation in a song tells you where the big thoughts are. As with written and spoken text, periods indicate complete thoughts and commas point to lists and auxiliary phrases. Punctuation indicates an opportunity to take a breath, so a song's punctuation can help you with phrasing and interpretation.

A series of questions in a song provides you with a different task than a series of commas. In your everyday speech, the inflection of your tone of voice usually goes up when you ask a question and goes down when you make a statement. By singing a song that has a list with a series of commas, you want to reflect that continuing thought. You can practice this by taking a breath in a middle of a sentence when you're speaking. Notice how the inflection of your voice stays up. That same idea happens when you sing; the inflection of your voice tells the listener that you're continuing on the same train of thought. In contrast, a period needs a sense of finality. Say the following two sentences: You did that. You did that? Notice the change in the tone of your voice when you read the question. This inflection is the same kind that helps the listener know that you have just made a statement as you sing.

Breathing in a series of commas takes a little planning. You can breathe after every comma but you may not need to. You can take a slight pause just like you do in speaking when you pause in the middle of a sentence but don't take a breath. A series of questions is very similar; breathe where you need, and use a very slight pause for those places where you don't need a breath.

You can breathe after a comma, as long as you remember that your train of thought doesn't stop as you take the breath. The same train of thought continues just like when you take a breath between phrases in a conversation.

The places where you don't want to breathe are between syllables in the middle of a word, in the middle of a grammatical phrase that should be kept as one thought, or between a noun and modifier. Look at the text to determine where you would take a breath if you were speaking the words. If it doesn't sound logical to breathe when you're speaking the lyrics, try to find another place to take the breath when you sing.

If you're struggling with a phrase because you need a breath, cheat the last note of a phrase rather than trying to hurry in on the first note of the next phrase. If the last note is a half note, you can cut the note off a half beat early to catch your breath. In "Simple Things," you can take a little time away from the word "me" to make sure you have enough breath to sing the next phrase.

Catching your breath

If you're singing an up-tempo song with quick moving words, you have to know exactly how to get the breath in quickly to make the next line come out clearly.

Remember that the release for the next breath has to happen very quickly. Release your abdomen to allow the breath to drop into the body and exhale slowly. Opening the throat quickly prevents gasping. Gasping doesn't allow you to get the air in as fast, and it feels more like a struggle. For more help with breathing, see Chapter 3.

Explaining intro, interlude, and postlude

The *introduction* is the beginning of the song. The accompanist plays it on the piano before you start to sing. An introduction is important, because the first word and note grows out of the introduction.

The *interlude* is a segment of music in between sections of a composition. In songs, the interlude usually occurs between segments of the song, and the pianist plays alone.

The *postlude* is the song's ending that concludes the musical and dramatic thoughts. The song isn't over until the pianist releases the last note of the postlude.

Timing your breathing from the beginning

Take a look and listen to your musical introduction, the part before the lyrics come in. Before you sing that first note, you need to be ready — you need to time your breath. Sometimes, timing your breath just right so you can begin the first phrase with enough air is tricky. The best way to get the breath is to practice breathing two beats before you sing. Get your song's tempo in your head. When you have that tempo set in your mind, count one, two, breath, breath, (breathe for two counts) and then begin to sing. If you find that's too much time for breath, practice taking the breath in one count. What you don't want to do is to take the breath, hold it for a few counts and then sing. Holding your breath only gets you locked up in your upper body. Remember that breath is always in motion whether moving in your body or out. For "Simple Things," you want to start taking your first breath about two beats before you sing the first word, "Sometimes."

Changing the tone for each section

Each section of a song should have a distinct feel or tone. To convey different tones in different sections, you need to make a change of thought to create a change of tone. In "Simple Things," you have an opportunity to change your thought as you begin the second verse. Look through your song and determine how many sections it has. You know it's a new section because one of these things happens: a piano interlude (a solo section for the piano in between the vocal section) often leads to a new section, the music changes and adds different rhythms or moves to a new key, or the text changes and a new topic is introduced.

If you ever studied poetry, you discovered that each *poem,* or grouping of words, had a certain rhythm to it, called *meter.* After you found the meter, you may have looked further to find the rhyme scheme. Knowing the rhyme scheme gave you a clue as to how many sections were in the piece.

The form of a song tells you how many sections you can expect to find.

- **Strophic,** which is similar to a hymn, means that the same music is repeated for each section of text or each *stanza*.

- **Two part AB** means that two main sections may occur in order as AB or ABA with the first section repeating. An example of an AABA song is the *Flintstone's* theme and AB "(Baby You Can) Drive My Car" by the Beatles. You may think of other songs that fit because they have a verse and a chorus.

- **Through composed** means that the entire piece is new with no repeats of any sections in any stanza. Examples of through composed songs include "Yesterday" by John Lennon and Paul McCartney, and "Stairway to Heaven" by Led Zeppelin.

If a section repeats, speculate about what made the composer or lyricist repeat those words? What reason could they have had for saying it again? After you think about those reasons, you can discover how to create changes in your tone by changing what you're thinking. The fact is that you need to sing a repeated part differently the second time than you did the first time. (And if it repeats a third or even a fourth time, each repetition should be distinct from the others.)

Finding the minimum number of sections to a song tells you the minimum number of changes.

Chapter 19

Acting the Song

In This Chapter
▶ Telling a song's tale
▶ Who's the character behind the song?
▶ Selling your song with appropriate nonverbals

*I*f you think about the movie musicals that you've seen on television, you remember the choreography, the great scenery, the graceful dancing partners singing their duet — all the pizzazz. What if you have to stand on stage and sing a song by yourself with only the piano for company? You have to the right chapter for some ideas on making your solo routine a stellar performance.

Your biggest job as a singer is to say something when you sing. Standing up and singing memorized words is just the beginning. Apply your acting skills to a song for a powerful performance. Give your audience a reason to look and listen to your performance.

Seeing the Song as a Story

Every well-written song takes the listener on a journey. The journey involves the use of text and music to tell the story. In this section, you'll find information about how to work with the text of your song to understand it as a story, how to work with your voice to portray that text with emotion, and how the music and text can work together.

Chatting it up before I sing

Well-written songs offer you an opportunity to create a partnership with the words and music. Songs that aren't so well written give you the opportunity to work harder and make sense of the jumble. By working the text as a speech or monolog, you may find that the song doesn't mean what you thought it did.

Just like reading a poem for the first time, you may not absorb all the meanings the first time. The second time around, you may find several new things that jump out at you. The more you work it, the more you can enhance the relationship between your singing and the words coming out of your mouth.

You may think that just singing the song well is enough — a wonderful start but you want to take it a step farther. Saying words out loud forces you to decide what the words mean. For example, you can emphasize the words "I had a cat" in three different ways:

- If you say the words and emphasize the first word, you're saying that you had a cat and probably you alone.
- If you emphasize the second word *had,* that may mean the cat is no longer with you.
- Emphasizing the last word may mean that you had a cat instead of a dog.

Playing with the various words makes you think about what you're trying to say and how best to say it. As you speak through the text of your song, make specific choices about what you think the text means, as you did above when you said, "I had a cat." Your specific choices give the listener an opportunity to really focus on your story so the listeners hear the words and not just the glorious sounds of your voice.

When you begin to work your text as a monolog or add expression to your singing, you may find that your eyebrows tend to go up. If you find that your eyebrows push up to your hairline (not a good thing), put a piece of clear tape on your forehead to convince them to go back down. You can put electrical tape up if that's all you have, but it may leave a sticky film. Put the tape down or vertically on your forehead, so you can feel each time your eyebrows flex. The tape wiggling on your forehead is quite distracting in the beginning, but eventually, you can find a way to express your thoughts without tightening up anything on your face.

Voicing the text

Think of some of the famous singers from the past or present. One singer that just about everyone remembers as a great operatic actress was Maria Callas (1923–77). She was quite a character, and her voice was the subject of hot debate, but her commitment to her text was remarkable. It didn't matter if she was singing in English or not. Everybody in the audience knew what she was saying and what was being expressed with her voice. Say something and sing at the same time. It's such a rewarding experience. By working on the text of your song as a speech, you explore the meaning of the words. The next step is to deliver that same precise understanding of the text with your singing voice. You too can be a great singing actor.

Musical responses

In songs, the music has something to say about the character and the text. The music is a vehicle for the voice to tell the story. As you listen to your song (the piano part recorded by your pianist or a recording of you singing the song), what does the music have to say about the story? Often the setting of the text with the music enhances the delivery of the text. In the song "Wouldn't it be loverly" from *My Fair Lady*, Eliza Doolittle's text is at the same pace as a person might speak the text. By setting the text at a normal speaking pace, the music helps you sound as if you are talking and telling a story with music. In the song "Ya Got Trouble" from *The Music Man*, you know just by hearing the sound of the accompaniment that Harold Hill is not going to sing about what a beautiful morning it is. The short, detached sounds from the accompaniment tell you that trouble is brewing. You'll also find times in songs that the singer gets to rest. During these times the music is talking and you want to respond to the music and your upcoming text. Read on for suggestions for what to do during an interlude.

Accounting for interludes

If the song has an *interlude,* a passage in the music when you're not singing, you need to figure out how to handle that period of time. Interludes can be perplexing. What in the world do you do to kill that time? You think specific thoughts called *subtext*. Subtext is thoughts that support the plot and continue the plot during musical interludes of a song. Subtext can take you from the musical introduction right to the song's first line.

The interlude may be really simple but you still want to hear the music and let it be part of your story. Think of the piano as your scene partner. Even if you are onstage alone singing a song, the piano is offering you some feedback within the structure of the music. You don't even have to read music to figure it out. You just need to listen to the music and decide how it's helping to tell the story.

Exploring Character

You want to make your performance well rounded and interesting to the audience. So you need to do some detective work on your song. Song detective work includes taking a close look into the character singing the song.

Tidbits of information from the script provide you with answers to questions about the character you're portraying. By answering these questions, you know the basic information about what this character is made of.

Getting into character means temporarily inhabiting the life and circumstances of a character for a story. In this case, the story is presented in the lyrics of the song. If the lyrics are from a play or musical, your song and your character have an entire life for you to explore.

If you just can't find the answers to some of the questions about the character singing the song, make a good guess based on the other details that you have read in the script, or create a story or scenario that supports the words of the song. Making up the missing details of your character's life helps you create a complete picture of exactly who this person is. As long as your scenario leads you to say and sing the words on the page, it can work. If your scenario is so far fetched that it distracts you and you're too busy to sing, make it a little less complicated for now. Simple is good.

Characterizing your character

Answering fundamental questions about the character singing your song leads you to some specific details about the character and how to portray that character when you're alone on stage.

You want to find out the dirt on your character. Some basic questions to answer include:

- ✔ What's the character's name?

- ✔ How old is the character? Your character's age and physical condition plays into how you interpret the song. Young characters move differently than older characters.

- ✔ What is the character's occupation or station in life? Knowing that your character is the local sheriff means he dresses, carries himself, and behaves differently than the town drunk who lives in the alley behind the gas station. The drunk may slur his words but the sheriff may be well spoken.

- ✔ What does the character look like? Knowing the character's occupation gives you your first clues on what the character might look like and how he would carry himself. The town drunk would probably be disheveled with wrinkled clothes and a red face from too much alcohol. The rest of the details you can glean from the text. Often, the other characters in the show say things about your character and you can use this information to help you further decide what your character might look like because of his occupation and because of what others say about him.

- ✔ How does your character change during the course of the show, and what stage is the character in during this song? If you think of *The Sound of Music*, Maria changes during the course of the story and Eliza

> Doolittle changes drastically during the course of *My Fair Lady*. By knowing the story, you'll know what stage of character development she's in when you sing the song.

Where does this song take place? Knowing where the story takes place can also change how you sing a song. If the setting of your song is the middle of a hot summer afternoon, that's very different than singing a song as you watch a blizzard outside your window. Neil Sedaka sang about "Laughter in the Rain," which gives a clear picture of where the song is taking place. Even if it's not spelled out in black and white, you can make a choice about where the song is set and picture that place in your mind.

Knowing your character's background gets you to dig for the basic information available about your character. Allow yourself some time to digest the script as you're working on the song. See the big picture first. Summarize the details and then move on to the smaller details. You want to know about the inner life of the character as well as the outer life.

If you know this basic information about your character, you know if this person is similar to yourself or the exact opposite. By the way, I just love playing characters that are the opposite from my own personality. It allows me a chance to pretend to be someone else entirely. I get to live someone's life onstage and then be myself when I go home at night. What better way to live a secret life?

Discovering your character's motivation

Singing is a way of expressing huge heightened emotions. A song conveys feelings so big that the character can't just say it; he has to sing about it. Just in case you don't rush into song every few minutes in your everyday life, keep reading to discover how you can get to that huge, heightened sense of awareness that makes you just want to burst out singing.

Before singing a song, you want to know a few things. You want to know what happened just before this song to motivate your character to sing and say the words, why does your character sing, and how does your character intend to overcome any obstacles ahead of them. In this section you can find the answers to these questions about some familiar songs so you can answer the same questions about your song. Some songs are not from a musical or opera. For these songs, you need to do enough work with the text that you can use your imagination to lead you to the answers to these questions.

An event usually occurs that motivates the character to this song. The character has a problem to overcome, is in a predicament he wants to change, or wants to help someone. Knowing the events that led up to the story gives you insight into your character's predicament. You have to have some sort of predicament, good or bad, to sing. The obstacles that the character encounters are pretty important. Without the obstacle, everyone in the show may be so content that they don't need to burst out singing. Mother Abbess sees Maria's frustration and is motivated to sing "Climb Every Mountain" in *The Sound of Music*. Aunt Eller in *Oklahoma!* sings, "The Farmer and the Cowman Should be Friends," because the men are all fighting, and she wants them to stop fighting and get along. A song that's not from a musical with specific motivation is "Return to Sender," which you may have heard Elvis Presley sing. He's motivated to sing the song, because his letters keep coming back, even though he said he's sorry, and it's breaking his heart. In the movie, *The Wizard of Oz*, the Lion is motivated to sing "If I Were The King of the Forest" because he wants courage and he's tired of being afraid. His buddy the Tin Man sings, "If I Only Had a Heart," because he wants to feel.

As you sing during a concert or other performance, you want to be living in that moment without worrying about what just happened or the note coming at the end. Face the task at hand and conquer it before moving on or looking back. Let go of what just happened and focus on the phrase you're singing. The next phrase is waiting. By focusing on your process and preparation, you don't have to worry about the outcome, because the outcome is something to analyze *after* the performance. Shooting for the outcome prevents you from being in the moment.

Planning actions to get something done

You want to plan an action that helps your character get what he wants. An action sounds like something that you have to leap around the stage to accomplish, but it's not. You can stand still and have a plan of action. After you decide why you're singing the song, you create a plan to get what you want and overcome the obstacle. An example of a song or aria from an opera that illustrates a specific action is from the opera *Carmen*. Carmen is arrested and Don José is supposed to take her to prison. She sings the aria "Seguidilla" to entice Don José into letting her go. Her plan of action is to get him to release her and she gets her way because she entices him by using her body and voice to seduce him.

Finding the character's tempo

For each character you play, you want to find their beat or their tempo. Many things, such as age, physical condition, and state of being, affect the tempo. For example, an old person has a slower pace than a teenager does. However, the state of being of the older person may cause them to be a live wire on the stage. If the person is hot and bothered, they may not be sitting idly watching the sunset. Their energy may be flying around the room.

As you explore your character, look at what can affect the pace:

 ✔ The preceding action in the song or in the story: If the character was just mugged, the pace is much faster than for someone who just woke up on a lazy Saturday morning.

 ✔ The environment: The pace in the middle of the woods in a national park protected area is much slower than in a major city.

 ✔ The type of song: Is the song a ballad? If so, the character must be slowing down for just a moment or two so the pace may not be as frantic as in an up-tempo song. See Chapter 21 for more information about ballads and up-tempo songs.

When you know your character's tempo, you may want to read on to find out how to move appropriately around the stage as you play your character.

Getting Physical

Most singers feel stiff if they just stand still and sing a song. Knowing how to move, where to move, and what to move when you sing keeps you looking good as you sing. When singing a song your choices are to stand still or move around the stage. You can find some advice on how much to move in the "Movin' and groovin' with my song" section, later in this chapter, and help with gesturing as you're singing in the "Hands up" section, coming up later in this chapter. Because focusing your eyes is important for your song, you'll find out just ahead what you need to know about who to look at and why you shouldn't close your eyes while you sing.

Figuring out where to focus

When singing a song, you can sometimes look in one spot and sometimes look around. Knowing the story of your song gives you an opportunity to understand the type of song that you're singing, and this understanding tells you where to focus your eyes. If you're talking to just one person, you may focus on the back wall or a place out in front of you. An example of a song in which you may talk to just one person is "I Can't Make You Love Me." If that person isn't in the room, but you're daydreaming of them, you may gaze out into the distance as you long for them. An example of this would be when Elton John sang for Princess Diana's funeral. She wasn't present, but you knew that he was singing to her. Your eyes may move around when you're talking to a group of people, but not move like you're watching a tennis match. In the opera, *Così fan tutte,* Guglielmo talks to all the women in the audience when he sings, "Donne mie, la fate a tanti," which translates, "I would like a word with all you lovely women."

If you notice other people as they're telling a story, their eyes automatically look around in different ways. When you're trying to remember something, you may look up at the ceiling. This is a common reflex when you're trying to dig something out of your memory bank. When you're watching one person, you may hold your gaze on that person and not look away. If you start to think about what you're saying, you may look away from your audience as you think. These are all natural and normal movements of your eyes. When singing a song, you can also have this same natural movement of your eyes moving away from the person you're addressing and then back.

Closing your eyes is a not an option when you want to act and sing. In every-day conversations with other people, you keep your eyes open. You wouldn't have a conversation with someone and close your eyes unless you're lying on the couch talking to someone across the room. Singing a song is about having a conversation with someone and telling a story. You want your eyes open to talk to your audience. Closing your eyes cuts off your biggest means of communicating with your audience. They're left out because, by closing your eyes, you are only communicating with yourself. Give your audience a reason to look at you and watch you when you sing.

If you choose to look at the people as you perform and get distracted looking someone in the eye as you're singing, try this tip. Look at their hairline. Try it out sometime on a friend and ask them if they can tell if you're looking them in the eye. More often than not, they probably have no idea. Ask your friend to do the same to you so you can see what you look like. Try this until you're comfortable singing your song and maintaining your focus on your task.

Hands up

Most beginning singers want to move their hands a lot when they sing because they assume that gesturing makes their song more interesting and exciting. It can but it can also look like you are flipping burgers on a grill if you don't allow your arms to open out as you gesture. First, you want to figure out how to move your hands and arms to gesture, and then you want to know when and why you move them. The following exercise gets your hands in the right moves for gesturing and then you can read the information about when to gesture in the "Gesturing appropriately" section, coming up next in this chapter.

1. Put your hands down by your side.

2. With your thumbs leading the way, move your hands up toward each other and then out in a big arc with your elbows away from your body and your palms up and open.

3. If you know what the Chanel logo looks like, two back-to-back Cs,)(, start with your hands down at your side, trace your hands from the bottom right hand of each C, until your hands are out to the side of your body with your hands about as high as your shoulders. To make the gesture look natural, you'll want distance between your elbows and the sides of your body.

As you practice this movement, you'll be able to do it faster and vary it slightly using just one arm or moving your arms higher for those times you need a big emphasis for your text.

Gesturing appropriately

The big question people ask is what to do with their hands. Well, what do you do with your hands as you speak? If your hands normally move when you speak, then you may feel stiff if they remain frozen at your side during your song. Work the song as a monolog to discover what's happening and how the character would react to the actions in the story. Basically, you gesture when you react. For example, think about how you'd move in reaction to "Whoa! Don't bring that spider any closer to me!" Or how would your hands gesture if you were saying, "I wanted to buy that doll, but the woman snatched it out of my hand," "Here I am!" or "When are you going to clean up this incredibly messy room?" If you recognize the same kind of opportunities in a song, you feel more like yourself gesturing with your hands rather than trying to plan something interesting to do during your song just to fill the dead space.

Following are some things to avoid:

✔ **Pantomiming:** Pantomimic gestures only mime the text. For example, if you plan out specific movements without thinking about why they help your story, such as lifting your hand to the sky when you say the words, "Moon and stars," or place your hand on your chest when you say the word, "heart," you're not doing your job as an actor. You want to see the bigger picture beyond the moon and stars. What roles do those two elements play in your story? That's what's important to demonstrate. Your audience knows exactly where to find the moon and stars. Try to avoid pantomimic gestures if at all possible. Pantomime may work if you're creating a comic character, and pantomime is one way to play the character. However, serious songs work best when the gestures come from what you're saying and thinking about the song and not from pantomime.

✔ **Choreographed moves:** If your song is fun and spunky, please allow your pleasure and joy of singing the song reflect through your story and not through choreography. You don't need to plan out any movements before you do your work on the text of your song. If you have chosen a dance number for your song, you can assume that some movement is in order. Think twice about what you are trying to show off when you start moving. If you want to show off that you are a great dancer, keep in mind that you want to sing well at the same time and not distract your listeners. You want to attract their attention but not distract from your singing. If your story is really strong and you are truly committed, you won't need to dance around the room.

Movin' and groovin' with my song

When you sing for an audience, you want the story to come through and the listener to see and hear you connect your story and singing. Whatever movements you make around a stage or around the room should enhance your singing and the story. Being able to move and sing is important, yet starting small is best. Here are some tips on coordinating movement with music:

✔ At home, practice moving around and singing, doing simple tasks as you sing just to practice doing two things at once.

✔ When you're comfortable moving and singing, speak through your song lyrics and notice what gestures you make. Knowing how you gesture when you speak helps you to figure out how to move when you're singing.

✔ Some songs don't require much movement at all. Err on the busy side at first when you're practicing and then pare down the movements until you're sure that you're moving in response to what you're saying. Just moving around for its own sake when you're singing doesn't really enhance your song. In what kind of song should you park it? Classical songs don't require much movement and usually not many gestures; take a few steps but don't stray too far from where you started.

If singing is new to you, adding some sort of movement may just be too much for you right now. Taking it one step at a time is a good idea when you're figuring out how to put your new technique and a new song before the public. When you're ready to go from just good technique to coordinating that technique while telling a story, you need to know how to move. You need to know where to look and how much to move when you sing. You can also read Chapter 21 for more information about how to tell a story and sing a song at the same time.

If you try to plan out your feelings, you may get bogged down with your feelings and forget to do something and make a plan of action. Doing something advances you toward your goal. It's better to do something as you feel rather than just explore your feelings. In life, you think about what you are going to do. When someone makes you mad, you think about what you are going to do to get him back, but you probably don't sit around when you're mad, thinking only about your feelings. You think about action.

Translating a song that's in a foreign language

Singing in another language is common in classical music. Just because the song is in another language, you aren't off the hook on your responsibilities as an actor. You want to know exactly what's happening in each word, so you can deliver each word with conviction.

✔ **Create a word-for-word translation.** The first step is to look up each word, so you know exactly what you're saying. It's tough to find the operative word in the line if you aren't sure what half of the words mean. After you find the definition for each word, create a paraphrased version of the text in English. If the word-for-word translation turns out to be, "To you with love I only," it can be paraphrased to "I love only you," which makes perfect sense.

✔ **Compare the word-for-word translation with a paraphrased version of the text.** You may find the paraphrased version on the copy of your song underneath the foreign language text. Remember that you can't really commit to the paraphrase until you know which word means what in the original language. Sometimes the poetic translation found underneath the original text has

very little to do with the original meaning of the poem. Always do your own translation as well just to check.

✔ **Practice speaking the word-for-word translation in English, the paraphrase in English, and the text in the foreign language.** After you do all your homework, you want to prepare your text just as if it were in English. You want to work the text as a monolog, both in English and the foreign language. Finding the operative words in the English language may not be in the same order as in the foreign language. Strive to be a great actor and singer no matter what the language or style of music.

Some of the newer books being published for classical songs or songs from operas, called *arias,* include word-for-word translations and paraphrases of the text. What a nice gift the publisher offers you. They did your homework for you. If you want to sink your teeth into the language, get a good dictionary with a pronunciation guide as well as the definitions of the words. If you buy the dictionary with the pronunciation guide, you save yourself so much time looking up the diction rules.

Chapter 20

Confronting Your Fear of Performing

In This Chapter

▶ Naming the root of the anxiety

▶ Tackling the anxiety by preparing

▶ Evaluating your progress at each performance

*P*erformance anxiety is a big problem among performers of all kinds and at all levels of experience. Finding ways of dealing with anxiety and turning nerves and adrenaline into positive forces in your performance are just as important as great technique. Whenever those butterflies in your stomach get out of hand, this chapter offers some dependable methods for working through your anxiety.

Facing the Symptoms

Knowing what you're afraid of is half the battle. After you pinpoint the source of your fear, you can take charge of it.

The most common fears are

- ✔ Cracking during the performance and not being able to hit the high note
- ✔ Looking stupid in front of friends
- ✔ Forgetting the words to the song
- ✔ Fearing success or failure, rejection, or the unknown

Naming the fear enables you to go after the problem and beat it. Throughout this chapter, you can read about the common concerns and determine whether that's what's scaring you. After you find the source, move forward and find a solution to eliminate it and not just the symptom.

TIP

Running in place simulates adrenaline

A rush of adrenaline brings about a racing heart. You can duplicate that feeling by running in place until you're out of breath . . . then sing your song.

Being out of breath while you practice helps you get used to singing phrases where you desperately want to just exhale and not sing.

Breathlessness is similar to what happens when anxiety strikes during the performance.

Every time you take the breath, you can feel it falling into your body. As it falls in your body, realize that you can sing even when your heart is pounding. It's just not easy.

You may find comforting the knowledge that thousands of other singers face the same icky anxiety you feel right before a performance. The symptoms include butterflies in your stomach, shaky knees, dry mouth (sometimes called cottonmouth), a sudden urge to cry or run away, trembling hands, a racing heart rate, nausea, runny nose, cold hands but sweaty underarms, and the urge to pee no matter how many times you visit the bathroom. Did you find any of your symptoms on that list? I certainly see mine.

News Flash: Adrenaline isn't the enemy! In all honesty, you want a little adrenaline to boost your performance.

Assuming that you must be calm before a performance is the same as setting yourself up for huge pangs of anxiety when you don't turn out to be as cool as a cucumber. Expecting to be nervous and jittery, on the other hand, can enable you to sing through your anxiety. In fact, you can use the fight-or-flight excitement of adrenaline coursing through your body to enhance your performance. By reframing your thoughts about the performance, you change from fight-or-flight adrenaline to a rush of excitement to seize an opportunity.

Alleviating Anxiety through Preparation

Your symptoms are out in the open, and now you can talk about how to relieve your anxiety. Make a choice to change your thoughts about your performance. If you continually dread the symptoms that you know are going to arise, you won't get past the first paragraph without thinking that this tactic won't work. So remind yourself that you're anxious because you fear something; the symptoms don't just randomly appear.

Practicing well

The biggest key to alleviating anxiety is preparation. *Preparation* isn't the same as *overpracticing* or aiming for perfection. Over-practicing means that you practice so much that you lose sight of the joy of singing and only focus on singing perfectly. Aiming for perfection takes the joy out of singing because everything becomes a contest, if only with yourself.

The following pointers can help get you prepared and ready for performing.

- **Staying positive and motivated as you practice.** Figure out a way to motivate yourself. What kind of reward do you need to get yourself to practice regularly? People who don't like being alone oftentimes don't like to practice. You must recognize that and then be even more disciplined to do your work. Your positive thinking during your practice sessions carries over into your performing.

- **Setting goals for each practice session.** The first practice session goal may be to successfully sing the song through without words to find consistent breath flow (see Chapter 3). The second practice session goal may be to keep that same easy flow of breath as you sing the words. Trying to tackle too many things at once causes frustration.

- **Practicing at the level you intend to perform.** That means you have to practice all the details of your song separately, and then gradually put them all together until you consistently create the sounds that you want to create in your performance.

- **Setting a deadline for memorizing the song.** The melody and words of the song need to be in your long-term memory. When you attempt to memorize the song the night before the performance, you may be overwhelmed trying to deal with the excitement of performing and remembering the words at the same time.

  I recommend having the song memorized at least one week before a performance. That gives you seven days to work on the song without looking at the music. If you're singing a group of songs, you may want to have them memorized earlier so you have time to work with the accompanist and work on your acting objectives (see Chapter 19) as you use your singing technique.

- **Speed-reading through your text to help you remember the words.** Forgetting the words of a song that you've memorized usually happens because your concentration momentarily slips. For example, you may start thinking about being happy that the high note sounded good and suddenly, as you're getting back to business, you realize you haven't any idea where you are in the song. Practicing your concentration and speed-reading through the text on a regular basis helps you put the text into your long-term memory and not just short term.

Playing to your strengths

Doing things that you know you're good at builds confidence and relieves anxiety. Setting yourself up for success by playing to your strengths makes even more sense when you're nervous about performing. Use the following tips to put yourself in a winning frame of mind:

- ✔ **Choosing pieces that enhance your strengths.** Singing one song in a performance means that you have an opportunity to find a piece that really enables you to show your areas of expertise. When you need to choose ten minutes of music, the task naturally gets harder, but finding the appropriate material is part of the preparation. Chapter 17 deals with choosing music.

- ✔ **Focusing on your strengths.** Singing songs that require agility is a great goal when that is something you feel confident doing. If not, make the performance about your fabulous tone, breath control, or any other aspect that you feel confident sharing.

Managing your thoughts

Performers who don't experience performance anxiety may tell you to just get over it and stop being afraid. I like to call those people adrenaline junkies. They love that rush of adrenaline that hits just before the performance. But trying to stop being afraid may only frustrate you. You have to deal with your anxiety, which is different than adrenaline. Anxiety adds a sickening sensation on top of the adrenaline. You don't want to stop the adrenaline, but rather eliminate the underlying fear that leads to anxiety about performing.

Anxiety brings negative thoughts into your head. Negative thoughts may try to convince you that you're going to forget the words even though you know the song cold. Just hearing so much busy talking inside your head can ruin your concentration and make you forget the words.

Sometimes you can use negative practice to find the extremes of your symptoms. Try making the symptoms worse the next time you practice. By visualizing or imagining a critical audience, you may experience some symptoms of anxiety. Notice what those symptoms are and how you feel about the audience. As you feel that sense of dread, sing through your music. Visualize yourself being able to complete your task regardless of how grumpy your imaginary audience looks.

Making a list of the negative thoughts that frequently pop into your mind is a way to manage your thoughts. By facing those thoughts you can recognize that they aren't helpful and can therefore switch to positive thoughts instead. Making a list of affirmations to counter your negative thoughts also can help you retrain your mind to focus on the positive. Affirmations include saying things such as: "My singing is improving each day. I am confident that my breath control gets better with each practice session."

Getting up the nerve

Your thoughts may turn to the audience whenever you become concerned about what they think of you and your singing.

You can't get rid of the audience; after all, an audience is a necessity for your performance. You can, however, pretend that the members of the audience aren't really in the audience — an option that works for some people. You don't have to sing directly to the audience or look them in the eyes. You can look over their heads and not have to worry about reading the expression on their faces when you look them right in the eyes.

Doing your job as you sing means that you must tell a story. Insecurity can lead you to believe that everyone is looking at you harshly. Reframing your thoughts so that you accept the audience and let go of the hostile image you may have of the audience can go a long way toward overcoming your doubts. You've probably heard this suggestion for overcoming stage fright: Imagine that all the people in the audience are sitting in their underwear. You can also remind yourself that the audience chose to attend your performance, and they want to hear you sing well.

Building performance focus

Have you ever been so focused on a task that you lost track of time or were startled when someone came up behind you? That's the kind of focus that you want as you sing. Focus totally on your task at hand, leaving the rest of the stuff for later. To help you practice concentrating, try

- ✔ **Staging some distractions.** Practice in front of an audience of friends and ask them to randomly whisper, rustle paper, drop a book, or stand up and walk around while you're singing. The first few times you may lose your composure, but just laugh it off and keep trying until you can hold your concentration and ignore the distractions.

- ✔ **Practicing concentration.** Set a timer for five minutes and practice focusing totally on your singing for those five minutes. Five minutes may seem like a short amount of time — until you have to fill it with only one task. You may find your mind wandering and thinking about something else after a few minutes. That's okay. Set the timer and try again.

Working up to concentrating for the full five minutes may take a few days. You can also practice focusing and then intentionally letting your mind wander so you can tell the difference.

✔ **Leaving distractions at the door.** That fight you had earlier in the day, the report that's due tomorrow, your upcoming vacation — any number of everyday concerns may occupy your mind. Create a ceremony that enables you to leave those distractions at the door.

Put a basket outside your practice room door and mentally dump all your worries and frustrations into it before you enter the room. You can also write a to-do list before your session, so you know exactly what you need to think about right after you practice. Acknowledge that you still have to resolve those issues in your mind and then move to the current task at hand.

One of my colleagues gave me some great advice a few years ago: "Never let anyone live in your head rent free," and "Only have conversations with people who are in the room." That means tabling those kinds of conversations in your head when that person isn't in the room with you. What great advice!

Performing to Build Confidence

What you may not want to hear is that you must perform to get over performance anxiety. You must put yourself in the hot seat on a regular basis to find your groove. Basketball players practice their shots so their bodies remember those sensations in the heat of the moment. You too must put your skills to the test in the heat of the moment. You know you're ready to take it public when:

✔ You have a burning desire to move past the anxiety.

✔ Your technical skills are polished enough that you can depend on them.

✔ You find a song that complements your current abilities.

Find a small gig to get you started. By *gig,* I mean anywhere you can sing. Sing for one friend, then for your family, and then for a small gathering such as at a nursing home. Sing in the church choir with the group and then sing a solo for a Sunday school class before singing it for the entire congregation. The same is true of the community chorus. Sing with the chorus, then sing small solos, and then shoot for the solo in front of the community.

Cracking isn't the end of the world

The number one reason for *cracking* (when the singing muscles stop working properly just long enough for the sound to stop) isn't maintaining a steady flow of air especially on high notes. Sometimes singers crack when they're suffering from severe allergy problems or other ailments that make their voices feel different. Young singers may crack as they figure out how to sing higher notes. Young men may experience some cracking during puberty and afterward as they discover how to sing higher notes without too much pressure in the throat.

Giving yourself permission to experience the crack enables your body to release some of the tension associated with the fear. Ninety-nine percent of the time, whenever I give my students permission to crack, or ask them to please let the note crack just to know what it feels like, they don't crack. Give yourself permission to not be perfect. It's impossible to be perfect. Take the one note that isn't so perfect and average it with the other hundred notes in the song, and you have pretty slim odds for cracking.

Cracking on a high note isn't the end of the world. I've seen singers crack, and members of the audience didn't boo, because they understood that it was just part of the growing experience for that singer. The first time I saw a professional crack in a concert I was secretly thrilled, not because the singer cracked but

because he kept going with the understanding that his voice wasn't working properly at that one moment in time. The rest of the notes in the concert were glorious, but the cracked one gave me hope.

The fear of cracking may disappear after you sing the same phrase several times without any problem. Make a list of the things that you have to do when you sing and keep practicing them until you can do them all at the same time. You may have to practice doing two things at once before trying to do four. Practicing these things helps prevent cracking: keeping a steady flow of air moving as you sing (see Chapter 3), opening your throat (see Chapter 6), and knowing your capabilities by understanding what your voice can do in each area, such as your head voice (see Chapter 11). Enabling yourself to do several things at one time takes courage and determination. Most people are capable of multitasking, and so are you. You can drive your car, change the station on the radio, and have a conversation with the person in the passenger's seat all at the same time. You can certainly apply this same process to singing.

You may find that acting helps you sing the high note without cracking. You may get so caught up in the heat of the moment that you want to sing the high note and the breath just moves for you. How cool is that!

Devising a game plan

For each and every performance, make a plan of action for success. Assuming that you're going to succeed means that you will. Assuming that you're going to fail is the same as giving in to those voices in your head.

Reframe from those stupid things that people have said to you in the past about your performing abilities. Being critical is human nature, but remember that it's only one person's opinion. If I'd listened to things people have said,

I'd never have written this book or dared to be a singer in New York. Take these five steps to get your game plan in place.

- ✔ **Making a specific timeline to get yourself ready to sing at the time of your performance.** See Chapter 10 for more on creating a practice routine. After developing your practice routine, you'll know how long it takes for your voice to be ready to sing at your best. You can plan your warm-up time for the day of your performance to get you ready. Some suggestions include:

  - Taking time to vocalize or warm up the notes you'll sing in the performance.

  - Vocalizing long enough for your voice to be singing at your peak when you walk on the stage.

  - Singing through your song on the performance day enough that you feel confident but not so many times that your voice feels tired.

- ✔ **Inviting someone who helps boost your confidence to each performance.** Do you know someone who can encourage you as you walk out for the performance? Discuss your fears with this close friend or confidant and then discuss your feelings after the performance. You may find that your perception of that awful note isn't what your friend heard. By having a support system with you, you can quiet negative thoughts that may creep into your head.

- ✔ **Looking at each performance as an opportunity to succeed.** You have to expect success before you can achieve it. Success doesn't just happen, but you can make it happen.

- ✔ **Practicing what you intend to do.** If you plan to take a moment and take a breath before beginning to sing your song, practice it that way. Taking that moment to quiet your mind and settle your racing heart is worth it. By practicing and visualizing your success, you can more easily make it happen.

- ✔ **Charting your improvement.** Make a list of what you want to accomplish and with each performance shoot to accomplish one more task on the list.

  For example, the first task may be remembering all the words. By practicing with distractions at home, you can boost your ability to concentrate. When you remember all the words at your first performance, you may want to try remembering the words and breathing consistently at the second performance. Just getting the breath in your body and then using it helps many other technical problems that can creep onto your list. Give yourself a gold star when you achieve each goal.

Before singing your song in public, try it out in front of some friends. By trying it out a few times before your big performance, the song may seem familiar and not so scary.

Evaluating your performance

Progress happens because of each step that you take. After every performance, look at how you did and how you felt using the lists in the following sections. Because everything in your life affects your singing, decide what steps worked well for you and toss the ones that didn't.

Looking at preparation and performance issues

Check the technical aspects of your performance to discover what you can improve upon. Look at what did and didn't work well and make adjustments for next time. Ask yourself these questions after your performance:

- ✔ Did I rehearse enough with the accompanist?
- ✔ Did I work the song enough from memory?
- ✔ What did I do well during the performance?
- ✔ Did I get enough sleep the night before or in the days before the performance?
- ✔ Was my warm-up long enough, high enough, early or late enough in the day?
- ✔ Was I focused on the moment (or on the audience's reaction to my singing)?
- ✔ Did the steps in my preperformance routine work well?
- ✔ Did I leave enough time for dressing?
- ✔ Did I take time to visualize the performance in my mind?

Be fair when charting your progress. Seeing your gradual improvement in your quest to manage adrenaline and fear is important. Several months may pass before you feel comfortable singing in public, so give yourself some time. After each performance, take the time to make a list of the things that you did well. When you accomplished more than what was on your list, recognizing that accomplishment is important. Taking consistent steps toward your goal is the key.

Be brave. Take a risk. You won't know until you dare to try.

Checking your anxieties

As for your anxiety, you can make a checklist by answering the following questions to help you remember how you felt.

✔ How did I feel right before the performance? If this performance is the first one you evaluate, the answer to this question may be, I felt unprepared, terrified, or nauseous. By recognizing these symptoms, you may realize that the symptoms aren't debilitating and may ease up over time.

✔ What were my symptoms of anxiety, if any? The symptoms may include sweating, racing heart, and the urge to run away. By naming the symptom, you can see that it lessens with each performance or that you just make the choice not to run away, because you enjoy the performance after you get to the stage.

✔ What was the level of anxiety at the beginning of the performance? In the middle of the performance? At the end of the performance? After the performance? Many singers say their anxiety is worse just before the performance, but it goes away as they begin singing. If the anxiety hits in the middle of the performance, you were probably anticipating the high note and worrying about how to sing it. Continuing to work on your technique allows you to gain more confidence in your technique to alleviate the stress over that part of your voice. Stress after the performance may mean that you're worried about what people may say to you after the performance.

By asking these questions, you can see your progress over the course of a few weeks or months.

Chapter 21

Auditioning a Song for Musical Theater

. . . .

In This Chapter

▶ Getting the lowdown on musical theater auditions

▶ Picking a winning number to cash in on

▶ Preparing for the big day and more

▶ Finding out who and what to expect

. . . .

Want to audition for the local theater company? A Broadway show? Before planning your debut, you need to know how to prepare for a musical theater audition. In this chapter, you explore how to choose and prepare an appropriate song for the audition. You also find out about what to expect at an audition, so you're prepared to knock their socks off!

Getting Some Tips on Musical Theater

Daydreaming of hitting the stage? For those of you who've only auditioned for local choirs and rock bands, the musical theater audition has some quirks of its own. Keep reading to find out what you need to know.

Strutting your stuff

Singing at the audition means that you're prepared to sing a song using a musical theater style of singing. This style of singing is a bit different from classical singing.

You need to choose songs that are typical *ballads* (slower songs), and *up-tempos,* which are faster songs. Within these two basic types of songs, you want to find variety that shows off all your skills and abilities.

It's also fair to assume that, in addition to singing, you may be asked to dance and perform a monolog or read from a script at some point during your audition.

You can find some auditions that are geared toward singers where you won't have to dance, but you may be asked to "move." For example, singers who audition for shows like *The Sound of Music, Phantom of the Opera,* and *The King and I* aren't expected to dance as they would at an audition for *Oklahoma!, 42nd Street,* and *Grease.* So it's okay if you don't know any dance steps, but you should be able to move easily enough or be coordinated enough to follow along if someone at the audition instructs you.

Doing your homework

If you want to audition for a musical in your area, you'll need to find out some things before you head to the audition. An ad may have the answers to these questions — if not, you can just call the theater office or contact person and ask. All this depends on the company, who wrote the ad about the audition, and the person listening to them sing. In many cases, you have to just show up with several things in your notebook and make some decisions on the spot.

- ✔ **What kind of song should I sing?** In the ad for the audition, it may or may not tell you what kind of song to prepare for the audition. Sometimes the ad tells you to sing something from the show you're auditioning for and sometimes it tells you *not* to sing something from the show. You'll want to choose a song that is similar to the show you're auditioning for *and* similar to the character that you would like to play. See the sections "Selecting Your Songs" and "Avoiding the wrong song," later in this chapter.

- ✔ **Do I need to bring a resume?** If the answer is yes, and you don't have a singing resume prepared for auditions, see the sidebar in this chapter "Finding the right auditions" for some help with your resume.

- ✔ **Do I need to bring a photograph of myself to the audition?** At most auditions, singers bring a photograph called a *headshot.* This headshot is usually an 8-x-10 inch, black-and-white photograph of just their head or upper body. The photo also usually has the singer's name printed on the bottom in the border. For more information about headshots, see the sidebar in this chapter "Finding the right auditions."

- ✔ **Can I get some advice from a pro?** You may also want to get some advice from someone who understands the audition process such as a voice teacher, acting teacher, or coach. This person can help you choose your song, hone some basic skills of how to present yourself at the audition, and help you decide if your material is good for your voice.

Selecting Your Songs

Choosing songs to practice is different than choosing songs for an audition. You want to practice songs that expand and challenge your vocal technique. But songs for the audition should highlight your strengths and accomplishments from all those hours of practice.

When you audition, you need at least one ballad and one up-tempo song. Within your choice of songs, you need variety of stories, acting choices, and range. (For more on range, see Chapters 5 and 12.) The following sections explain in more detail.

I find that singers are usually either ballad lovers or ballad haters. Those singers that only love up-tempos usually agonize over their choice of the ballad. If you are an up-tempo lover, find a ballad that suits you and really dig into it as an actor to find a reason to croon those words, and then the slow tempo won't seem so eternally long.

The hardest part of auditioning is choosing the songs to sing. Choosing songs that are really perfect for you and that show off your talents is an art. This artful skill takes time to develop, so keep looking at songs to continue expanding your book of songs. (See the "Preparing your book" section, later in this chapter.)

Adding variety to spice up your style

Yes, variety is the spice of life, and your choice of songs should offer variety. A little variety gives you an opportunity to show off a well-balanced set of skills. Song number one can be a song that shows off glorious high notes and song number two may have a sassy belt that shows off your ability to change gears quickly.

Find songs that show off your strengths as a singer, and try to find variety within each song. If each of your songs has a narrow range, search for songs that allow you to show off some high notes right after you sing your belt song or show off a *legit* sound — a sound similar to the sound opera singers make but with a little more emphasis on the text instead of the singing (see Chapter 16 for information about singing in different styles of music). Remember that range is the highest and lowest note that your voice can get to and all the notes in between. The biggest thing that you want to avoid is having every song be the same kind of character and same kind of vocal sound coming out of your mouth, because the auditioner won't get to see that you're a skilled actor who can sing and play different kinds of roles and can add variety and spice to your character's life throughout the show.

At many musical theater auditions, you may be asked to sing a pop song, but to show a variety of song styles, you want to have early musical theater songs (not just the shows that have been written in the last ten years), later songs, and pop/rock songs, too. Often, singers confine themselves to singing contemporary songs. That's a great start, but keep on looking for songs that are written in and/or are also meant to portray an earlier time period. For example, Leonard Bernstein wrote the music for *Candide* (1956) in the latter 20th century, but Voltaire's story, on which this musical is based, dates back to 1759.

To get you started, choose songs from the top three broad categories: musical theater songs written before 1960, after 1960, and pop/rock. If you have one song from each of these three periods, then branch out and add more songs to your repertoire from the following categories:

- Pre-'30s musical comedy songs by such composers as George M. Cohan, Jerome Kern, Irving Berlin, George and Ira Gershwin, and early songs of Cole Porter.

- Songs from '40s and '50s musicals written by Richard Rodgers and Lorenz Hart, Richard Rodgers and Oscar Hammerstein, Leonard Bernstein, Frederick Loewe, Jule Styne, Frank Loesser, Jerry Bock and Sheldon Harnick, Hugh Martin, Richard Adler, Bob Merrill, and Meredith Willson.

- Songs from '60s musicals written Stephen Sondheim, John Kander and Fred Ebb, Charles Strouse, Cy Coleman, Jerry Herman, and Harvey Schmidt.

- Contemporary musicals that are more pop oriented, such as those written by Andrew Lloyd Webber, Stephen Schwartz, William Finn, Stephen Flaherty, Marvin Hamlisch, Alan Menken, and Maury Yeston. You can find more, but these few names can get you started on the search.

- Songs within the pop, rock, folk, country, and jazz styles.

- Selections from operettas by such composers as Victor Herbert, Rudolf Friml, Sigmund Romberg, and Gilbert and Sullivan.

- Classical music selections from operas.

As much as you may like the music of Steven Sondheim, his music is often really tough to read. Have an alternative song prepared just in case you arrive at the audition ready to sing your Sondheim piece and see that the pianist's right hand is in a cast, even though he's willing to play anything with his left hand.

Dramatizing your lyrics

You can't just choose a song because you sing it well. If you just sing it well, you can sell a recording instead of asking an audience to watch you sing it.

For those songs that you sing really well, figure out how to make it work for you as an actor. Keep these things in mind:

- Don't sing a song if you don't like the words. If you search long and hard, you can find songs that have great lyrics that you just can't wait to put to music.

- Make sure that you can relate to the story. Take the time to really hone in on a great story that supports the song and gives you a reason to sing it. Check out Chapter 19 for some help on telling a story while singing.

- The stories in the songs must be varied to show different aspects of your personality and acting abilities. After you find that wonderful ballad about your long lost love, find a funny song that shows off your comic timing. But don't get off the bus yet. Stay on and keep searching for a song that shows off fire and determination.

Avoiding the wrong song

It's the wrong audition song if

- You don't like it.

- It's out of your league as a singer or musician. By that I mean that the song is out of your range, the majority of notes sit too high, or it's too difficult musically.

- The song needs a band to make it work. You'll likely only have a pianist backing you up, so stick to songs that work with this type of accompaniment.

- The song makes the listener think of the famous person that made the song a hit. You want the listener to hear you and focus their attention on you. It's hard to find great songs that no one famous has performed but be aware of this as you are choosing your song. If you remember that famous performance, chances are someone else will too.

- You couldn't sing the song on your worst day. If you constantly have to be aware of your singing technique when you sing it, choose something else.

- Making the 16-bar cut is impossible.

- You can't get through the song without crying.

- Every accompanist has trouble sight reading it.

- The song is really negative.

Another audition song to avoid is the one that's *overdone*. The eternal question is "What's overdone?" Each year the answer to this question can change. Assume that if it's a song that everyone knows and loves to sing, it's probably done quite a bit. If you have a copy of the song in a popular music book, so do several thousand other people. If you see the show listed in the trade paper *Backstage* all the time, your song is probably super popular. You don't have to find obscure songs, but if ten other people sang your favorite song at the last audition, it may be overdone.

Getting Yourself and Your Music Ready

Okay. So you've got your songs, and you know you can sell 'em. Now, what? In this section, I help you get ready for an audition by giving you tips on how to prepare your music thoroughly as well as prepare yourself personally so that you audition with confidence, regardless of whether it's your first time or fiftieth.

Adjusting the key if you need to

I highly recommend that you try to find the song in the key that you want to sing it in. If you sing a song that's way out of your range, you may end up sounding more like Kermit the frog than Maria Callas or Barbara Cook on those high notes. See Chapter 17 for Web sites that allow you to find out what key sheet music is in before you purchase it.

Still, if you finally find a wonderful song that's *almost* perfect for you, you can get it transposed if you need to. *Transposed* means that someone — you or someone you hire — puts the song in a key other than the one it was originally written in — so the melody sounds higher or lower. So if the song is just the one you want to sing, but the notes are a tad too low or a little too high for you, then you can have it transposed.

If you aren't sure about the original key, look at the range and *tessitura* (where most of the notes sit in the song). Or you can try some of the newer Web sites that allow you to check the key of the song before you purchase it.

If you transpose your song (or have someone else do it), keep these things in mind:

> ✔ **You may want the beginning of the song much higher but that also means the middle section that's tricky for you also gets higher.** It's one thing to have some really cool high notes and quite another to sing those

cool high notes over and over when you raise the key. Practice the song in the new key, whether higher or lower, to make sure that you can manage all the notes in the new key.

✔ **You can't assume that your audition accompanist can or will transpose by sight (put the song in a higher or lower key as she's playing).** So purchase the song in the key you want to sing it in, or have someone transpose it for you before the audition. An accompanist may refuse if the song is just too difficult, and it's her choice. You don't want her to sight read something at your audition if she thinks she may mess it up. You need the piano to sound really good as you sing.

If you choose to mark the chords on the original or to create a lead sheet, which would have just the melody and chords, make sure that you have an accompanist read from your copy before the audition. She may find some spots that you overlooked. Fixing it beforehand can save you plenty of heartache.

✔ **Hiring someone to transpose an entire song is expensive.** Transposing means the person has to copy the music by hand or with their computer program into another key, which can be time consuming and costly. You can expect to pay way more to have a song transposed than what it would cost you to purchase one in the right key for you. A song in sheet music that costs you less than $10 may cost well over $50 to transpose.

✔ **Make sure that you have an accompanist read the transposed copy of your music before the audition.** Don't assume that the person who transposed it didn't make any mistakes. It won't take long for someone to play through it, and then you'll know exactly how it sounds in the new key and if this key really does fit your voice.

Making a 16-bar cut

In the beginning of your audition quest, you may not be given the opportunity to sing your entire song. So for each song that you choose to sing at your audition, know 16 bars or 8 bars in advance and have it prepared. (Still, knowing the entire song is best, just in case you're asked to sing it. Many local community auditions, for example, may allow you to sing the whole song. That's great for you, but even in these situations, be prepared with a cut just in case they start to run late.)

A *bar* or *measure* is what's between the bar lines. Notice the vertical line going down through the five lines on the musical staff. That's a bar line and what's in between two bar lines is a *measure* (which is also known as a *bar*).

When you cut the song, you can count out the measures or assume that you have about 30 seconds to sing. That's a short amount of time, so make the most of it. When deciding on the 16 bars, keep these points in mind:

- ✔ The 16 bars (or 16 measures) need a sense of completion. The cut should make sense lyrically, and the music should have a sense of completion.

- ✔ When counting out the bars, the introduction before you sing doesn't count. The biggest mistake is assuming that you can start at the beginning and just go until the end. You're going to be cut off and that cutoff may happen right before the best part of the song.

- ✔ It's difficult to choose which section to sing in the heat of the moment. Making the decision before the audition gives you time to think about the cut, practice the cut to make sure you really get to say something, practice hearing the note, and then starting on that phrase.

- ✔ Choose a section that really shows off your vocal range and your acting abilities.

Marking the music

As you rehearse and prepare your music, highlight whatever an accompanist may find tricky in the song. If you're taking it to a pianist to play it for you, ask her to mark it. Assuming that you're on your own and have seen some of the directional markings in Chapter 18 and feel confident that you can find them yourself, use a highlighter and highlight the following:

- ✔ **Directional symbols,** such as a repeat sign, DS al Coda, or a double bar. (See Chapter 18 for an explanation of these markings.) Highlight them so the accompanist can see them ahead of time. You can also point out the marking, so she knows how to map out the page turns.

- ✔ **Tempo changes** that are important and that may not be well marked in the music. You can give them your starting tempo, but any changes need to be marked so they can easily follow along.

- ✔ **Places where you ad-lib what's on the page.** If you're singing a section very freely, mark it so the accompanist can follow you or create chords to support you while you ad-lib.

Preparing your book

Preparing music for auditions is a tricky game. Keep searching for songs to fill in those repertoire gaps. The biggest rule of all is that whatever is in your notebook or in your bag is fair game at the audition. They'll most likely ask you what you would like to sing first. If you sing your most favorite song and they ask to hear something else, be sure an unprepared song is not in your notebook of audition songs. You'll be giving your notebook to the audition pianist to play from and he may flip through your notebook and suggest one of those unprepared songs as you're handing out your resume or talking to the other people in the room. You don't want to have to say it's not ready. Keep all your songs that are ready in one notebook and the songs that are works in progress in another. To prepare your songs for your audition notebook, follow these guidelines:

- **Photocopy the song and tape it so it stands up easily.** Taking songs to an audition requires a bit of preparation. As long as you own the original, it's legal for you to make a photocopy to sing from at an audition. After you make the copy, tape the pages like an accordion or put the music in nonglare see-through sheets. Some people like to tape the sheets onto file folders, so they stand up easily. That's a good system, but it's much harder to keep up with your songs and keep them in a logical order. If you're taping the song to stand up on the piano, alternate the tape so the first page is taped on the front of the sheets between the pages and the second page is taped from behind. Then folding the sheets like a book is easier.

- **Punch holes in the music and insert in a three-ring notebook.** Put the sheets back to back just like they appear in a book and punch the holes. By turning the page, the accompanist should see two new pages of music just like a book. Tape the sheets together on the top and bottom right corners.

- **Original scores written by hand are hard to read.** When the earlier musical theater shows were written, the composer wrote out the music by hand. Older copies of original scores done by hand are hard to read. If you have to err on the safe side, I suggest that you find a copy of the music that's a little easier to read.

- **Bring a full copy of the song and not a copy from a fake book.** Newer books that offer 1,000 songs in one book are usually fake books. A *fake book* has only the words, the chord symbols, and the melody line. The accompaniment part isn't shown. Don't take a fake book copy to an audition. You may be lucky and get an accompanist who reads well and can make up the accompaniment part. If it's not your lucky day, however, you may be surprised at what the accompanist comes up with. Be safe; find a copy of the song that includes the piano part.

In addition to your collection of songs for audition purposes, keep a journal or notebook of auditions. You can keep a record of what you sang, who was at the audition, where the audition was held, who helped you get the audition, what kind of audition it, did you get a callback or a job offer, any comments that were made during the interview, and the names of the people you met. It's surprising how fast you can forget these details. When you go back to sing for the same company at a later date, you want to refresh yourself on what changes they asked you to make to your song to see if you're easy to direct, who was there so you can say hello to them, which songs they liked or didn't like, so you can choose something else if necessary, and any other information that may improve this audition.

Taking your songs to an accompanist

Hearing a pianist play your song before you take it to an audition is very important. If you don't read music, this is even more important. You may erroneously assume that your song is the exact same version that you heard on the radio, so it'll come as quite a shock when you hear your song for the first time at an audition and have no earthly idea what those sounds are. Remember that publishing companies usually publish songs in keys that are easy to play. If the singer on the radio sings the song in a really hard key with many *accidentals* (sharp, flat, or natural signs placed before individual notes to indicate that they're a half-step higher or lower), the publishing company may change the key to make it more accessible to beginning pianists.

By having a pianist read your music for you before an audition, you get an opportunity to check the key to make sure it's exactly in the range where you want to sing. The following sections explain what an accompanist can do for you.

Taking the lead

Your voice teacher may have been playing the song for you, and you may be comfortable with that version. By taking it to someone else to read it for you, though, you have to be much more specific when you lead.

A good pianist waits to hear the consonant on the downbeat before playing the chord. If you wait to hear the chord from the pianist, you may be waiting a long time. You may get an audition pianist that wants to lead you but that usually happens because you're not leading, or they feel like you're in trouble. Sometimes, the pianist speeds up if they hear you struggling to maintain the longer phrases. By speeding up, they assume that you won't struggle so much with maintaining airflow. You have to be confident enough to lead and know that when you lead, they follow.

The speed that you take your first breath also indicates your tempo. If you take a quick breath, they assume that the song is going to move out. If the breath is slow and deliberate, they can assume that the piece is going to move slowly.

Getting help with musical notation

He can also check the cuts you made or new directional markings you inserted. If he has trouble following the markings, ask him how to write it out to make it clear to someone who's never seen the song before.

If you have changed the key and put new chord symbols over the line to indicate the new sequence of chords, make sure the pianist checks these out for you. One tiny little error can lead you to the wrong high note at the end.

You may also want to ask the pianist to help you mark the song to make your needs clear. If you want to slow down at the end or get louder in one section, ask him to help you mark the piece so any accompanist can read ahead and see those changes coming. If your tempo is really important, you may want to ask the pianist to write in a metronome marking to indicate exactly the speed you would like to sing. (See Chapter 10 for more on metronomes.) The audition pianist won't have a metronome on the piano, but they can see the marking and estimate the tempo that you desire.

What do you wear?

At your audition, remember that they're looking at you from the minute you walk in the door and not just when you sing. You want to show your body and look great in your outfit. Think about what the character looks like. You want to suggest the character but not dress exactly like the character.

Also remember that you may not be cast the first time you audition, but you need to make a good impression. Sometimes, directors ask you back to audition again to make sure that you're outstanding every time you audition and not just on a good day. Though your mother may not like it, wear the same outfit for the callback. Check out *Breaking Into Acting For Dummies* by Larry Garrison and Wallace Wang (Wiley Publishing, Inc.) for more advice on your wardrobe.

What Goes On at an Audition?

After you make it through the doors, you may be *typed*. Typing at a musical theater audition doesn't mean that your fingertips fly across a keyboard. *Typing* refers to whether you're the right *type* for the role. The *casting panel* (usually made up of the casting director, director, musical director, and choreographer) look at you to determine if you're physically right for the role. If you physically fit what they're looking for, you get to stay at the audition and sing and dance the night away.

Who'll be there

For every musical, a producer, musical director, stage manager, choreographer, director, casting director, and general manager run the show. These are theatre bosses who hold the line. You may see any or all of them at your audition.

- **Producer:** The person with the money or the one who finds it, so the show can go on.
- **General manager:** The budget man who keeps up with how the money is spent.
- **Casting director:** Calls in the actors or talks with their agents to audition for the parts in the show.
- **Director:** Guide and traffic cop for all the actors on the stage.
- **Musical director:** Responsible for the quality of the music in the production. That may involve everything from working on arrangements for specific numbers to playing the piano at performances. When the musical director isn't available, the rehearsal pianist is called in.
- **Choreographer:** Creates the staging or the directions of who moves when and where during the show.
- **Conductor:** Waves her arms in time to the music, so the musicians in the orchestra pit and singers on stage can follow along.
- **Stage manager:** Keeps everybody and everything in order.

Be nice to everyone at an audition. You never know whom you're talking to. That person may be the director's assistant or they may end up directing the next show you audition for.

Working with the audition pianist

The audition pianist can be your friend or foe based on how you behave. Most of the time, the pianist who is at the audition is a really swell person who plays like a dream.

A few simple actions that seem harmless to you can really set an accompanist off. Please allow me to share a few tips as follows:

- Never snap your fingers to give the accompanist the tempo. It may be an easy way to describe your tempo, but many accompanists take offense to it.
- Smile and address the pianist with respect when you give them your tempo or point out the roadmap in your song. Briefly, but very nicely, describe what you have highlighted or any tough spots.

✔ Explain how you plan to indicate that you're ready to begin. You can nod your head or look up to let him know that you're ready to begin.

✔ You can hope that the audition pianist can transpose at sight, but you can't assume. Feel free to ask if they can transpose, but if they hesitate or say no, choose something else to sing.

✔ Please don't try to shake hands with the audition pianist even if you think it's good manners to shake someone's hand. Shaking hands translates to squeezing someone's hands, no matter how gently. The pianist doesn't want swollen fingers after shaking hundreds of hands during a long audition day.

Reading music on the page and transposing at sight are two different skills. Unless someone is used to transposing a song, it may not be his strongest skill. You may also hear more wrong notes as they attempt to read it in your favorite key. Be safe and get the song transposed and written out well in advance of your audition. Better yet, choose a song that's already in the key you can sing well. See the "Adjusting the key if you need to" section, earlier in this chapter, for details on choosing a song in the right key.

✔ Thank the pianist just before you leave. You may not know the pianist personally and may assume that he's just a really cool person who only plays the piano. The truth may be that the pianist is the musical director. Be sure to read the suggestions on how to prepare your music for the audition, so the pianist enjoys meeting you and playing your song.

At an audition, you won't get to use a body microphone. You may get a body microphone during the show if it's in a big hall and the company has some money. However, at the audition you need to show that you can project your voice. Work on creating a resonant sound and use that to project your sound at the audition. Chapters 11 through 13 contain information about projecting sound in the specific areas of your range.

When do I need an agent?

You need an agent when you have enough performing experience that you need to get into the bigger, more prominent auditions. An agent helps you get performing jobs, but the agent doesn't do all the work. The agent can only get you the audition. You have to be good enough to land the gig. An agent usually takes 10 percent of your performance income whether they get you the gig or not. If you think you might be interested in an agent, start reading the articles in the trade paper *Backstage* about agents and managers to see if that kind of business relationship is what you're looking for. For more detailed information about agents, managers, freelancing, auditions, and contracts, pick up a copy of *Breaking into Acting For Dummies* by Larry Garrison and Wallace Wang (Wiley).

Finding the right auditions

For those of you who want to explore some auditions in cities with more theaters and more competition at the auditions, read this information just to know what you might encounter at an audition and what are some common types of auditions. An *open call* audition means that the theatre has no agreement with the union, and anyone with or without experience can show up. That means that there may be many people who also read about the audition in the local paper, or saw the ad in a trade paper like *Backstage*.

In New York City, if the audition is supposed to begin at 9 a.m., the line to sign up for an audition slot could be snaked around the block before 7 a.m. For the really exciting auditions, the line can begin the day before with people sleeping on the sidewalk just for a chance to be seen and heard. Persistence is key.

Auditions for members of the actors union, Actors Equity, aren't the same as open call auditions for the general public. Union auditions are called Eligible Principal Audition (EPA) and Equity Chorus Calls. The EPA is an audition to cast the principal or leading roles in an Equity show, and the chorus call is to cast members for the chorus. You can find information about the union at the Actors Equity Web site (www.actorsequity.org/home.html). At this site, you can find information about contracts, membership, auditions both principal and chorus, how an equity member sets up an audition, and you can find links to other sites for other similar unions.

Before you pack your bags and hop on the bus to go to the audition, check out the following list to be sure you're prepared.

- ✔ **Read the trade paper *Backstage* for at least one year** before hopping on the train. You want some time to get used to the audition listings and to prepare your *audition book* (a notebook that has photocopies of all the songs you're prepared to sing for auditions) for any type of show. As you're preparing, set some goals — both short term and long term — so you have a plan of action.

- ✔ **Get that resume ready.** For musical theater auditions, you don't have to pick an exact *fach* or voice category, such as baritone, bass, or tenor, like the classical singers do. Be specific about your voice, but casting directors want to know if you're versatile for singing in the theater, not the opera house. List your important credits, such as theatre credits divided into regional, stock, tours, and so on, but don't try to list them all. Assume someone will only spend about 30 seconds looking at your resume or give it a quick scan. If you list every single thing you've done, they may miss the credits you really want them to see. You also want your resume to be only one page. Don't fib or stretch the truth on special skills. You can check out *Breaking Into Acting For Dummies* by Larry Garrison and Wallace Wang (Wiley) for more information about performance resumes and headshots.

- ✔ **Get your headshot ready.** Do your homework to make your package really catch the eye. Your photo needs to look like you at the audition. Staple the headshot and resume together with the staples facing the resume side.

- ✔ **Pick up audition skills** from classes or advice from teachers.

- ✔ **Prepare your speaking voice** for the variety of demands in roles onstage and your off-stage role in life. See Chapter 14 for help with your speaking voice.

Directing your focus

At an audition, your choices of where to direct your eyes are similar to where you direct your eyes if you're just telling a story. The only decision you have to make is whether to look at the person you're singing to or not. Most of the time the answer to that question is to *not* look at them. However, if you have a fun song that has spunk and character, then do look at them. The songs that are addressing your invisible scene partner are best directed to that imaginary partner on the wall directly in front of you.

Assuming that the casting director for whom you're auditioning is sitting near the middle of one wall in the audition room, focus your eyes a few feet on either side of him (or them if there's more than one person). Most acting teachers tell you to keep your eyes centered on the wall, so you don't have any odd body angles in an audition. That's really good advice in the beginning of your training. As you get more accustomed to different kinds of focus and multitasking, you can widen your focus.

Good luck at your audition. Remember that the word *no* is just a small little word. Keep honing your technique as a performer and keep auditioning. It may take a while to find your niche in the performance world, but don't give up. Check out Chapter 17 on beginning a new song, Chapter 19 on dramatizing the lyrics, Chapter 16 to drill your song, and Chapter 15 if you want to find a teacher or coach to help you in your quest.

Part V
The Part of Tens

"Very nice audition, Vince. Let's talk a minute about that little thing you do at the end with the microphone."

In this part . . .

Famous performers don't always have great technique, but the ten singers in Chapter 22 do. Check
it out to see if the hot singers you like are listed. Those
questions that you wanted to ask about singing but just
didn't know who to ask are probably in Chapter 23. In this
chapter, I answer ten of the most frequently asked questions about singing. See if you know the answers. Then if
you'd like to find out about vocal health, see Chapter 24.

Chapter 22

Ten Performers with Good Technique

In This Chapter
▶ Finding out who has versatility and range
▶ Meeting a few of my favorites

Who are the singers with good technique? You can find some great performers with great vocal technique and some great performers that are still working on their technique. Check out this list of ten singers to see if I list your favorite singer. The list includes pop/rock, country, musical theater, and classical music performers.

Although the number of singers with great vocal technique in this list is limited to ten, you can be sure that the actual number of wonderful singers with great technique is much higher. The eclectic nature of this list just goes to prove that good technique crosses the line of style, gender, age, race, and song.

Eileen Farrell

The American dramatic soprano, Eileen Farrell (1920–2002), was known for her varied style but consistent technique — no matter what the style. You can check out her jazz albums to hear her belting and crooning and then listen to her sing the roles of some operatic heroines. Signature roles include Gioconda in *La Gioconda,* Maddelena in *Andrea Chenier,* Leonora in both *La Forza del Destino* and *Il Trovatore.*

Frederica von Stade

A lyric mezzo, American Frederica von Stade, has the range of a soprano, the light quality of a lyric voice, the flexibility of a coloratura, and the most amazing ability to mesmerize an audience. Her voice fills the air with electricity, and her acting is compelling, whether she's singing an aria in a recital or leaning against a post in the opera. Signature roles include Cherubino from *Le Nozze di Figaro,* Chérubin in *Chérubin* by Massenet, Mélisande in *Pelléas et Mélisande* by Debussy, Charlotte in *Werther* by Massenet, Cenerentola in *La Cenerentola* by Rossini, and cross-over albums, such as *On the Town, Showboat,* and *The Sound of Music.* More information is available online at www.fredericavonstade.com.

Luciano Pavarotti

Italian tenor, Luciano Pavarotti, is known worldwide as one of The Three Tenors. His remarkable technique and beautiful tone are two of his most well-known trademarks. He's one of those tenors that can carry a full sound up to the highest notes with ease. (If it were only as easy as he makes it sound.) His singing debut was in 1961, and his recordings often fill half the shelf in the record store. You can find out more about Pavarotti online at www.lucianopavarotti.com.

Audra McDonald

Soprano Audra McDonald was classically trained at Juilliard, but she's made a name for herself in the musical theater world. Her ability to sing long lines contrasts her easy agility. By choosing to sing musical theater, she has found a perfect outlet for her easy style changes while maintaining her solid technique. Signature roles include Sharon in *Master Class,* Carrie in *Carousel* (cast recording), Sarah in *Ragtime* (cast recording), and Marie in *Marie Christine* (cast recording). You can find out more about her online at www.audra-mcdonald.com.

Brian Stokes Mitchell

Brian Stokes Mitchell is making a huge name for himself on Broadway. His rich baritone voice carries well within a theater and easily moves from high to low. His control over his range, breath, and articulation is just as inviting as his handsome command of his characters. Signature roles include Fred in *Kiss Me Kate,* Coalhouse in *Ragtime,* Valentin in *Kiss of the Spider Woman,* and Don Quixote in *Man of La Mancha.* Stokes' Web site is www.brianstokes.com.

Karen Carpenter

Karen Carpenter (1950–1983), my all-time favorite female singer, studied music along with her brother Richard in college at Cal State. They went on to earn 11 gold albums and 10 gold singles in their bright career in the 1980s. The world of music suffered a great loss when she died from the complications of anorexia. Her tone was rich, rounded, and spoke volumes about the text just by the inflection of her words and the line she spun with the melody. Signature songs include "Close to You," "Rainy Days and Mondays," "Top of the World," and "We've Only Just Begun."

Elvis Presley

Elvis Presley (1935–1977), the King of Rock and Roll and my favorite male singer, brought simple songs dancing off the page. His voice moved easily from high to low. Throughout his movie and singing career, he made a huge success out of being a sexy singer. His career spanned 33 movies and 140 albums and singles, and his music crossed the lines between gospel and rock and roll with a blues feeling. Growing up in Memphis, he was surrounded by famous gospel and blues singers who made a lasting impression on the young singer. Signature songs include "Love Me Tender," "Jailhouse Rock," "Blue Christmas," and "Viva Las Vegas." Go online to www.elvis.com to find out more about him.

Luther Vandross

A successful R&B/Pop singer, tenor Luther Vandross, has proved that good technique enhances a long singing career. He moves easily throughout his range, and his tone is crystal clear by choice or scratchy and emotional. The vast amount of information that's available about him on his Web site (www.luthervandross.com) proves that he's a powerful musical force in the entertainment world. His signature hits include "Here and Now," "Power of Love," and his duet with Mariah Carey, "Endless Love."

LeAnn Rimes

A singer from the time she could walk, LeAnn Rimes, has been showing off her vocal chops anywhere that she can perform. Her early recordings reveal her smooth country style, but her later recordings sound more and more like pop. She has agility, flexibility, a high belt, and intentionally flips registers on ascending intervals in her country songs. She uses riffs, which are described in Chapter 12, in her pop songs. Signature songs include "How Do I Live" and "Blue."

Garth Brooks

What a handsome splash tenor Garth Brooks has made in the world of country music. He not only has good technique but also maintains that technique solidly with each passing year. His power ballads have some pop flavor, and his rodeo songs are a country mix of accordions and humor. Majoring in advertising at Oklahoma State University probably hasn't hurt his successful career. His signature songs include "The Thunder Rolls," "Unanswered Prayers," "The Dance," and humorous rounds, such as "Friends in Low Places." More information is available about him online at www.garthbrooks.com.

Chapter 23

Ten FAQ about Singing

In This Chapter

▶ Belting out a tune even if you're a soprano

▶ Eating and drinking before you sing

*I*t's not a stupid question if you don't know the answer. Most new singers ask the same questions, so see the answers to ten Frequently Asked Questions (FAQ) about singing that follow in this chapter. Read through the following questions and answers to help with your singing.

Is belting bad?

No, belting isn't bad for you if you do it right, and sopranos can certainly belt. In fact, sopranos often have an easier time with belting than mezzos. Belting is bad for you if you use a heavy chest voice to create the belt sound. Check out Chapter 14 for information about working with your speaking voice and creating a healthy belt sound. You can also hear a singer on the CD demonstrate belting for you.

Why doesn't my voice work sometimes?

Plenty of things can cause your voice to not work right. Thinking too much about how you sound as you sing may make you nervous and your voice may not sound your best. Check out Chapter 20 for some help with performance anxiety or Chapter 19 for help with acting and singing. Not getting enough sleep can cause your voice to feel sluggish and not respond as easily as it normally does. Singing too much the day before or the day of an audition can cause your voice to get tired. The singing muscles are like other muscles in your body. Working out is just fine, but they need a rest after the workout. Emotions also affect your singing voice. Crying can make the cords swell and feel puffy, too. So, wait until after the performance to watch that sad movie.

What's the difference between a coach, voice teacher, and an accompanist?

A *coach* is someone who plays the piano well and can help you or give you tips on your singing. During a work session with a coach, you may practice hearing the piano cue for your entrances in your song, work on the pronunciation of the words, get tips on how to sing with the correct style, and find good places to breathe within the text. A coach helps with some basic tips on technique and supports the work of your voice teacher.

A *pianist* or *accompanist* is someone who plays the piano for you to practice singing but doesn't offer advice. An accompanist usually charges less than a coach does, because their role isn't as demanding.

The *voice teacher* is the technique specialist. Although the coach may have knowledge of technique, the voice teacher should be the pro and expert. The voice teacher may not play the piano so well but should make up for it in knowledge and advice on your technique. In your voice lesson, you can expect to work at least half of the session on technique and the other half applying that technique to repertoire. For more information about finding a voice teacher and what to expect in lessons, check out Chapter 15.

If my voice is scratchy, do I have nodes?

It takes quite a bit of abuse to get nodes. You can't get nodes from yelling for your favorite team for only one day. The cords may swell or be mad at you the next day, but you have to abuse your voice for a longer period to develop nodes. Just remember that nodes are like calluses. If you don't rub the cords the wrong way, you won't have the problem. If the scratchy sounds continue, try vocalizing high in your range. Nodes usually affect the higher part of your voice. If the sound is husky only in the middle part of your voice, you probably have another kind of swelling other than nodes. Check out Chapter 24 for more information on vocal health and Chapter 14 for help with your speaking voice.

Do I have to be fat to have a big voice?

Nope. Your voice's size isn't related to your waistline's size. If that were true, then all great singers would be big and every large person would be a great singer. Actually, having extra weight around the middle makes it harder to move your body to breathe. If you're used to that movement, then it's not a problem. The size of your throat and head make a bigger difference in your voice than your girth.

What's the best singing method?

The best singing method is the one that works best for you. You can find singers and teachers who are quick to recommend their method, claiming, "It's the best." As long as the method introduces you to breath and breath management, tone and resonance, articulation that allows you to be understood without causing tension, and the general principles of good singing, then it's a good method. My method of teaching is a combination of all the teachers that I've studied with. You may hear singers talking about the "bel canto" method of singing. *Bel canto* literally means *beautiful singing* in Italian and implies the use of smooth, open tones. This method of singing and teaching began early in the 18th century. Today, *bel canto* implies beautiful singing in a more classical style.

Do I have to speak Italian to sing well?

No. Speaking Italian never hurt anyone, so it can only enhance your singing. However, Italians aren't the only people making beautiful sounds in the concert halls. Singers of every nationality can sing well. Enjoy your native tongue, whatever it is, and sing your little heart out.

Can I have a few drinks before the performance to calm my nerves?

Drinking alcohol and singing isn't a great combination. You can read in Chapter 24 about how alcohol dehydrates you. Alcohol also slows down your reactions. You want a clear head for singing and performing. Chapter 20 has some tips for dealing with performance anxiety. You may find those tips so helpful that you can save the drink for the celebration party after the performance.

Why can't I eat ice cream before I sing?

Ice cream causes phlegm and mucus to build up. That mucus is thick and makes you want to clear your throat too much. Unless dairy products don't bother you, I suggest that you avoid ice cream and any other dairy product before singing. Make the mad dash to the ice cream store after practicing. What should you eat or drink? Water is a safe bet. Some singers say they don't like cold water right before they sing. You can experiment with it to see if it makes your voice feel different. Other singers may have told you to drink water with lemon or fruit juice to clean out your throat. It won't do any harm if you want to try it, but I don't find it beneficial. Experiment with any drinks before the day of a performance, so you know exactly how your throat feels afterward.

Eating a couple of hours before a performance gives your body a chance to digest the food and gives you some energy for the performance. Some people like to sing on a full stomach, but you need to experiment singing right after eating to know if it affects you. On the day of a performance, eat familiar foods. You don't want any surprise digestive problems during the show.

What do I do if my voice is husky, breathy, strident, muffled, and hooty?

The first thing that you can do is read about *onset of tone* in Chapter 6. If after working on onset of tone, your voice still isn't clear, take some time to read about healthy speaking habits in Chapter 14. If you're abusing your speaking voice, you can also be making your singing voice work much harder to make gorgeous sounds. Husky tones are usually from some sort of abuse of the singing voice or the speaking voice. Medications may cause your throat to be dry and scratchy. You can read Chapter 24 for more information about medications and their effect on the singing voice. Breathy tones are usually the result of the cords not closing firmly, allowing too much air to escape. Strident tones are usually from too much physical pressure or not enough balance of sound in the resonators. Try the exercises in Chapters 3 and 6 for opening the throat to feel the release of the added physical pressure. Muffled or hooty tones are usually from not making specific vowels or allowing the resonance to live too far in the back of your throat. Read Chapter 8 on vowels and the shape of vowels and then read Chapter 4 and 6 for some help with tone.

Chapter 24

Ten Tips to Maintaining Vocal Health

In This Chapter

▶ Speaking in a way that's good for your voice

▶ Figuring out how to nourish your voice

▶ Getting the lowdown on vocal problems

*L*ong-term *vocal abuse* — any activity that causes strain on your voice — can change the quality of your singing. And your voice may not always be able to repair itself. Although most singers can minimize long-term problems with vocal rest, you should avoid continued vocal abuse. Make your vocal health a priority now.

Regardless of whether you sing in your church choir or tour endlessly, maintaining healthy habits is essential to maintaining your vocal health.

Figuring Out Everyday Abuses

The following list is by no means all-inclusive. You may find other factors that greatly affect your vocal health over a period of time. What's important is that you recognize problems and keep them at bay before a big performance. But keep these common everyday factors in mind:

✔ **Alcohol:** Alcohol dilates blood vessels in your body, which is not such a good thing for your vocal cords if you plan to sing. When the blood vessels dilate, the blood thins and comes to the surface, which makes you more susceptible to a hemorrhage on your vocal cords. Limit your intake of alcohol to those days that you don't have to practice or perform and drink plenty of water on those days that you do choose to drink, because alcohol dehydrates you.

✔ **Cigarette smoke:** The smoke often causes inflammation of the tissues in the throat and that makes it more difficult to sing. Avoid smoking and secondhand smoke at all times. You especially want to avoid smoke for several days before a lesson or performance.

✔ **Clearing your throat:** If you're a habitual throat clearer, now is the time to break that habit and find out the root of the problem. Excessive throat clearing can be caused by mucus buildup from postnasal drip or acid reflux. Swallow instead of clearing your throat and talk with your doctor about the cause. For many singers, throat clearing is just an unconscious habit that results from trying to clear the vocal cords for singing. Singing with a little mucus won't hurt.

✔ **Food:** Certain foods can irritate your voice. Dairy products often cause mucus to build up, which causes you to clear your throat frequently. Some people claim that spicy foods don't enhance their singing. Pay attention to how your body reacts to certain foods, so you know what to avoid the day before or day of a big concert or performance.

✔ **Pollen or dust:** Sensitivities to allergens, such as pollen or dust, may cause the vocal folds and throat to swell. Ask your doctor for suggestions to help with allergy problems. In the meantime, take some basic precautions: Clean your house on a regular basis to prevent dust bunnies from collecting and bothering you; choose non-allergenic materials for your bed linens; use a vacuum cleaner that removes all of Fluffy and Fido's hair and avoid areas with large quantities of dust. Listen to the local weather report to find out the pollen count. Most areas have higher pollen counts in the early morning or early evening. If you limit outdoor activities to the middle of the day, you're less likely to encounter the highest levels of pollen.

✔ **Medications (such as antihistamines):** The problem with most over-the-counter drugs is that just about anything you can find to help you with the symptoms of a runny nose or watery eyes dries out your throat. If you need to take the medications, compensate by drinking more water, so you don't get dry when you sing. You may also want to avoid the medications on the days that you have to do plenty of singing. Look for more information about medications in the "Medicating a Sore Throat" section, later in the chapter.

Incorporating Healthy Speech into Your Singing

Your speaking voice directly affects your singing. By taking good care of your voice while speaking, you ensure better health for your singing voice. (Just in case you missed it, Chapter 14 tells you about the speaking voice.) Try making your speaking habits more healthy by

✔ Using full volume when you need to be heard (usually at sports events, parties, or clubs), but not screaming.

✔ Talking at a reasonable volume, not speaking loudly all the time.

✔ Noticing your articulation as you speak to prevent tension — not speaking with tension, such as jaw tension, tongue tension, or glottals.

✔ Applying your knowledge of breathing while talking on the phone and avoid talking on the phone until your voice hurts due to lack of breath support.

✔ Finding your optimum speaking pitch, rather than speaking on a pitch that's too low for you, which usually causes a grinding sound.

✔ Practicing the speaking exercises in Chapter 14 to work on your speaking habits.

Getting the Skinny on Weight

Though it may not be your personal issue, a body that is too lean may have trouble finding the stamina to sing and sustain the higher pitches. Make sure you're nourishing your body on a regular basis for stamina. Many singers wait until late in the day to eat, but your body needs something to get it started. Try to find a routine that enables you to get food in your body early in the day, so you aren't snacking well into the night when your body finally feels hungry.

Keeping Yourself Hydrated

Your body is 50 percent to 65 percent water. Your lungs depend on water to keep the tissue moving easily. Muscle tissue is made up of 75 percent water. So keeping your body well hydrated helps your singing voice work better.

Some people get bored just drinking water. You can balance out your hydration with other liquids as long as you realize that the sugar content in most drinks doesn't help your waistline and that caffeine actually dries you out. Because caffeine is a diuretic, which means that it makes your body get rid of water, you can't rely on that morning cup of coffee to keep your voice in good working order.

Getting Plenty of Shut-Eye

Not getting enough sleep doesn't give the tissue in your body — in your throat — time to heal. Depriving yourself of sleep only makes your voice feel sluggish and harder to sing at your best. You may survive on just a few hours sleep at night but is your voice also just surviving? You want the voice to *thrive* and not just survive. Try getting more sleep for a few nights and see if that makes a difference in your singing. Even one more hour can make quite a bit of difference for your tissues. You want to to recoup and regenerate during the night.

Those singers who dislike singing in the morning but who get stuck with that early morning audition need to make a game plan in advance. Get yourself to bed early for a few nights before the audition. I don't sleep as well the night before a big performance, but I compensate by sleeping plenty in the days before.

Making Sure You're Well-Nourished

You need to maintain a balanced diet — following guidelines of basic nutrition means getting a balanced amount of whole grains, fruits and vegetables, meats, and dairy products. Within this balanced diet, you find proper amounts of protein, carbohydrates, and fats. You may find that singing requires more energy, which means adding more protein to your diet to enhance your body's ability to sustain you through long rehearsals.

Also, if you aren't cooking in the kitchen with Julia Child, take some vitamins to make up for what you don't get from the drive-through window. You don't have to spend a fortune on vitamins but find a multivitamin that fits within your budget and fills in the nutritional gaps for the big essentials.

Preventing a Sore Throat or Infection

A few simple little remedies to keep on hand for those times when you feel that tickle coming on can make all the difference in the world. My favorite is a bottle of nasal saline spray, which is just salt and water. You can find this at your local drug store right next to all the other medicated nasal sprays. By spraying the salt water up into your nose, you can wash out the germs that are lingering around waiting for your immune system to get pooped, so they can attack. You may even feel that slight tickle when the drainage begins. By flushing your nasal passages, you can prevent the mucus from getting too thick and hopefully sidetrack those germs.

Or try gargling with warm salt water. Adding a few teaspoons of salt to a half cup of warm water and then gargling helps wash away any germs that can lodge in the back of your mouth. If you have frequent infections around your tonsils, you may find that saltwater is one of your best friends. Additionally, swishing that saltwater around in your mouth makes those painful little canker sores stop right in their tracks.

Medicating a Sore Throat

It's going to happen sometime, so you may as well know your options: You *are* going to catch that cold or sore throat and you have to know how to deal with it. Use this advice for when your throat feels scratchy:

- ✔ **Avoid most nose sprays.** Nasal sprays that contain antihistamines or decongestants are habit forming and can cause symptoms to worsen when you stop. These types of sprays should only be used in emergencies.

- ✔ **Drink plenty of water with your medications.** Most of the over-the-counter medications cause you to dry out. As long as you're prepared for that and compensate with extra fluids, you won't be shocked. Read about the lowdown on three common cold medications:

  - • **Antihistamines:** These medicines make the flood stop when your nose starts running. The antihistamine dries out your upper respiratory tract secretions and probably makes you sleepy to boot. Use an antihistamine to get the flooding in your nasal passages to stop but know that the dryness affects your singing. Keep up with your fluids to counteract.

  - • **Cough medicine:** Most dry out your voice. Your best bet is to find dextromethoraphan with guaifenesin. The guaifenesin is a mucolytic that keeps the mucus flowing. Take the cough medicine but keep drinking fluids.

  - • **Decongestants:** They open up your nose but dry out your throat. When you feel that stuffy nose, you reach for your decongestant, which opens up the nasal passages. Don't be fooled though; your decongestant dries you out. Keep the fluids incoming even with decongestants. They may be less drying than strong antihistamines, but the decongestant can produce a tremor, make you hyper, or leave you with insomnia. Don't experiment with any medications right before a performance or concert. Try out medications ahead of time to know how your body reacts.

- ✔ **Keep some nasal saline spray handy.** As your body tries to wash out the germs (runny nose), you can use a nasal saline solution to help fight against the infection. Using the spray when you're sick means you need to be careful to not get all your germs on the nozzle of the bottle and then put the lid on only to have the germs welcome you back the next time you use the spray. Place the nozzle close enough to your nose to get in a good squirt but not so close that the cold germs from your nose get on the nozzle. You may get a little on your face, but you'll just feel like you dunked your face in a tiny ocean.

- ✔ **Steam it up with a humidifier.** The winter heater may dry out your home, so keep the humidifier running, especially at night. Make sure you rinse it out daily to prevent growing a mold farm in the leftover water. The water condensation on the windows will dry, but feel free to turn off the humidifier if it looks like it's raining on the inside of the house.

- ✔ **Thin out your mucus.** If you suffer from postnasal drip, you probably have mucus that's too thick. Use the nasal saline solution or other medications from your doctor to help dry up the drip without drying out your throat.

- ✔ **Try throat lozenges without sugar.** Use throat lozenges to help with those dry coughs from a dry throat. Most lozenges are just comforting candy on the same aisle with the other cold medicines. You may find that drops without sugar prevent that sugary film from attaching to your teeth and having a big party on your expensive dental work. Beware of lozenges with menthol, which can dry out your throat.

Keeping Your Emotional Life in Check

If you're having trouble with your singing voice, the problem may be more than just technique. A good voice teacher can help you with styles of singing and technical feats that enable you to sing the high notes with ease. But if you're locked up inside, the voice can't respond. Think about those times that you have been afraid. It was difficult to speak. Your voice and body were reacting to internal stimuli. So keep in mind that your emotional health can affect your singing just as much as your physical health does.

Just in case you're wondering, crying isn't the best thing for your voice. The tension and pressure from the emotional release doesn't exactly make the cords happy little campers. Even though your life may be stressful and hectic, find ways to release aggression or pent-up emotions regularly, so you aren't holding them inside. Many times, singers have walked in the door for lessons and just couldn't sing due to emotional traumas hanging over their heads. By finding reliable friends or confidants, you have an outlet for those emotions, and you can use your singing as a means of expression. If you find yourself too tight and frustrated to sing, call someone for help, so you can keep singing through the good times and the bad.

Paying Your Voice Teacher

Okay, so it doesn't really affect your vocal health, but it's a great idea!

Chapter 25

Ten Tips for Performing Like a Pro

. . . .

In This Chapter

▶ Picking the right accompaniment, clothes, and mic

▶ Looking 'em straight in the eye: Stage presence

. . . .

Knowing how to behave when you're singing for an audience is important. Whether you're singing solo at Carnegie Hall, at a talent show in Tallahassee, Florida, with other performing artists in a local revival of *West Side Story,* at a Renaissance festival, or singing at a wedding ceremony, you want to get your ducks in a row and sing with confidence and gusto. Being a hick is okay, but be a hip hick with great stage presence. Read these tips for some answers to the why and how of performing. I start with first things first and then proceed on down to your last exit off the stage.

Rehearsing to Beat the Band

If you're a seasoned pro, you may not need to sing the music with an accompanist if you've been practicing on your own. However, I suggest at least one dress rehearsal and several more practice rehearsals before a performance. At the first couple of rehearsals, you can sing while reading from the music. For the last rehearsal and the dress rehearsal, sing the music from memory. Under pressure, it's shocking how quickly the words leave your short-term memory under pressure. By rehearsing the song from memory, you get even more opportunities to test out your wonderful technique while using your acting skills. At the dress rehearsal, you also want to practice walking on stage and off before your song, so you know how winded you are after climbing up the stairs for your entrance, walking around the stage, or down a long hallway.

Wearing the Right Duds

You may not have much choice in the matter of what you wear when you perform if you're singing in, say, a musical theater production. The director usually decides for you, and costumes are made to fit. But if you're a soloist at a wedding or maybe you just got a gig as a lead singer in a local jazz band, the outfit you wear for the performance can make or break your evening. Platform shoes may be *in,* but you can't feel a forward flow of energy. Spike heels are also tricky, because you may have a long walk across the stage or up to the choir loft. Practicing in the shoes that you plan on wearing for the performance gives you a sense of familiarity on the day of the concert. Noisy jewelry is going to distract your audience. It may look really cool at home with your new outfit, but if you can hear it when you move, leave it at home.

When you practice, wear the outfit that you plan to wear for the performance. If you can't move your arms or can't breathe well while wearing it, choose something else. Moving your body enough to breathe is important. The support hose that you plan to wear may also cut off your breath. Practice singing while wearing your pantyhose, so you can get used to moving against the elastic.

Short skirts may be sexy, but if the stage is much higher than the audience is, the audience may also get a glimpse of the intimate details of your undies. Unless you want someone to look up that sexy skirt, save it for the party after the concert. The same is true for clingy materials that may show every little blemish under bright lights and every little drop of sweat when the big moment arrives.

If you're performing in a concert or musical production that involves others, such as a chorale, musical drama, church choir, or local rock band, please don't use perfume, cologne, or personal product that gives off a fragrant odor. The smell of perfume causes some singers to have allergic reactions, such as sneezing, watery eyes, and itchy throats. Unless you're trying to sabotage the other singers, you may want to make friends instead of enemies and arrive fragrance free for the concert.

Finding Your Stance

After you know where to stand, you want to practice walking into place. This may sound silly but knowing how to walk across the stage and land in place isn't as easy as it sounds. Looking like a pro takes a bit of thought and practice. Even if you can't practice on the stage, choose a designated landing spot and practice walking across the room to find your position. You want to stop in place but also find your posture as you stop. Find your alignment (see Chapter 2), walk across the room, and maintain that posture. If you can maintain the alignment, you can sense your alignment as you walk across a stage.

Singing with a Piano, Organ, or Band

Singing with an organ is different than singing with a piano. The pipes that create the sound often aren't near the organ console whereas the sound from the piano comes out the back of the instrument. An organ may be harder to hear, depending on the stops that the organist is using. After singing with an organ a few times, you get used to the difference in the sound. Just expect to have to listen more, and you won't be surprised.

Singing with a band can be really cool, but the first time may be a bit confusing. If the speakers are pointed away from you and they usually are, you may have trouble hearing yourself. Ask if it's possible to have a speaker turned toward you. Remember that bands often play pretty loud, and turning the speaker toward yourself can be distracting if you have a huge wall of sound coming at you. If a specific instrument plays your melody line, you may have to get used to picking out that sound from all the other instruments.

You may find yourself bonding with the band when you sing a new song. Sometimes, instrumentalists in the band add solos as they play. Ask one of the band members to nod to you when it's time for you to come back in if the instrumentalists start adding extra measures. You can also ask the bandleader how you'll know when to come back in. It's also a good idea to take along your tape recorder to the rehearsal, so you can tape it. If you only get one shot at rehearsing with the band, you can always review your tape to get used to the timing. Sometimes, the band plays songs in different keys. If the song seems uncomfortable for you to sing, you may need it lowered or raised. If you do need it raised or lowered (in a different key), you want to know how to ask for the change. You can ask that the key be a few steps higher or just one step higher. The band members should know what you mean.

Making Your Entrance

As you enter the stage from a doorway or wing, look out at the audience and smile. You appear far more confident if you look straight at your audience as you walk across the stage. Practicing this is important. Your smile needs to look genuine even if you don't want to be out on stage. After you reach your position on the stage, pause in place to bow. Other performing venues may require you to be a bit more subdued. Singing for a church service would require a different approach than a pop concert. For a church service, you may not get applause as you stand up to sing. That doesn't mean the audience doesn't like you. Their focus isn't on your performance but rather on your message in your performance.

Roping in Your Audience

When singing in a concert, knowing whether to acknowledge your audience or stick to your own little world is tricky. Singers can't always sing intimate songs in an intimate locale, but you can imagine being in an intimate locale by imagining a fourth wall. The fourth wall just means that you pretend to be in a room alone with a wall in front of the audience. If your song is one that addresses a group, then use the audience as part of your story. Using the audience as part of your story means that they're part of the story within the time period of the song. If you think of them as contemporaries living in this year, you may get too familiar and less like your character.

To get a feel for whether to include the audience as part of your song, watch the seasoned pros. The casual atmosphere at a pop concert is different than the more formal atmosphere of a classical performance. Know your audience and behave appropriately. When in doubt, watch the others performing before you. Waving to your sister isn't okay when you're singing with the symphony in a big concert hall, but it may be just fine at the children's concert in the park. When in Rome . . .

Ignoring That Mosquito

In a normal concert, people cough, enter late, or leave right in the middle of your song. People in the audience don't think about how it distracts the performer. When you practice at home, you may want to intentionally stage some distractions. Ask a friend to drop a book or walk into the room as you're singing, so you can practice concentrating even while they're bopping around. What may distract you at the performance?

- ✔ **Lights:** You want the light to be on your face, so the audience can see you. That may seem blinding, but it also prevents you from seeing the audience, which is good. If you're nervous, you can pretend that no one is out there. Or you can visualize all the happy faces looking at you, delighted to see you. After you see the stage, you want to mark the spot where the light is the best on your face. Too far forward and the light may miss you entirely. You want them to see you if you got all dressed up for the show. The next thing that you want to do is practice walking into the light. I know it sounds silly, but you want to know where the best light is so you can make it look natural that you're suddenly brilliantly illuminated. Otherwise, you may be looking up to find the best light as the audience is waiting for you to sing. Ask a friend to come to the rehearsal to check the lighting for you.

- ✔ **Flashing photos:** It's better if your devoted fans or family wait until after you finish singing. If you see Aunt Shirlene lugging around the family camera, ask her to wait until the applause, because she may not know how distracting it can be. If you find that someone does start taking photos in the middle of your song, try to focus on an object in front of you so you aren't looking right into the flashing light. Blinking lights from camcorders can be mesmerizing or maddening.

- ✔ **Other performers:** In the wings, you may see many people milling around waiting for their entrance. Focus on your task and ignore them. You can ask them to not move around the sides while you sing, but you may just have to figure out how to ignore them if they forget.

Handling Those Hands

Putting your hands down at your sides is safest. It may not be the most interesting place for them, but you won't go too wrong by erring on the side of calm and still. If you choose to gesture, make it a complete gesture and make sure that your elbows move out away from your body. You may look like you're flipping burgers if you just move your hands and not your arms. Of course, if you're using a hand-held microphone, your gestures need to accommodate it. (See the "Using the Mic" section, coming up next in this chapter.)

Clasped in front of you is another option for your hands. Clasping your hands at your waistline is cool, but wringing your hands isn't. Being nervous at a performance is okay, but try not to show it. Don't let 'em see you sweat, as they say. Pretend that performing is the easiest thing in the world. Your hands can also rest on the piano if it's near enough to you and if the lid is closed. If the lid is open on a baby grand or grand piano, please don't put your hand on the lid or inside the lid. It makes your audience nervous to see your hand right where the lid may fall.

You don't want to put your hands behind you and wiggle them or clasp them right in front of your zipper. Little kids usually put their hands at their zipper when they have to go to the bathroom, so you don't want your audience to make that assumption. Little kids also put their hands behind them to pick their seat before the show.

Using the Mic

Microphones (*mics* for short; pronounced like the name *Mike*) are on a stand, hand held, hanging from the ceiling above the stage, sitting on the floor, or hooked onto your collar. Knowing how to handle this bundle of electronic wizardry takes a little practice. Ask if you can practice a bit with the microphone before the instruments start playing. That way, you can hear the difference between too close and too far. Consider the following list of microphones and how you're going to work with the particular type that you'll be using:

- ✔ **Body mic:** You may have seen body microphones on television: A microphone cord goes through your clothing, and a small box packs under your clothes or your belt. If you don't get a chance to use one before the show, just visualize the sensation of having the box attached to you, so you won't be shocked to feel something hanging on your back.

- ✔ **Floor level:** If the microphones are on the floor, remember that the audience is going to hear the sound of your walking across the stage.

- ✔ **Hand-held:** If you're using a hand-held mic, hold it far enough away from your mouth that you don't touch it with your lips but close enough that the sound of your voice reaches the microphone.

- ✔ **Stationary:** If your mic is on a stand, you can move around to adjust the sound. You can check out the stand before the concert. The height of most microphone stands can be adjusted. Look at the middle of the stand, and you'll probably see a ring that you can twist to adjust the height. If you have to turn on the microphone, practice walking out to the stand and finding the button, so you feel confident that you can turn it on with your hands shaking. It's okay if your hands shake. You just have to know that it's going to happen and adjust your movements to feel confident.

If you don't use a microphone, use your knowledge of resonance from Chapter 7 to help your voice carry over the instruments.

Taking Your Bow

First and foremost, the manner in which you take your bow depends on the concert. If you're a famous diva, you may do a curtsy, which is bending the knees and bowing down deeply. But I think it's better to wait on that until you arrive at one of the big opera houses. Until then, use the tried and true standard bow: Bend from the waist and bow your head to the audience.

✔ After you find your spot on the stage, stop in place and lean forward from the waist. You want your head down, looking at the floor momentarily. Otherwise, it looks like you're looking up to make sure that everyone is clapping.

✔ Your hands can be along the sides of your legs or clasped in front. Allow your hands to slide down your leg as you bend over. Remember that little rule about not putting your hands in front of your zipper if you choose to clasp them?

✔ Slowly count to two and raise back up. After you bow, acknowledge your accompanist. If the piece was a huge ensemble number, you may bow with your accompanist. You want to make that decision in advance and plan who bows when and after whom. Some people like to turn and extend their arm out to acknowledge the accompanist. If the pianist isn't leaving the stage with you, that's appropriate. But if you're a team, plan bows separately and then together.

Exiting the stage is also an art. After you finish singing and take your bow, head toward the exit. Look at your audience again and smile as you exit the stage. If the audience just loved what they heard, they may continue clapping, so you can take another bow. Wait for the peak of the applause and then go back onto the stage. If you had an accompanist playing for you, ask the accompanist to bow with you again or bow with you at the next curtain call.

Depending on the situation, you may want to prepare an encore. How will you know when to sing the encore? Finish your last number, hear the applause, exit the stage, return to the stage for your bow, exit the stage again, return to the stage and sing the encore, or return for another bow and then come back out to sing the encore. An encore is appropriate for a recital where you were the main attraction, or performance with a group such as the band or symphony. When you start to do more performing, you figure out when an encore is appropriate and what to prepare for the encore.

Part VI
Appendixes

The 5th Wave   By Rich Tennant

"Well, that's the last time we hire a high soprano to sing at the glass-blower's convention."

In this part . . .

You can pick from a list of songs that are arranged according to your voice type in Appendix A. I also let you know whether the song is upbeat or slow and moving before you even hear it.

Then don't forget to look through Appendix B to find out more about how you can use the super CD that comes with this book to flesh out the musical notation and some of the exercises that I recommend throughout the book.

Appendix A

Suggested Songs to Advance Your Singing Technique

*T*his list of suggested songs is designed to advance your singing technique. As you practice the exercises and techniques that you're reading about in the book, you can use this list of songs to practice and apply your new skills.

A beginner song is one with easy rhythms, narrow range, and melody that often moves in stepwise motion with the piano accompaniment, and at a comfortable tempo.

An intermediate song, however, has more difficult rhythm, wider range, and melody that skips in larger intervals, is somewhat independent of the piano accompaniment, and moves at a faster pace.

Belt songs are typically much more difficult due to the technique demands, big stories to tell, and difficult music. Work with the exercises in Chapter 14 until you feel confident that your belt is healthy.

I mark the tempo of the classical songs with *slow, medium,* and *fast.* The musical theatre songs are marked as a ballad or an up-tempo.

Classical: Ten songs for soprano

Five beginner-level songs for soprano

- ✔ "All Through The Night," an Old Welsh Air (slow)
- ✔ "Come Again, Sweet Love" by John Dowland (medium)
- ✔ "Now is the Month of Maying" by Thomas Morley (fast)
- ✔ "The Daisies" by Samuel Barber (medium)
- ✔ "Come Unto Him" from *The Messiah* by G.F. Handel (slow)

Five intermediate-level songs for soprano

- ✔ "Go 'Way From My Window" arr. by John Jacob Niles (slow)
- ✔ "I Attempt from Love's Sickness to Fly" by Henry Purcell (fast)
- ✔ "Come Ready and See Me" by Richard Hundley (medium)
- ✔ "Wiegenlied (Cradle Song)" by Johannes Brahms (slow)
- ✔ "Come and Trip It" from *L'Allegro* by G.F. Handel (medium)

Classical: Ten songs for mezzo

Five beginner-level songs for mezzo

- ✔ "Drink to Me Only With Thine Eyes" Old English Air (slow)
- ✔ "He Shall Feed His Flock Like a Shepherd" from *The Messiah* by G.F. Handel (slow)
- ✔ "The Black Dress" by John Jacob Niles (medium)
- ✔ "The Little Horses" by Aaron Copland (medium)
- ✔ "Tu lo sai (You know full well)" by Giuseppe Torelli (slow)

Five intermediate-level songs for mezzo

- ✔ "O rest in the Lord" from *Elija* by Felix Mendelssohn (slow)
- ✔ "Long Time Ago" by Aaron Copland (slow)
- ✔ "Dream Valley" by Roger Quilter (medium)
- ✔ "Wie Melodien zieht es (Like a Melody It Passes)" by Johannes Brahms (medium)
- ✔ "Le charme (The Charm)" by Ernest Chausson (medium)

Classical: Ten songs for tenor

Five beginner-level songs for tenor

- ✔ "Bright is the Ring of Words" by Ralph Vaughn Williams (medium)
- ✔ "Jeannie With The Light Brown Hair" by Stephen Foster (medium)
- ✔ "O Mistress Mine" by Roger Quilter (medium)
- ✔ "Where'er You Walk" from *Semele* by G.F. Handel (medium)
- ✔ "As Ever I Saw" by Peter Warlock (fast)

Five intermediate-level songs for tenor

- "Black is The Color of My True Love's Hair" by John Jacob Niles (medium)

- "Ave Maria" by Franz Schubert (slow)

- "Bist du bei mir (Be Thou With Me)" by J. S. Bach (medium)

- "Le Colibri (The Hummingbird)" by Ernest Chausson (slow)

- "Serenade" from *The Student Prince* by Sigmund Romberg (medium)

Classical: Ten songs for baritone or bass

Five beginner-level songs for baritone or bass

- "Passing By" by Edward Purcell (medium)

- "At The River" by Aaron Copland (slow)

- "When I Was One-and-Twenty" from *A Shropshire Lad* by George Butterworth (fast)

- "O Mistress Mine" by Roger Quilter (medium)

- "Caro mio ben (Dear One Believe)" by Giuseppe Giordani (slow)

Five intermediate-level songs for baritone or bass

- "O Ruddier Than the Cherry" from *Acis and Galatea* by G.F. Handel (fast)

- "Nina" by Giovanni Battista Pergolesi (slow)

- "The Twins" by Michael Head (fast)

- "Lydia" by Gabriel Fauré (slow)

- "An die Musik (To Music)" by Franz Schubert (medium)

Musical theater: Ten songs for soprano

Five beginner level songs for soprano

- "Till There Was You" from *The Music Man* by Meridith Willson (ballad)

- "How Lovely to Be A Woman" from *Bye Bye Birdie* by Charles Strouse and Lee Adams (ballad)

- "I Could Have Danced All Night" from *My Fair Lady* by Alan Jay Lerner and Frederick Loewe (up-tempo)

✔ "I'll Know" from *Guys and Dolls* by Frank Loesser (ballad)

✔ "Love, Look Away" from *Flower Drum Song* by Richard Rodgers and Oscar Hammerstein (ballad)

Five intermediate-level songs for soprano

✔ "One Kiss" from *The New Moon* by Sigmund Romberg and Oscar Hammerstein (ballad)

✔ "A Quiet Thing" from *Flora, The Red Menace* by John Kander and Fred Ebb (ballad)

✔ "One More Kiss" from *Follies* by Stephen Sondheim (ballad)

✔ "Show Me" from *My Fair Lady* by Alan Jay Lerner and Frederick Loewe (up-tempo)

✔ "Art is Calling for Me" from *The Enchantress* by Victor Herbert and Harry B. Smith (up-tempo)

Musical theater: Ten songs for mezzo

Five beginner-level songs for mezzo

✔ "My Romance" from *Jumbo* by Richard Rodgers and Lorenz Hart (ballad)

✔ "Mira" from *Carnival* by Bob Merrill (ballad)

✔ "Anyone Can Whistle" from *Anyone Can Whistle* by Stephen Sondheim (ballad)

✔ "Blue Skies" by Irving Berlin (ballad)

✔ "I Enjoy Being a Girl" from *Flower Drum Song* by Richard Rodgers and Oscar Hammerstein (up-tempo)

Five intermediate-level songs for mezzo

✔ "Much More" from *The Fantasticks* by Harvey Schmidt and Tom Jones (up-tempo)

✔ "Ribbons Down My Back" from *Hello Dolly* by Jerry Herman (ballad)

✔ "Climb Ev'ry Mountain" from *The Sound of Music* by Richard Rodgers and Oscar Hammerstein (ballad)

✔ "I Had Myself a True Love" from *St. Louis Woman* by Harold Arlen and Johnny Mercer (ballad)

✔ "You'll Never Walk Alone" from *Carousel* by Richard Rodgers and Oscar Hammerstein (ballad)

Musical theater: Ten belt songs for women

Five belt songs for soprano

- ✔ "You Can't Get a Man with A Gun" from *Annie Get Your Gun* by Irving Berlin (up-tempo)

- ✔ "If I Were a Bell" from *Guys and Dolls* by Frank Loesser (up-tempo)

- ✔ "I Cain't Say No" from *Oklahoma!* by Richard Rodgers and Oscar Hammerstein (uptempo)

- ✔ "As Long As He Needs Me" from *Oliver!* by Lionel Bart (ballad)

- ✔ "Rags" from *Rags* by Stephen Schwartz and Charles Strouse (up-tempo)

Five belt songs for mezzo

- ✔ "The Love of My Life" from *Brigadoon* by Alan Jay Lerner and Frederick Loewe (up-tempo)

- ✔ "Shy" from *Once Upon a Mattress* by Mary Rodgers and Marshall Barer (up-tempo)

- ✔ "Ooh, My Feet" from *The Most Happy Fella* by Frank Loesser (up-tempo)

- ✔ "On My Own" from *Les Misérables* by Alain Boublil, Claude-Michel Schönberg, and Herbert Kretzmer (ballad)

- ✔ "The Miller's Son" from *A Little Night Music* by Stephen Sondheim (up-tempo)

Musical theater: Ten songs for tenor

Five beginner-level songs for tenor

- ✔ "Ten Minutes Ago" from *Cinderella* by Richard Rodgers and Oscar Hammerstein (up-tempo)

- ✔ "On A Clear Day" from *On A Clear Day You Can See Forever* by Alan Jay Lerner and Burton Lane (ballad)

- ✔ "It Only Takes A Moment" from *Hello Dolly* by Jerry Herman (ballad)

- ✔ "The Only Home I Know" from *Shenandoah* by Gary Geld and Peter Udell (ballad)

- ✔ "He Loves and She Loves" from *Funny Face* by George and Ira Gershwin (ballad)

Five intermediate-level songs for tenor

- ✔ "Love, I Hear" from *A Funny Thing Happened on the Way to the Forum* by Stephen Sondheim (up-tempo)

- ✔ "Come to Me, Bend to Me" from *Brigadoon* by Alan Jay Lerner and Frederick Loewe (ballad)

- ✔ "We Kiss In A Shadow" from *The King and I* by Richard Rodgers and Oscar Hammerstein (ballad)

- ✔ "Maria" from *West Side Story* by Leonard Bernstein and Stephen Sondheim (ballad)

- ✔ "Race You To The Top of the Morning" from *The Secret Garden* by Lucy Simon and Marsha Norman (up-tempo)

Musical theater: Ten songs for baritone/tenor

Five beginner-level songs for baritone/tenor

- ✔ "Edelweiss" from *The Sound of Music* by Richard Rodgers and Oscar Hammerstein (ballad)

- ✔ "My Defenses Are Down" from *Annie Get Your Gun* by Irving Berlin (up-tempo)

- ✔ "Marianne" from *The Grand Tour* by Jerry Herman (ballad)

- ✔ "A Fellow Needs a Girl" from *Allegro* by Richard Rodgers and Oscar Hammerstein (ballad)

- ✔ "Try to Remember" from *The Fantasticks* by Harvey Schmidt and Tom Jones (ballad)

Five intermediate-level songs for baritone/tenor

- ✔ "Me and My Girl" from *Me and My Girl* by Noel Gay and Douglas Furber (up-tempo)

- ✔ "Almost Like Being In Love" from *Brigadoon* by Alan Jay Lerner and Frederick Loewe (uptempo)

- ✔ "Johanna" from *Sweeney Todd* by Stephen Sondheim (ballad)

- ✔ "All I Need Is The Girl" from *Gypsy* by Jule Styne and Stephen Sondheim (up-tempo)

- ✔ "Some Enchanted Evening" from *South Pacific* by Richard Rodgers and Oscar Hammerstein (ballad)

Musical theater: Ten belt songs for men

Five belt songs for tenor

- ✔ "Proud Lady" from *The Baker's Wife* by Stephen Schwartz (up-tempo)

- ✔ "Mister Cellophane" from *Chicago* by John Kander and Fred Ebb (up-tempo)

- ✔ "Corner of The Sky" from *Pippin* by Stephen Schwartz (up-tempo)

- ✔ "High Flying Adored" from *Evita* by Andrew Lloyd Webber and Tim Rice (ballad)

- ✔ "Steal with Style" from *The Robber Bridegroom* by Alfred Uhry and Robert Waldman (up-tempo)

Five belt songs for baritone/tenor

- ✔ "She Loves Me" from *She Loves Me* by Jerry Bock and Sheldon Harnick (up-tempo)

- ✔ "I, Don Quixote" from *Man of La Mancha* by Mitch Leigh and Joe Darion (up-tempo)

- ✔ "Everybody Says Don't" from *Anyone Can Whistle* by Stephen Sondheim (up-tempo)

- ✔ "I Don't Remember Christmas" from *Starting Here, Starting Now* by David Shire and Richard Maltby (up-tempo)

- ✔ "Where Is The Life That Late I Led?" from *Kiss Me, Kate* by Cole Porter (up-tempo)

Country: Ten songs for women

- ✔ "Can I See You Tonight?" by Deborah Allen and Rafe Vanhoy as sung by Tanya Tucker

- ✔ "Could I Have This Dance?" by Wayland Holyfield and Bob House as sung by Anne Murray

- ✔ "Daddy's Hands" by Holly Dunn as sung by Holly Dunn

- ✔ "I Can't Make You Love Me" by Mike Reid and Allen Shamblin

- ✔ "I Fall to Pieces" by Hank Cochran and Harlan Howard as sung by Patsy Cline

- ✔ "Paper Roses" by Janice Torre and Fred Spielman as sung by Marie Osmond

- "Pledging My Love" by Don Roby and Fats Washington as sung by Emmylou Harris

- "These Boots Are Made for Walkin'" by Lee Hazlewood as sung by Nancy Sinatra

- "When You Say Nothing At All" by Paul Overstreet and Don Schlitz as sung by Alison Krauss and Union Station

- "You Needed Me" by Randy Goodrum as sung by Anne Murray

Country: Ten songs for men

- "All The Gold in California" by Larry Gatlin as sung by The Gatlin Brothers

- "Are You Lonesome Tonight" by Roy Turk and Lou Handman as sung by Elvis Presley

- "By The Time I Get to Phoenix" by Jimmy Webb as sung by Glen Campbell

- "Can't Help Falling in Love" by George David Weiss, Hugo Peretti, and Luigi Creatore as sung by Elvis Presley

- "Forever And Ever, Amen" by Don Schlitz and Paul Overstreet as sung by Randy Travis

- "Kiss An Angel Good Morning" by Ben Peters as sung by Charley Pride

- "Look at Us" by Vince Gill and Max D. Barnes as sung by Vince Gill

- "Rocky Mountain High" by John Denver and Mike Taylor as sung by John Denver

- "Take Me Home Country Roads" by Bill Danoff, Taffy Danoff, and John Denver as sung by John Denver

- "What A Difference You've Made in My Life" by Archie P. Jordan as sung by Ronnie Milsap

Pop: Ten songs for women

- "Break It to Me Gently" by Diane Lampert and Joe Seneca as sung by Juice Newton

- "Breathe" by Holly Lamar and Stephanie Bentley as sung by Faith Hill

- "Breathe Again" by Babyface as sung by Toni Braxton

- ✔ "Colors of The Wind" from *Pocohontas* by Alan Menken and Stephen Schwartz as sung by Vanessa Williams
- ✔ "Don't Cry Out Loud" by Carole Bayer Sager and Peter Allen as sung by Melissa Manchester
- ✔ "The Rose" by Amanda McBroom as sung by Bette Midler
- ✔ "Torn Between Two Lovers" by Phillip Jarrell and Peter Yarrow as sung by Mary MacGregor
- ✔ "Touch Me in The Morning" by Ronald Miller and Michael Masser as sung by Diana Ross
- ✔ "We've Only Just Begun" by Roger Nichols and Paul Williams as sung by The Carpenters
- ✔ "When Will I Be Loved" by Phil Everly as sung by Linda Ronstadt

Pop: Ten songs for men

- ✔ "A Groovy Kind of Love" by Toni Wine and Carole Bayer Sager as sung by Phil Collins
- ✔ "All I Have to Do is Dream" by Boudleaux Bryant as sung by The Everly Brothers
- ✔ "Beyond the Sea" by Jack Lawrence and Charles Trenet as sung by Bobby Darin
- ✔ "Bye Bye, Love" by Felice Bryant and Boudleaux Bryant as sung by The Everly Brothers
- ✔ "For Once In My Life" by Ronald Miller and Orlando Murden as sung by Stevie Wonder
- ✔ "If" by David Gates as sung by Bread
- ✔ "You've Got A Friend" by Carole King as sung by James Taylor
- ✔ "Raindrops Keep Fallin' On My Head" by Hal David and Burt Bacharach as sung by B.J. Thomas
- ✔ "Stand By Me" by Ben E. King, Jerry Leiber and Mike Stoller as sung by Ben E. King
- ✔ "I Write The Songs" by Bruce Johnston as sung by Barry Manilow.

Appendix B

About the CD

. . . .

*A*ll the musical examples included in *Singing For Dummies* are recorded on the CD that comes with this book. On the CD, you can find 65 exercises to improve your singing along with the technical aspects, which I discuss in the chapters. In the chapters, next to the "On the CD" icon, you can find an explanation and helpful instructions for each of the tracks on the CD.

No singing experience is necessary to enjoy this book or the CD. Just follow the suggestions in the chapter to make consistent progress with your singing technique.

Finding the "On the CD" Icon

You can scan the text for the "On the CD" icon and follow along with the instructions for every exercise on the CD. Within the chapters, even more information is available about other efforts you can make to improve your singing, but the CD is always ready to sing along with. Use the CD as a cool tool to sing with at home, in your car, or wherever you find space to practice.

Each track begins with the piano playing the melody or musical pattern you see printed on the page. After the piano plays the pattern, you hear a singer demonstrate the sounds of the pattern. The first time through, listen to the singer and then sing by yourself on the following repetitions of the pattern. Each pattern is repeated several times in several different keys, so you can practice extending your range. You can hear both male and female singers throughout the CD. Feel free to sing along with any of the tracks. If the demonstration is a male voice, look at the text in the chapter that corresponds with that track for tips on how to make the pattern work for a female voice.

If some of the patterns are too high for you, read the text in the chapter for help on getting your voice ready for the higher notes or other technical skills being addressed. You can also find suggestions on dropping down and singing the pattern lower until you're ready for the higher notes.

As you listen to the CD, you may notice that the patterns gradually get harder. You don't have to sing every track today. You can work on the first few tracks until you're really comfortable applying all the suggestions in the text. When you're really cooking, move on to the next group of exercises. You can also check out Chapter 10 for help designing a practice routine. Skipping some of the information you already know is always an option. If you're an advanced singer with some experience, you may want to skip to some of the harder patterns in the latter chapters. Go for it! If you find yourself struggling with some of the later patterns, back up and work on some of the earlier patterns a little longer. The CD is designed to keep you singing and practicing for quite some time.

Finding the tracks on the CD

After inserting the CD, you can use the track skip control button on your CD player to move between tracks. The cue/review function is also a fast-forward or rewind feature, which allows you to fast forward through a specific track to get to just the right repetition of the patterns. You can find the exact timing of each track in the chart in this chapter.

You can use the track-skip control to move to the track you need to practice today. After you find the track, use your cheat sheet or practice chart to get yourself all ready and aligned for proper posture and breathing.

Be sure to keep the CD with the book. The suggestions and instructions in the chapters add even more helpful information to go with your listening pleasure as you sing along. The plastic envelope protects the CD surface to keep it in tip-top shape. Finding the CD in the book is also easier than hunting through your CD collection each time.

Tracks on the CD

You can see a list of tracks on the CD along with the timing of each track and figure number within the chapter. A figure number has two numbers; the first is the chapter number, which helps you locate the chapter that corresponds with the track. Some of the tracks don't have a musical example printed in the chapter. On these tracks, singers demonstrate specific skills that you can work within that chapter.

Track	Time	Figure Number	Pattern Description
1	1:33	n/a	Introduction to *Singing For Dummies*
2	1:07	3-1	Lip and tongue trills
3	:34	n/a	Sliding on pitch (Chapter 4)
4	1:27	4-1	Bouncing the tongue and jaw
5	:59	6-1	Creating a legato line
6	:55	6-2	Trilling a long, legato line
7	1:23	6-3	Managing long phrases
8	:35	n/a	Straight tone and vibrato (Chapter 6)
9	1:09	8-1	Alternating vowels for precise lip shapes
10	:58	8-2	Arching the tongue while alternating vowels
11	1:39	9-1	Singing tip consonants
12	:58	9-2	Singing soft palate consonants
13	1:20	9-3	Singing lip consonants
14	:57	9-4	Combining your consonants
15	1:05	11-3	Taking it down
16	1:37	11-4	Descending by step
17	1:09	11-5	Gliding through the middle
18	:47	11-6	Moving along the four in middle voice
19	1:50	11-9	Singing fourth
20	1:31	11-10	Bringing chest voice up
21	:39	11-13	Working with close vowels
22	:44	11-14	Spinning out in head voice
23	1:20	11-15	Smoothing the transitions
24	1:21	11-16	Creating a legato line in and out of chest voice

(continued)

Track	Time	Figure Number	Pattern Description
25	1:14	11-17	Working from middle voice up to head voice
26	:49	11-18	Spinning down
27	1:25	12-1	Staccato along the scale
28	1:16	12-2	Skipping around on staccato
29	1:12	12-3	Messa di voce
30	1:26	12-4	Mixing up registers
31	2:22	12-5	Descending down
32	1:08	12-6	Stepping between registers
33	:49	12-7	Laughing it up on three notes
34	:57	12-8	Flexing out on five notes
35	1:09	12-9	Sliding up the scale
36	:55	12-10	Tripping along the scale
37	1:05	12-11	Spicing it up
38	1:40	12-12	Bouncing on thirds
39	:38	12-13	Checking out pop riffs
40	:33	12-14	Descending pop riff
41	1:38	n/a	Improvising with chords on the piano (Chapter 12)
42	:55	n/a	Improvising with a pop tune (Chapter 12)
43	:45	n/a	Improvising by yourself on a pop tune (Chapter 12)
44	:13	n/a	Demonstration of falsetto (Chapter 13)
45	:46	13-1	Checking out your falsetto
46	:54	13-2	Getting the hang of falsetto
47	:44	13-3	Flipping out of falsetto

Track	Time	Figure Number	Pattern Description
48	:55	13-4	Gliding down out of falsetto
49	1:08	13-5	Sliding up to falsetto
50	1:01	13-6	Sliding into a mix
51	:20	n/a	Fry tones (Chapter 13)
52	1:27	13-7	Mixing it up
53	:30	13-8	Soaring above High C
54	:37	n/a	Rap Song (Chapter 14)
55	:37	n/a	Nya (Chapter 14)
56	:22	n/a	High energy speaking sounds (Chapter 14)
57	:48	n/a	Speaking on up the scale (Chapter 14)
58	:18	n/a	Demonstration of chest voice and belt (Chapter 14)
59	:09	n/a	Male belting demonstration (Chapter 14)
60	:51	n/a	Beginner belt tune: "That Ain't It Man" (Chapter 14)
61	:32	n/a	Intermediate belt tune: "Take Shelter, I'm A Belter" (Chapter 14)
62	:34	n/a	Advanced belt tune: "Let's Celebrate" (Chapter 14)
63	1:09	n/a	Speaking through the rhythms of "Simple Things" (Chapter 18)
64	1:16	n/a	Singing the melody of "Simple Things" on ah
65	2:28	18-1	"Simple Things" by Martha Sullivan © 2003

Troubleshooting

If you still have trouble playing the CD, please call the Customer Service phone number at 800-762-2974 (outside the United States: 317-572-3993) or send an e-mail to techsupdum@wiley.com. Wiley Publishing, Inc. will provide technical support only for installation and other general quality control items; for technical support on the applications themselves, consult the program's vendor or author.

Index

• *Numerics* •

16-bar cut from printed music, 255–256
42nd Street (musical theater), 250

• *A* •

abdominal muscles
 innie versus outie breathing, 30, 40
 movement during exhalation, 30, 38, 40
 producing vibrato and, 78
accidentals, 258
accompanists
 audition preparation with, 258–259
 for auditions, 260–261
 confidence for singing with, 203
 fake books used by, 209, 257
 recordings of, working with, 176
 rehearsing with, 281
 transposing abilities, 255, 261
 voice teachers use of, 176
acoustics
 echoing sounds, 108
 feeling the sound and, 47
acting the song
 character work, 229–233
 focus for, 233–234
 gesturing, 234–236, 285–286
 interludes, 229
 lyrics, working with, 228
 movement while singing, 236, 237
 music as story, 229
 planning actions, 232
 as story, 227–229
 translating a song, 237
Actors Equity (actors union), 262
adrenaline, 240, 242
advanced songs, 202–205
affirmations, 243
age
 puberty, male voice changes, 150, 191
 teenagers, 190–191
 voice changes with, 189, 191–192

voice type and, 60
 young singers, 189–190, 191
agents, 261
agility
 described, 137, 143
 interval expansion, 145–146
 for pop music, 146–147
 speed, 143–145
Aida (opera), 66
alcohol, cautions for, 273, 275
alignment
 correct, 17–19, 51
 moving into, 19
 overview, 51
 wall exercise, 19–21
allergies, 276
alveolar ridge, 96
Amazon.com (online store), 208
American English, 89
Anderson, Marian (singer), 63
Andrea Chenier (opera), 267
Andrews, Julie (singer), 62
Annie (musical theater), 63, 185
antihistamines, 276, 279
appoggio (outie breathing), 30, 32, 40
arias
 auditioning with, 184
 female mix, avoiding, 156
 for mezzo voice, 206
articulation, 204, 205. *See also* vowel
  sounds
articulators, 203
attention, accepting, 22
audience, performing for, 234, 243, 284
audition book (notebook of songs),
  256–258, 262
auditions
 agents for, 261
 being typed, 259
 casting panel, 259, 260
 country music, 186
 dancing at, 250
 finding, 262

auditions *(continued)*
  information needed for, 250
  journaling, 257–258
  microphone for, 261
  music preparation, 254–259
  notebook of songs (audition book),
      256–257, 262
  opera, 184
  overview, 16, 185
  photocopying songs for, 210, 257
  photographs, 250, 262
  pianists, working with, 258–259, 260–261
  procedure, 259–263
  professional help with, 250
  resumes, 250, 262
  song selection, 251–254
  style of singing for, 249–250
  union, 262
  visual focus, 233–234, 263
  wardrobe, 259

• *B* •

back
  hip position, tension from, 20
  tension release, 22
back phrasing, 188
back space
  creating, 71
  smiling and, 195
  soft palate consonants, shaping, 99
back vowels
  jaw position, 88
  lip position, 88, 89–90
  singing, 90
  tongue position, 88
Backstage (trade paper), 261, 262
ballads, 249, 251
bands
  auditioning for, 188–189
  singing with, 283
bar (measure)
  cutting, 255–256
  defined, 255
Barbershop quartet, 196
baritone
  belt songs for, 297
  classical songs for, 293
  described, 66

famous singers, 268
  personality, 61
baritone/tenor
  belt songs for, 297
  described, 64
  musical theater songs for, 296
Barnes and Noble (bookstore), 208
Baryshnikov, Mikhail (ballet dancer), 162
basketball granny shots warmup, 113
bass
  classical songs for, 293
  described, 65–66
  famous singers, 66
  performance roles, 66
  personality of, 61
  subdivisions, 66, 67
bass clef, 10
bass-baritone, 66
Beauty and The Beast (musical theater), 63
beginners
  belting, 165, 166, 168
  breathy tone, 73
  first sounds, 45–46
  gesturing, 234
  lessons, 177
  range, 202
  songs for, 202, 203–204, 213–216, 291
  voice endurance, 110
  young singers, 189–190, 191
bel canto method of singing, 273
bell register (whistle register), 156, 157–158
belting
  beginners, 165, 166, 168
  brassy sound, 127, 168
  breath and energy, coordinating, 167
  cautions for, 164, 165, 170, 271
  chest voice versus, 127, 165
  described, 164–165, 185
  gender differences, 166
  men, 166, 170, 297
  for musical theater, 185, 295, 297
  preparing for, 167–170
  resonance, feeling, 167–168
  singers as, 164, 185, 186, 187
  songs, 185, 291, 294–295
  women, 165, 166, 170, 294–295
Bernstein, Leonard (composer/
      conductor), 252

Black, Clint (singer), 186
"Blue" (song), 270
"Blue Christmas" (song), 269
bobbing head, correcting, 19
body, connecting with, 113, 163
body energy
  for clear tones, 162, 163–164
  described, 163
body language, videotaping, 118
body positions. *See* posture
bouncing the tongue and jaw, 53–55
bowing and exiting, 287–288
brassy tone, 86, 101, 127, 168. *See also*
    belting
Breaking Into Acting For Dummies
    (Garrison, Larry and Wang, Wallace),
    177, 259, 261, 262
breathing. *See also* breathing exercises;
    exhalation; inhalation
  anatomy of, 29
  basics, 27–33
  for belting, 167
  connecting to your song, 113
  coordinating with tone, 71–72
  jargon, 32
  mouth breathing, 84
  nose breathing, 83, 84
  overbreathing, 34
  overview, 10
  phrasing and, 221
  quick, 84, 223
  shortness of breath, 33, 240
  starting a tone, 70
  technique, 222–224
  tips for, 30, 33
  yawning and, 28
breathing exercises
  exhalation, 28–29, 35–39
  extending the breath, 39–40
  feeling breath, 30–33, 114
  on hands and knees, 31
  inhalation, 28, 33–35
  lying on the floor, 31
  opening your ribs, 40–41
  puffing like the magic dragon, 41–42
  slumping over, 33
  squatting down, 31
  tips for, 39, 41

breathy tone
  causes of, 73, 274
  whispering, 69, 70
Brightman, Sara (singer), 62
Brooks, Garth (singer), 186, 270

• C •

caffeine, 277
Callas, Maria (singer), 62, 228
Camelot (musical theater), 66
Candide (musical theater), 252
career, singing as, 173
Carey, Mariah (singer), 157–158, 187, 269
Carmen (opera), 63, 64, 66, 232
Carousel (musical theater), 268
Carpenter, Karen (singer), 44, 63, 187, 269
Carreras, José (singer), 64
carrying a tune. *See* matching pitch
Caruso, Enrico (singer), 64
Cash, Johnny (singer), 186
casting director, 260
casting panel, 259, 260
castrato, 65
CD with this book
  care of, 302
  tracks on, 302–306
  troubleshooting, 306
  using, 119, 301–302
CD with this book (exercises and
    demonstrations)
  agility, 143–145, 146
  belting, 167, 168, 169–170
  chest voice, 127–128
  consonants, singing, 98, 99–100, 101, 103
  falsetto, 151–153, 154, 155
  frying tones, 156
  head voice, 131–132
  improvising pop riffs, 148
  jaw bouncing, 54–55
  legato line, 75
  lip trilling, 37
  long phrases, 76
  matching pitch, 48
  melody on a single vowel, 217
  middle voice, 124–125
  mixed voice, 155, 157
  musical notes and rhythm, 216

CD with this book (exercises and demonstrations) *(continued)*
  optimum speaking pitch, 169
  placing the voice *(messa di voce)*, 140–141
  pop riffs, 147–148
  rapping, 162
  register transitions, 133–136
  registers, combining, 141–142
  "Simple Things" (song), 216
  staccato, 139–140
  straight tone, 77
  syncopation, 146
  tongue bouncing, 54–55
  trilling, 37, 75
  vibrato, 77
  vowel sounds, 90, 93, 217
  whistle register, 158
  words and music, putting together, 217
chanting, 161–162
Chappell, Jon *(Guitar For Dummies)*, 204
characters
  actions of, 232
  characterizing, 230–231
  getting into character, 230
  motivation of, 231–232
  tempo, 232–233
charting
  Daily Practice Chart, 115
  practice routines, 108, 115, 117, 118, 246
Chérubin (opera), 268
chest position, 20, 30
chest voice
  belting versus, 127
  described, 121, 126
  falsetto, transitions, 153, 154
  feeling, 127–128
  men, 126–127
  range, finding, 126–127
  transitions, 132–134
  women, 126–128
Chicago (musical theater), 64
chin position, 19
choir. *See also* training with a choir
  choosing, 195–197
  directors, 175, 196–197
  rehearsals, 195
  singing vibrato and, 194
  types of, 196
choral music teacher, 175

chords, pop riffs with, 148
choreographed moves, 236
choreographer, 260
church
  choirs, 196
  performing in, 284
cigarette smoke, 276
clarity of tone. *See* clear tones
classical music
  agility needed, 143
  arias, 156, 184, 206
  learning songs, 212
  opera, 183–184
  pop music versus, 147
  songs, list of, 291–293
  teachers, 175
  voice categories, 66–67
  voice resonance, 80
Classical Vocal Reprints (music distributor), 208
clear tones
  creating, 69, 72–73, 162, 163–164
  for projection, 73
  "Uh-huh" test for, 70
"Climb Every Mountain" (song), 232
Cline, Patsy (singer), 63
clock, practicing with, 111
"Close to You" (song), 269
closed vowels
  described, 94, 130
  head voice felt with, 130
colds, treating, 279–280
coloratura, 67
compilation music books, 209–210
conductor, 260
confidence
  building, 244, 246
  projecting, 17, 21–22
  in singing with others, 203
  in voice lessons, 178
connecting with your body, warmups, 113, 163
consonants
  breathing exercise, 41–42
  combination, 102–103
  exhalation exercises, 38
  lip, 100–101
  lisping and, 97
  overview, 95

R consonant, 97–98
soft palate, 98–100
TH consonant, 96, 97
tip, 96–98
unvoiced, 102
voiced, 102
contralto, 63
copyright information, 210
Così fan tutte (opera), 234
cost
of agents, 261
transposing a song, 255
voice lessons, 176–177
costumes. *See* wardrobe
cough medicine, 279
countertenor, 64
country music
auditions, 186
described, 185–186
famous singers, 186
songs, 297–298
training requirements, 185–186
twang in, 80, 186
cover (sound moves back), 166
cracking, 239, 245
creating tone
back space for, 71, 99, 195
clear tone, 69, 72–73, 163–164
coordinating breath with tone, 71–72
overview, 69–70
starting a tone, 70–71
credit cards, paying for lessons, 177
crescendo, 140, 164
criticism
constructive, 178
handling, 117
crooning, 80
crying, 271, 280
Customer Service, troubleshooting for
CD, 306
cycle of vibration (glottal cycle), 45

• **D** •

Daily Practice Chart, 115
dairy products, 273, 276
"The Dance" (song), 270
dancing while singing, 41, 236, 250
Debussy, Claude (composer), 268

decongestants, 279
demo recording, 188
Denver, John (singer), 64
diaphragm
described, 29
locking, 29
posture's effect on, 29
diction classes, 184
dictionaries
pronunciation guides, 237
pronunciation symbols, 88
Dion, Celine (singer), 187
diphthongs, 93
director, 260
distractions during performance, 243–244,
284–285
Domingo, Placido (singer), 64
"Donne mie, la fate a tanti" (song), 234
dramatic voice, 67, 267
Drescher, Fran (actor), 86
dropping the jaw, 52–53
dust allergies, 276
dynamics
crescendo, 140, 164
musical notations for, 218–219
for speaking voice, 164
varying, 140–141

• **E** •

echoing sounds, preventing, 108
"Edelweiss" (song), 204, 205
Eligible Principal Audition (EPA), union
auditions, 262
emotional health, 280
encores, 288
"Endless Love" (song), 269
endurance, 110, 184
energy flow
for belting, 167
body energy, 162, 163–164
correct posture for, 18
entrance, performance, 284
EPA (Eligible Principal Audition) union
auditions, 262
Equity Chorus Calls, union auditions, 262
evaluation
performance, 247–248
posture, 17–18

exercising your voice. *See also* CD with this
book (exercises and demonstrations);
practice routine
breaking it down, 116–117
choosing exercises, 115–116
discipline for, 116
exhalation. *See also* breathing; exhalation
exercises
discovering singing breath with, 28–29
innie versus outie breathing, 30, 40
posture, 35
exhalation exercises
blowing out a candle, 36
exploring exhalation, 28–29
moving air with consonants, 38
overview, 35
rib expansion, 38–39
trilling, 36–37
eyebrows, raising, 86, 195, 228
eyes
closing, 234
where to focus, 233–234, 263

• F •

face, front of (mask), 84, 167
fach, 184
facial tension, 23
fake books, 201, 209, 257
falsetto
ascending into, 153–154
descending from, 152–153
head voice strengthened with, 149, 150,
153, 154–155
mixed voice, 154–155
overview, 149–150
puberty and, 150
singing in, 151–152
songs using, 154
working with, 130
famous singers
bass, 66
contralto, 63
country music, 186
with good technique, 267–270
jazz, 189
mezzo, 63
musical theater, 185
opera, 184

pop and rock, 187
soprano, 62
tenor, 64
"The Farmer and the Cowman Should be
Friends" (song), 232
Farrell, Eileen (singer), 267
fatigue
during practice, 110
from singing high notes, 197, 202–203
voice, 187–188
feedback
asking for, 181
criticism, 117, 178
from teachers, 178
feeling
belting resonance, 167–168
breath movement, 30–33, 114
chest voice, 127–128
head voice, 130–132
middle voice, 121
sound, 47, 70–71, 85
feet
alignment exercise, 19
position, 20–21
Fitzgerald, Ella (singer), 189
flageolet (whistle register), 156, 157–158
flats, 12
Fleming, Renee (singer), 184
flute register (whistle register), 156,
157–158
focus
for acting a song, 233–234
for matching pitch, 86
for resonance, 85
folk songs, 61
food, 273–274, 276
For Men icon, 5
For Women icon, 5
Ford, Tennessee Ernie (singer), 66
forehead tension, 23
forgetting the words, 21, 241
Forrester, Maureen (singer), 63
42nd Street (musical theater), 250
Franklin, Aretha (singer), 187
"Friends in Low Places" (song), 270
front vowels
jaw position, 91
lip position, 90, 91
singing, 93

speaking, 92–93
tongue position, 90, 91, 93
vowel sounds, 90–94
frying tones
caution for, 156
defined, 155
men, 155–156
women, 156
full voice, 67

• *G* •

Garrison, Larry (*Breaking Into Acting For Dummies*), 177, 259, 261, 262
general manager, 260
gestures, 234–236, 285–286
getting into character, 230
glottal cycle, 45
"God Bless America" (song), 61
gorilla sounds, 73
Goulet, Robert (singer), 185
Grease (musical theater), 250
Grey, Joel (singer), 185
grunting, 70
Guitar For Dummies (Phillips, Mark and Chappell, Jon), 204

• *H* •

Hal Leonard (music distributor), 208
hand movements, 234–236, 285–286
"Happy Birthday" (song), 35, 37
"Happy Birthday, Mr. President" (song), 73
head
alignment, 19
bobbing movement, 19, 131
head voice
described, 121, 129
falsetto for strengthening, 149, 150, 153, 154–155
feeling, 130–132
head bobbing and, 131
men's range, 130
middle voice transitions, 134–136
range, finding, 129–130
sopranos, 62
women's range, 129

headshots, 250, 262
health issues. *See also* medications
alcohol, 273, 275
allergies, 276
belting, cautions for, 164, 165, 170, 271
emotional release, 280
healthy speech, using, 276
hydration, 181–182, 273–274, 277
nodes, 272
nutrition, 278
perfume, 282
sleep, 271, 277–278
sore throats/infections, 278–280
teachers experience with, 174
voice fatigue, 110, 187–188, 197, 202–203
voice pain, 110, 156
weight, 42, 227, 272, 277
"Here and Now" (song), 269
high notes
fatigue from singing, 197, 202–203
laughing and, 158
singing, 131, 141–142
whistle register tones, 156–158
hip position, 20
holding your nose
humming and, 83
singing while, 81
Horne, Marilyn (singer), 63
"How Do I Live" (song), 270
humidifier, 280
humming
holding your nose and, 83
starting a tone with, 70
for voice warmup, 114
husky tones, 274
hydration, 181–182, 273–274, 277

• *I* •

"I Can't Make You Love Me" (song), 233
icons in this book, 5–6
"If I Only Had a Heart" (song), 232
"If I Were The King of the Forest" (song), 232
Il Trovatore (opera), 267
imagery, 179. *See also* visualization
imitating other singers
resonance, 80
vibrato, 77–78

imitating sounds
 gorilla, 73
 Santa Claus laugh, 73
 sirens, 46
 snoring, 81–82
improvising, pop music, 146–148
inhalation. *See also* breathing; inhalation
   exercises
 correct versus incorrect, 33
 for releasing tone, 73–74
 for singing, 28
 throat openness during, 33
inhalation exercises
 dropping breath into your body, 34
 exploring, 28
 overview, 33
 panting like a pooch, 33–34
 singing "Happy Birthday," 35
 sipping through a straw, 34
innie breathing, 30, 40
intercostal muscles, 29
interludes, 224, 229
intermediate songs, 202, 204–205
International Phonetic Alphabet (IPA), 88
intervals, 202
interviewing teachers, 174–177
introduction of a song, 224
IPA (International Phonetic Alphabet), 88
Italian, 273

• *J* •

"Jailhouse Rock" (song), 269
jargon
 appoggio, 32
 singing on breath, 32
 support, 32
jaw
 back vowel position, 88
 bouncing, 53–55
 dropping, 52–53
 movement, 95
 releasing tension, 51
 yawning and, 52
jazz music
 band auditions, 188–189
 famous singers, 189
 scat, 188
 training requirements, 188–189

jewelry, caution for, 282
John, Elton (singer), 64, 234
Jones, Glendower (store owner), 208
Jones, Norah (singer), 73
journal
 audition, 257–258
 lesson notes, 180
joy, whooping with, 46

• *K* •

key. *See also* range
 choosing songs and, 205–206
 performing and, 283
 transposing, 254–255, 261
keyboards, piano/electric, 110
The King and I (musical theater), 250
Kiss Me Kate (musical theater), 268
Kiss of the Spider Woman (musical theater),
   268
knees
 position, 20
 unlocking, 20, 21
Krall, Diana (singer), 189

• *L* •

La Bohème (opera), 62, 64
La Cenerentola (opera), 268
La Forza del Destino (opera), 267
La Gioconda (opera), 267
Lang, K.D. (singer), 63
languages. *See also* jargon
 American English, 89
 Italian, 273
 learning, 184, 273
 translating songs, 237
larynx
 described, 45
 high notes, singing, 131
 male, 150
 muscles, 45, 47, 131
 position, 46–47, 145
 voice resonance and, 80
laughing
 coordinating breath and tone with, 72–73
 high notes and, 158
 on pitch, 143

Le Nozze di Figaro (opera), 268
learning a song
    breath control, 222–224
    making it your own, 220
    melody, singing without words, 216–217
    memorizing lyrics, 212, 241
    musical notation, reading, 213, 216,
        217–219
    phrasing, 221
    rhythm, tapping out, 213–216
    scanning, 211–212
    timing, 213, 216, 224
    tone, changing, 224–225
    vowel technique, 220–221
    words and music, putting together, 217
learning styles
    aural, 119
    kinesthetic, 119
    visual, 119
Led Zeppelin (band/composers), 225
ledger lines, 11
legato
    consonants sung with, 103
    sustaining tone with, 74–75
legit technique, 184, 185
Lennon, John (singer/composer), 225
lessons. *See also* practice routine; voice
        teacher
    beginners, 177
    cost, 176–177
    expectations for, 173–174, 178–179,
        180–181
    first lesson, success with, 181–182
    location, 176
    recording, 50, 180
    as tax deduction, 177
    tools, 110–111, 179
libraries, printed music from, 210
light voice, 66
lightening up the sound, 129
lighting for rehearsals and performance, 285
linguists, pronunciation symbols, 88
lip consonants
    shaping, 100–101
    singing, 101
lip trills
    for exhalation, 36–37
    for legato lines, 75
    for voice warmup, 114

lips
    combination consonants, 102
    consonants, 96–97, 99, 100–101
    focusing a pitch with, 86
    vowel sounds position, 87, 88, 89–90
lisping, 97
listening
    to singers' vibrato, 77
    as voice development tool, 179
The Little Mermaid (show), 62
"Love Me Tender" (song), 269
low tones. *See also* chest voice
    frying tones, 155–156
    singing, 138–139
lungs, 29
Lynn, Loretta (singer), 186
lyric voice, 66, 267–268
lyrics. *See also* songs
    dramatizing, 252–253
    forgetting, 21, 241
    memorizing, 212, 241, 281
    operative words, 212
    working with, 228

• M •

Man of La Mancha (musical theater), 268
Marie Christine (musical theater), 268
marking printed music, 256, 259
Martin, Mary (singer), 185
"Mary Had a Little Lamb" (song), 202
mask (front of face), 84, 167
Massenet, Jules-Émile-Frédéric
        (composer), 268
Master Class (musical theater), 268
Match Pitch (software program), 50
matching pitch. *See also* pitch
    described, 47
    focusing techniques, 86
    muscle memory for, 49
    recording yourself and singing along, 50
    sliding up and down on pitch, 48–49
McCartney, Paul (singer/composer), 225
McDonald, Audra (singer), 268
McEntire, Reba (singer), 186
McFerrin, Bobby (singer), 189
measure (bar)
    cutting, 255–256
    defined, 255

medications
  antihistamines, 276, 279
  cough medicine, 279
  decongestants, 279
  nasal saline spray, 279, 280
  nose sprays, 279
  throat dried out from, 274, 276
  voice irritated by, 276
  water with, 279
melody
  direction of, 211
  singing without words, 216–217
memorizing lyrics, 212, 241, 281
men. *See also* men, voice types
  belting, 166, 170, 297
  chanting, 161–162
  chest voice, 126–128
  country songs for, 298
  frying tones, 155–156
  head voice, 130
  middle voice, 122–124, 125
  mixed voice, 154–155
  pop songs for, 299
  puberty voice changes, 150, 189, 191
  register transitions, 133–136
  speaking voice, 159
men, voice types. *See also* falsetto; tenor
  baritone, 61, 66, 268, 293, 297
  baritone/tenor, 64, 296, 297
  bass, 61, 65–66, 67, 293
  bass-baritone, 66
  castrato, 65
menopause, 191
Merman, Ethel (singer/actor), 164, 185
messa di voce (place the voice), 140
methods of singing, 179, 273
metronome, 111
mezzo. *See also* Carpenter, Karen
  belt songs for, 295
  classical songs for, 206, 292
  described, 62–64
  famous singers, 63
  lyric, 267–268
  musical theater songs for, 294–295
  personality, 61
  register, 63
  subdivisions of, 63, 67

microphones
  auditioning with, 261
  performing with, 187, 286–287
  singing without, 79
  types of, 286–287
Middle C, finding, 11
middle voice
  chest voice transitions, 132–134
  described, 121
  falsetto transitions, 153–154
  finding, 122–125
  head voice transitions, 134–136
  men's range, 122–123
  singing in, 123–125
  transitions, when to make, 132
  women's range, 122
Midler, Bette (singer/actor), 164
The Mikado (operetta), 66
minidisc recorder, 111
mirrors, practicing with, 53, 111
Mitchell, Brian Stokes (singer), 268
mixed voice
  arias and, 156
  men, 154–155
  in pop and rock, 187
  women, 156–157
monotone, 169
Monroe, Marilyn (actor), 73
Morgan, Lorrie (singer), 63
Morris, James (singer), 66, 184
mouth
  open space in, 71
  opening wide, 85
  quick breaths through, 84
movement
  abdominal muscles, 30, 38, 40
  choreographed, 236
  dancing while singing, 41, 236, 250
  feeling breath, 30–33, 114
  gestures, 234–236, 285–286
  head bobbing, 19
  jaw, 95
  pantomime, 235
  soft palate, 81–82
  while singing, 236, 237
moving the tone forward. *See* projection
mucus
  from dairy products, 273, 276
  postnasal drip, 280

mumbling, 95
muscles
  abdominal, 30, 38, 40, 78
  diaphragm, 29
  intercostal, 29
  larynx, 45, 47, 131
  overview, 44–45
  vocal cords, 45, 150, 271
music distributors, 208
The Music Man (musical theater), 62, 229
musical comedy, 252
musical director, 260
musical notation. *See also* notes
  bar lines, 213
  bass clef, 10
  common time, 213
  dynamics, 218–219
  flats, 12
  intervals, 202
  ledger lines, 11
  measure (bar), 255–256
  octave, 12
  sharps, 12
  staff, notes on, 10–12
  tempo, 218–219
  time signature, 213, 216
  treble clef, 10
musical theater. *See also* auditions
  belting for, 185, 295, 297
  song categories, 252
  songs, list of, 293–297
  training requirements, 185
  using falsetto, 154
My Fair Lady (musical theater), 229, 231
"My Favorite Things" (song), 204–205

• *N* •

nasal consonants, 83
nasal resonance, 83, 165
nasal saline spray, 279, 280
nasality
  checking for, 81
  defined, 83
  eliminating, 81–83
National Association of Teachers of Singing
  (NATS), Web site, 173

neck
  lengthening, 19
  tension release, 22, 51, 53
Neely, Blake (*Piano For Dummies*), 50, 110,
  204, 213
neighbors, working practice time around,
  108
nervous ticks, 18–19
Newton John, Olivia (singer), 62
nodes, 272
noise, echoing sounds, 108
nose
  holding while humming, 83
  holding while singing, 81
  nose breathing, 83, 84
nose sprays, 279
notation. *See* musical notation
notebook of songs (audition book),
  256–258, 262
notes
  defined, 44
  high, 131, 141–142, 156, 157–158, 197,
    202–203
  holding, 213
  Middle C, 11
  pivot, 144, 145
  on a staff, 10–12
  stepwise motion, 202
  syllables matched with, 55
nutrition, 278
nyah sound, for belting, 167–168

• *O* •

octave, 12
Oklahoma! (musical theater), 63, 66, 232,
  250
On the CD icon
  described, 5
  finding, 301
On the Town (musical theater), 268
open call auditions, 262
open vowels, 94, 130
opera
  auditions, 184
  famous singers, 184
  training requirements, 183–184

operative words, 212
operettas, 252
optimum speaking pitch, 161, 162–163,
   168, 169
organ, singing with, 283
outie breathing (appoggio), 30, 32, 40
"Over the Rainbow" (song), 204
overbreathing, 34

● *P* ●

pantomime, 235
Parton, Dolly (singer), 62
Pavarotti, Luciano (singer), 64, 73, 268
payment policy, 177
Pelléas et Mélisande (opera), 268
perfect pitch, 48
performance. *See also* performance anxiety
   audience, acknowledging, 284
   bowing and exiting, 287–288
   distractions, 243–244, 284–285
   encores, 288
   entrance, 284
   evaluation, 247–248
   hand placement, 234–235, 285–286
   microphones, 187, 286–287
   with piano, organ or band, 283
   preparation, 241–244
   rehearsing for, 281, 285
   stance, 282–283
   success plan, 245–246
   by voice teachers, 175
   wardrobe, 282
performance anxiety. *See also* performance
   adrenaline and, 240, 242
   alleviating, 15–16, 240–244
   building confidence, 244
   checklist, 247–248
   group singing and, 193–194
   performance evaluation, 247–248
   in recitals, 181
   symptoms, 239–240
   voice cracking, 239, 245
performance roles
   bass, 66
   mezzo, 63
   soprano, 62
   tenor, 64

perfume, 283
Phantom of the Opera (musical theater), 250
Phillips, Mark (*Guitar For Dummies*), 204
Phillips, Pamelia (*Singing For Dummies*),
   1–6
photocopying sheet music, 210, 257
photographs
   for auditions, 250, 262
   performance, 285
phrasing technique, 221
pianists. *See also* accompanists
   for auditions, 260–261
   as teachers, 171–172, 175, 272
   transposing abilities, 255, 261
Piano For Dummies (Neely, Blake), 50, 110,
   204, 213
piano skills
   learning, 110
   voice teachers, 175–176
pitch. *See also* matching pitch
   chanting exercise for, 161–162
   defined, 44
   eyebrows, raising to stay on pitch, 86, 195
   focusing techniques, 86
   laughing on, 143
   monotone, 169
   optimum (central) speaking pitch, 161,
      162–163, 168, 169
   perfect, 48
   pitch pipe for, 111
   rapping exercise, 162
   relative, 48
pitch pipe, 111
pivot notes, 144, 145
place the voice (*messa di voce*), 140
poetry, rhythm of, 224
pollen allergies, 276
pop music
   agility for, 146–147
   auditions, 188
   characteristics, 147
   classical music versus, 147
   improvising, 146–148
   for men, 299
   patterns in, 147
   pop songs, list, 298–299
   riffs, 146, 148
   training requirements, 187–188

twang in, 80
for women, 298–299
Porgy and Bess (operetta), 66
positions. *See* posture
positive thoughts, 242–243
postlude, 224
postnasal drip, 280
posture
    alignment, 17, 18, 19–21
    chest position, 20, 30
    chin position, 19
    confidence projected through, 17, 21–22
    diaphragm affected by, 29
    evaluating, 17–18
    for feeling breath movement, 30–33, 114
    feet position, 20–21
    on hands and knees, 31
    hip position, 20
    knee position, 20
    lying on the floor, 31
    overview, 10, 18–19
    releasing tension, 17, 22–25
    shoulder position, 19, 20, 33
    slumping over, 33
    squatting down, 31
    for voice warmups, 114
    walking, 21
    wall exercise, 19–21
"Power of Love" (song), 269
practice routine. *See also* CD with this
        book (exercises and demonstrations)
    charting, 108, 115, 117, 118, 246
    choosing songs for, 201–202
    Daily Practice Chart, 118
    developing, 180
    echoing sounds during, 108
    exercises, applying, 119
    exercising your voice, 115–117
    flaws, overworking, 180–181
    goals, 108, 116, 180, 241
    location, 109
    overpracticing, 241
    performance preparation, 241
    planning, 108, 246
    progress, monitoring, 111, 179
    setting up, 109
    tape recordings, 111, 117–118, 180
    time, 109, 110, 173
    tools, 110–111, 179

video taping, 118
warming up, 108, 111–114
Presley, Elvis (singer), 232, 269
printed music
    compilation books, 209–210
    copies for lessons, 182
    downloading, 209
    fake books, 201, 209, 257
    from local libraries, 210
    marking, 256, 259
    photocopying, 210, 257
    retail outlets, 208
    16-bar cut, 255–256
    Web sites, 208, 209
producer, 260
projection
    clear tone for, 73
    dropping the jaw, 52
    optimum speaking pitch, 163
    resonators, 79–80
pronunciation
    dictionary guides, 237
    general rules, 102
    symbols, 88
    vowel sounds, 89
puberty, male voice changes, 150, 191
punctuation, breath control and, 222–223

• *Q* •

quick breaths, 84, 223

• *R* •

R consonant
    flipped, 97
    practicing, 97–98
    rolling, 97
    shaping, 97
Ragtime (musical theater), 268
"Rainy Days and Mondays" (song), 269
Raitt, Bonnie (singer), 187
Ramey, Samuel (singer), 66
range. *See also* key
    baritone, 66
    bass, 65
    bass-baritone, 66
    beginners, 202

range *(continued)*
  choosing songs and, 202, 205–206
  combining registers, 141–142
  defined, 137
  dynamics, varying, 140–141
  extending upward, 139–140
  frying tones, 155–156
  head voice, 129–130
  mezzo, 63
  middle voice, 122–123
  overview, 138
  for performing versus practicing, 137
  soprano, 62
  speaking voice, 168–169
  teenagers, 189, 191
  tenor, 64, 65
  tessitura and, 61
  voice type and, 60
  young singers, 189
rapping, 162
reading music, 15. *See also* musical
    notation
recitals, student, 176, 181
recordings
  accompaniment, working with, 176
  demo, 188
  matching pitch exercise, 50
  practice sessions and lessons, 50, 111,
    117–118, 180
  rehearsals, 283
  speaking voice, 160–161
  vowel sounds, 93
regional dialects, 89
register. *See also* chest voice; falsetto;
    register transitions
  combining, 141–142
  defined, 137
  head voice, 121, 129–132, 134–136
  middle voice, 121, 122–125, 132, 133–136
  voice type and, 60
register transitions
  bass, 65
  chest voice, 132–134
  falsetto, 152–154
  head voice, 134–136
  mezzos, 63
  middle voice, 132–135
  overview, 14
  sopranos, 62

space in front of mouth, closing down, 138
  tenor, 64
  vowels, for practicing, 138
rehearsals
  with accompanists, 281
  choir, 195
  choir directors and, 197
  lighting, 285
  recording, 283
  singing from memory, 281
relative pitch, 48
Remember icon, 5
repertoire
  notebook of songs, 256–258
  song categories for, 252
resonance
  belting, 167–168
  chanting for, 161–162
  defined, 79
  focusing a sound for, 85
  misconceptions, 84–86
  moving tone forward, 79–80, 86
  nasality, 81–83
  resonators, 79–80
  ringing it out, 81
  in sinuses, 84
  sympathetic, 84
  voices to imitate, 80
  vowel sounds, 80
resonators. *See also* mouth; throat
  exploring, 80
  moving the tone forward with, 79–80
resumes for auditions, 250, 262
retail outlets for printed music, 208
"Return to Sender" (song), 232
rhythm. *See also* reading music
  choosing songs and, 203–204
  common time, 213
  holding notes, 213
  of poetry, 224
  tapping out, 213–216
rib expansion, 38–39, 40–41
riffs, 146, 270
Rimes, LeAnn (singer), 186, 269–270
rock music. *See* pop music
Rodriguez, Daniel (the Singing Cop), 64
rolling R consonant, 97
Rossini, Gioacchino Antonio
    (composer), 268

• S •

Santa Claus laugh, 73
scales. *See also* musical notation
   agility exercises, 143–145
   nine-tone, 144–145
   sustaining tone exercise with, 75–76
scat (jazz singing), 188
scratchy voice, 272
screaming, 187–188
"Seguidilla" (song), 232
sharps, 12
sheet music. *See* printed music
shoes, caution for, 282
shoulders
   position, 20
   raised, 33
   rounded, 19
Showboat (album), 268
sighing
   clear tone developed with, 72–73
   first sounds with, 46
   for voice warmup, 114
sightsinging, 195
Simon, Carly (singer), 187
"Simple Things" (song)
   breath control for, 223, 224
   learning, 213, 216
   phrasing, 221
   printed music, 214–215
   vowels sounds, 220–221
Sinatra, Frank (singer), 80
singing
   dancing while, 41, 236, 250
   without microphones, 79
singing breath, discovering, 28–29
Singing Cop (Rodriguez, Daniel), 64
Singing For Dummies (Phillips, Pamelia)
   icons in book margins, 5–6
   organization, 2–5
   using, 1–2, 6
singing on breath, 32
singing voice. *See also* exercising your
      voice; register; voice types
   agility in, 137
   cracking, 239, 245
   difficulties with, 271, 272, 274
   endurance, 110, 184
   exercising, 114–117

female and male differences, 14, 121–122
   strengths, 60, 68, 207, 242
   warming up, 13, 113–114
singing voice categories
   coloratura, 67
   dramatic, 67, 267
   full, 67
   light, 66
   lyric, 66, 267–268
sinuses, tone resonating in, 84
sirens, imitating, 46
16-bar cut from printed music, 255–256
skiing (stationary) warm-up, 113, 163
sleep, 271, 277–278
slouching, effect on breathing, 29
slumping over posture, 33
smiling, staying on pitch and, 86, 195
Smith, Kate (singer), 164
snoring, 81–82
soft palate
   consonants, 98–100
   described, 81, 98
   movement, 81–82
   nasality and, 82–83
   resonance versus nasality, 81
   resonant tones with, 82–83, 86
software programs, Match Pitch, 50
Sondheim, Steven (composer), 252
songs. *See also* acting the song; learning a
      song
   advanced, 202–205
   for auditions, 251–254
   to avoid, 253–254
   beginning, 202–204, 213–216, 291
   belt, 294–295
   categories, 252
   choosing, 15, 173–174, 201–202, 205–206
   classical, 291–293
   country, 297–298
   cutting, 255–256
   by experience level, 201–204
   falsetto used in, 154
   folk, 61
   forgetting the words, 21, 241
   intermediate, 202, 204–205
   key and, 205–206
   list of, 205
   lyrics, 21, 212, 241, 252–253, 281
   musical theater, 252, 293–297

songs *(continued)*
  pop, 298–299
  for practice versus performance,
    201–202, 251
  sections of, 211–212, 224–225
  singing strengths, emphasizing, 207,
    242, 251
  story, 207
  translating, 237
soprano
  belt songs for, 295
  classical songs for, 291–292
  described, 61–62
  famous singers, 62, 267, 268
  musical theater songs, 293–294
  performance roles, 62
  personality, 61
  range, 62
  subdivisions, 62, 67
  tessitura, 62, 68
sore throats/infections, 278–280
The Sound of Music (musical theater)
  beginner songs, 204
  characters, 230, 232
  dancing, 250
  tenor role, 64
  von Stade, Frederica in, 268
"The Sound of Music" (song), 204, 205
sounds
  feeling in your body, 47
  imitating, 46, 73, 81–82
speaking voice. *See also* pitch
  belting developed with, 164, 165
  chanting, 161–162
  clear tone for, 163–164
  front vowels, 92–93
  optimum pitch, 161, 162–163, 168, 169
  range, increasing, 168–169
  recording, 160–161
  singing voice benefited with, 276–277
speed. *See* tempo
staccato, 139
stage fright. *See* performance anxiety
stage manager, 260
"Stairway to Heaven" (song), 225
stance, performance, 282–283
starting a tone, 70–71
"stationary" skiing warm-up, 113, 163

staying on pitch. *See* matching pitch
stepwise motion, 202
story songs, examples, 207
straight tone
  defined, 76–77
  moving to vibrato from, 77
  vibrato and, 76–77
  whining as, 77
Streisand, Barbra (singer), 157
stress, breathing affected by, 33
stretching
  like a rubber band, 24–25
  warmup, 112–113
strophic form, 225
Sullivan, Martha (song writer), 214–215
supporting the note, 32
sustaining tone
  ascending and descending with scales,
    75–76
  with legato, 74–75
  trilling the lips or tongue, 75
Swayze, Patrick (actor/dancer), 162
Sweet Adelines (female Barbershop
    quartet), 196
syllables, matching with notes, 55
symbols, 88. *See also* musical notation
sympathetic resonance, 84

• T •

tape recorder/player, 111
tax deduction, lessons as, 177
teachers. *See also* voice teacher
  choir directors, 175
  experience of, 174
  overworking flaws, 181
  pianist, 171–172, 175, 272
  student recitals, 176, 181
  vocal coach, 171, 172, 272
  what to expect from, 178–179
Technical Stuff icon, 6
technique. *See also* agility; range; register
  breath control, 222–224
  exemplary singers, 267–270
  jazz, 188
  musical theater, 185
  opera singers, 184
  phrasing, 221

pop and rock, 187–188
songs for advancing, 291–299
strengths, emphasizing, 207, 242
teenagers, 190–191
tone changes, 224–225
voice teacher for, 172
vowel sounds, 220–221
teenagers
range, 189, 191
technique, 190–191
training, 190
tempo. *See also* agility
of characters, 232–233
choosing songs and, 203
musical notation for, 218–219
of songs, 212
tenor
belt songs, 297
classical songs, 292–293
described, 64–65
famous singers, 64, 268, 269, 270
musical theater songs, 295–296
performance roles, 64
personality, 61
range, 64–65
subdivisions, 64, 67
The Three Tenors, 268
tension. *See also* tension release exercises
back, 20, 22
facial, 23
forehead, 23
from overbreathing, 34
overview, 17
tongue, 51
watching for, 53
tension release exercises. *See also*
warming up
jaw, 51, 52–55
limbering up, 23–24
melting into the floor, 22–23
neck, 22, 51, 53
overview, 50–51
shaking, rattling 'n' rolling, 24
stretching like a rubber band, 24–25
tongue, 53–55
Terfel, Bryn (singer), 184
tessitura
defined, 61, 62
determining voice types and, 61

mezzos, 63, 68
sopranos, 68
TH consonant, 96, 97
"Three Blind Mice" (song), 161
The Three Tenors, 268
throat
clearing, 276
creating back space in, 71
dried out from medications, 274, 276
openness, 33, 160
releasing a tone and, 74
sore throat/infection, 278–280
water for, 181–182
through composed, 225
"The Thunder Rolls" (song), 270
tight tones, 70, 274
timbre, 68
time
length of practice, 110, 173
for noticing voice changes, 179
when to practice, 109
time signature, reading, 213, 216
timing, for breathing, 224
tip consonants, 96–98
Tip icon, 6
TIS Web site (music distributor), 208
"Tomorrow" (song), 185
tone. *See also* creating tone; nasality;
resonance
of basses, 65
brassy, 86, 101, 127, 168
breathy, 69, 70, 73, 274
changing, 44–45, 224–225
clear, 69, 70, 72–73, 162, 163–164
of mezzos, 63
moving tone forward, 79–80, 86
overview, 12, 43–44
placing in the same location, 84–85
releasing, 73–74
of sopranos, 62
straight, 76–77
sustaining, 74–76
of tenors, 64
tension release and, 50–55
tight, 70, 274
voice type and, 60
tongue
back vowels position, 88
bouncing, 53–55

tongue *(continued)*
consonants, shaping, 96, 97, 99–102
flexibility, 51
front vowels position, 90, 91, 93
jaw movement and, 95
keeping completely flat, 85
nasality and, 82–83
tension release exercises, 53–55
trills, 75
vowel sounds position, 87, 88
tools for practicing, 53, 110–111
"Top of the World" (song), 269
training requirements
country singers, 185–186
jazz singers, 188–189
musical theater, 185
opera singers, 183–184
pop and rock singers, 187–188
teenagers, 190
young singers, 189–190
training with a choir
benefits of, 192–194
choir directors, 196–197
choosing a choir, 195–197
going solo versus, 194–195
types of choirs, 196
transitions. *See* register transitions
translating songs, 237
transposing songs, 254–255, 261
treble clef, 10
tremolo (fast vibrato), 76
trills
for exhalation, 36–37
lip, 36–37, 75, 114
for sustaining tone, 75
tongue, 75
troubleshooting for CD, Customer
Service, 306
Twain, Shania (singer), 186
twang
of country singers, 80, 186
of pop singers, 80
twitches. *See* nervous ticks

• U •

"Uh-huh" test
for clear tones, 70
for optimum speaking pitch, 162–163
"Unanswered Prayers" (song), 270
union auditions, 262
unvoiced consonants, 102
Urkel, Steve (TV character), 44. *See also*
White, Jaleel (actor)

• V •

Van Dam, José (singer), 66
Vandross, Luther (singer), 269
Verdon, Gwen (dancer/singer), 185
vibration. *See also* vibrato
glottal cycle, 45
middle voice, 122
vibrato
bouncing your abdomen and, 78
choir singing and, 194
defined, 76
imitating other singers, 77–78
moving from straight tone to, 77
in pop and rock music, 187
straight tone and, 76–77
tremolo (fast), 76
vibration rate of, 76
wobble and, 76, 192
videotaping, body language, 118
visual focus, 233–234, 263
visualization
for moving tone forward, 79–80, 86
for performance anxiety, 242
as voice development tool, 179
vitamins, 278
"Viva Las Vegas," 269
vocal coach, 171, 172, 272
vocal cords
crying and, 271
described, 45
growth during puberty, 150
vocal slides, voice warmup, 114
voice. *See* singing voice; speaking voice

voice changes
  with aging, 191–192
  menopause, 191
  at puberty, 150, 191
voice pain, 110, 156
voice teacher. *See also* lessons
  accompanist used by, 176
  background, 175
  cancellation policy, 177
  constructive feedback from, 178
  cost, 176–177
  expectations for, 173–174
  finding, 14, 172–173
  interviewing, 174–177
  location for lessons, 176
  music used, 176
  payment policy, 177
  performances by, 175
  piano skills, 175–176
  singing methods of, 179, 273
  student performances, 176
  as technique specialist, 172
  voice type worked with, 175
voice types. *See also* mezzo; soprano;
    tenor
  baritone, 61, 66, 268, 293, 297
  baritone/tenor, 64, 296, 297
  bass, 61, 65–66, 67, 293
  bass-baritone, 66
  castrato, 65
  categories, 66–67
  contralto, 63
  countertenor, 64
  determining, 12, 59–61, 67–68
  four basic, 61–66
  personality of, 61
voice warmups, 113–114. *See also*
    humming; lip trills; sighing
voiced consonants, 102
voiced sound, 102
volume. *See* dynamics
von Otter, Annie Sofie (singer), 184
von Stade, Frederica (singer), 267–268
vowel sounds
  back vowels, 88–90
  closed, 94, 130

diphthongs, 93
front vowels, 90–94
for learning a song, 220–221
nasality, avoiding, 83
open, 94, 130
overview, 13, 87
pronunciation, 89
resonance, 80
stream of, 220–221
swallowing, 86

• *W* •

walking posture, 21
wall exercise, for alignment, 19–21
Wang, Wallace (*Breaking Into Acting For
    Dummies*), 177, 259, 261, 262
wardrobe
  auditions, 259
  performance, 282
warming up. *See also* tension release
    exercises
  duration, 111–112
  jerky movements, avoiding, 113
  overview, 111–112, 114
  stretching your body, 112–113
  voice, 113–114
water, 181–182, 273–274, 277, 279
Web sites
  Actors Equity (actors union), 262
  Brooks, Garth (singer), 270
  copyright information, 210
  Match Pitch (software program), 50
  McDonald, Audra (singer), 268
  Mitchell, Brian Stokes (singer), 268
  Pavarotti, Luciano (singer), 73
  Presley, Elvis (singer), 269
  for printed music, 208, 209
  Vandross, Luther (singer), 269
  voice teacher, finding, 172–173
  von Stade, Frederica (singer), 268
Webster's dictionary, pronunciation
    symbols, 88
weight, singing affected by, 42, 227, 272
Werther (opera), 268

West Side Story (musical theater), 64
"We've Only Just Begun" (song), 269
whining, 77
whispering, 69, 70
whistle register, 156, 157–158
White, Barry (singer), 66
White, Jaleel (actor), 80. *See also* Urkel,
    Steve (TV character)
whooping with joy, 46
Williams, Hank (singer), 186
Wilson, Ann (singer), 187
The Wizard of Oz (musical theater), 204,
    205, 232
wobble, 76, 192
women. *See also* mezzo; soprano
    belting, 165, 166, 170, 294–295
    chanting, 161
    chest voice, 126–128
    country songs for, 297–298
    frying tones, 156
    head voice, 129
    high notes (whistle register), 156–158
    laughing up high, 158
    lightening up the sound, 129
    menopause, 191

middle voice, 122–125, 161
    mix voice, 156–157
    pop songs for, 298–299
    register transitions, 133, 134, 135, 136
    speaking voice, 159, 169
Wonder, Stevie (singer), 61, 64
words. *See* lyrics
"Wouldn't It Be Loverly" (song), 229
Wynette, Tammy (singer), 186

"Ya Got Trouble" (song), 229
yawning
    breathing and, 28
    creating back space with, 71
    for dropping the jaw, 52
Yearwood, Trisha (singer), 186
yelling on pitch, 164, 167. *See also* belting
"Yesterday" (song), 225
young singers. *See also* beginners
    range, 189
    technique, 191
    training, 189–190

Notes

Notes

Wiley Publishing, Inc.
End-User License Agreement

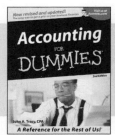
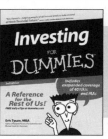

FOR DUMMIES®

A world of resources to help you grow

HOME, GARDEN & HOBBIES

0-7645-5295-3

0-7645-5130-2

0-7645-5106-X

Also available:

Auto Repair For Dummies
(0-7645-5089-6)

Chess For Dummies
(0-7645-5003-9)

Home Maintenance For
Dummies
(0-7645-5215-5)

Organizing For Dummies
(0-7645-5300-3)

Piano For Dummies
(0-7645-5105-1)

Poker For Dummies
(0-7645-5232-5)

Quilting For Dummies
(0-7645-5118-3)

Rock Guitar For Dummies
(0-7645-5356-9)

Roses For Dummies
(0-7645-5202-3)

Sewing For Dummies
(0-7645-5137-X)

FOOD & WINE

0-7645-5250-3

0-7645-5390-9

0-7645-5114-0

Also available:

Bartending For Dummies
(0-7645-5051-9)

Chinese Cooking For
Dummies
(0-7645-5247-3)

Christmas Cooking For
Dummies
(0-7645-5407-7)

Diabetes Cookbook For
Dummies
(0-7645-5230-9)

Grilling For Dummies
(0-7645-5076-4)

Low-Fat Cooking For
Dummies
(0-7645-5035-7)

Slow Cookers For Dummies
(0-7645-5240-6)

TRAVEL

0-7645-5453-0

0-7645-5438-7

0-7645-5448-4

Also available:

America's National Parks For
Dummies
(0-7645-6204-5)

Caribbean For Dummies
(0-7645-5445-X)

Cruise Vacations For
Dummies 2003
(0-7645-5459-X)

Europe For Dummies
(0-7645-5456-5)

Ireland For Dummies
(0-7645-6199-5)

France For Dummies
(0-7645-6292-4)

London For Dummies
(0-7645-5416-6)

Mexico's Beach Resorts For
Dummies
(0-7645-6262-2)

Paris For Dummies
(0-7645-5494-8)

RV Vacations For Dummies
(0-7645-5443-3)

Walt Disney World & Orlando
For Dummies
(0-7645-5444-1)

Available wherever books are sold. Go to www.dummies.com or call 1-877-762-2974 to order direct.

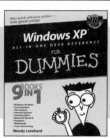

FOR DUMMIES®

Helping you expand your horizons and realize your potential

INTERNET

The Internet FOR DUMMIES
0-7645-0894-6

The Internet ALL-IN-ONE DESK REFERENCE FOR DUMMIES
0-7645-1659-0

eBay FOR DUMMIES
0-7645-1642-6

Also available:

America Online 7.0 For Dummies
(0-7645-1624-8)

Genealogy Online For Dummies
(0-7645-0807-5)

The Internet All-in-One Desk Reference For Dummies
(0-7645-1659-0)

Internet Explorer 6 For Dummies
(0-7645-1344-3)

The Internet For Dummies Quick Reference
(0-7645-1645-0)

Internet Privacy For Dummies
(0-7645-0846-6)

Researching Online For Dummies
(0-7645-0546-7)

Starting an Online Business For Dummies
(0-7645-1655-8)

DIGITAL MEDIA

Digital Photography FOR DUMMIES
0-7645-1664-7

Photoshop Elements 2 FOR DUMMIES
0-7645-1675-2

Digital Video FOR DUMMIES
0-7645-0806-7

Also available:

CD and DVD Recording For Dummies
(0-7645-1627-2)

Digital Photography All-in-One Desk Reference For Dummies
(0-7645-1800-3)

Digital Photography For Dummies Quick Reference
(0-7645-0750-8)

Home Recording for Musicians For Dummies
(0-7645-1634-5)

MP3 For Dummies
(0-7645-0858-X)

Paint Shop Pro "X" For Dummies
(0-7645-2440-2)

Photo Retouching & Restoration For Dummies
(0-7645-1662-0)

Scanners For Dummies
(0-7645-0783-4)

GRAPHICS

PowerPoint 2002 FOR DUMMIES
0-7645-0817-2

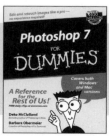

Photoshop 7 FOR DUMMIES
0-7645-1651-5

Macromedia Flash MX FOR DUMMIES
0-7645-0895-4

Also available:

Adobe Acrobat 5 PDF For Dummies
(0-7645-1652-3)

Fireworks 4 For Dummies
(0-7645-0804-0)

Illustrator 10 For Dummies
(0-7645-3636-2)

QuarkXPress 5 For Dummies
(0-7645-0643-9)

Visio 2000 For Dummies
(0-7645-0635-8)

Available wherever books are sold. Go to www.dummies.com or call 1-877-762-2974 to order direct.

FOR DUMMIES®

The advice and explanations you need to succeed

SELF-HELP, SPIRITUALITY & RELIGION

0-7645-5302-X

0-7645-5418-2

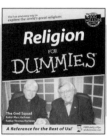
0-7645-5264-3

Also available:

The Bible For Dummies
(0-7645-5296-1)

Buddhism For Dummies
(0-7645-5359-3)

Christian Prayer For Dummies
(0-7645-5500-6)

Dating For Dummies
(0-7645-5072-1)

Judaism For Dummies
(0-7645-5299-6)

Potty Training For Dummies
(0-7645-5417-4)

Pregnancy For Dummies
(0-7645-5074-8)

Rekindling Romance For Dummies
(0-7645-5303-8)

Spirituality For Dummies
(0-7645-5298-8)

Weddings For Dummies
(0-7645-5055-1)

PETS

0-7645-5255-4

0-7645-5286-4

0-7645-5275-9

Also available:

Labrador Retrievers For Dummies
(0-7645-5281-3)

Aquariums For Dummies
(0-7645-5156-6)

Birds For Dummies
(0-7645-5139-6)

Dogs For Dummies
(0-7645-5274-0)

Ferrets For Dummies
(0-7645-5259-7)

German Shepherds For Dummies
(0-7645-5280-5)

Golden Retrievers For Dummies
(0-7645-5267-8)

Horses For Dummies
(0-7645-5138-8)

Jack Russell Terriers For Dummies
(0-7645-5268-6)

Puppies Raising & Training Diary For Dummies
(0-7645-0876-8)

EDUCATION & TEST PREPARATION

0-7645-5194-9

0-7645-5325-9

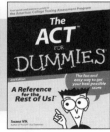
0-7645-5210-4

Also available:

Chemistry For Dummies
(0-7645-5430-1)

English Grammar For Dummies
(0-7645-5322-4)

French For Dummies
(0-7645-5193-0)

The GMAT For Dummies
(0-7645-5251-1)

Inglés Para Dummies
(0-7645-5427-1)

Italian For Dummies
(0-7645-5196-5)

Research Papers For Dummies
(0-7645-5426-3)

The SAT I For Dummies
(0-7645-5472-7)

U.S. History For Dummies
(0-7645-5249-X)

World History For Dummies
(0-7645-5242-2)

Available wherever books are sold. Go to www.dummies.com or call 1-877-762-2974 to order direct.

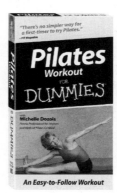

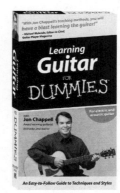